New Models of Financing and Financial Reporting for European SMEs

Eva Kaili • Dimitrios Psarrakis
Raz van Hoinaru
Editors

New Models of Financing and Financial Reporting for European SMEs

A Practitioner's View

Foreword by Valdis Dombrovskis

palgrave
macmillan

Editors
Eva Kaili
European Parliament
Brussels, Belgium

Dimitrios Psarrakis
European Parliament
Brussels, Belgium

Raz van Hoinaru
European Parliament
Brussels, Belgium

Queen Mary University of London
London, UK

ISBN 978-3-030-02830-5 ISBN 978-3-030-02831-2 (eBook)
https://doi.org/10.1007/978-3-030-02831-2

Library of Congress Control Number: 2019930471

Cover credit: Getty Images/MarioGuti/Tjaša Krivec

This Palgrave Macmillan imprint is published by the registered company Springer Nature Switzerland AG
The registered company address is: Gewerbestrasse 11, 6330 Cham, Switzerland

Foreword

Small and medium-sized businesses (SMEs) are the backbone of the EU economy. Not only do they employ two out of every three employees. They also produce 57 percent of value added in Europe. Start-ups in particular play an important role in job creation. Young firms account for an average of only 17% of employment, but they create 42% of new jobs. Finally, smaller companies working on innovative business models and new technologies today are the seeds that will ensure Europe stays competitive also in the future. For all these reasons, the success of start-ups, scale-ups, and other small and medium-sized firms is crucial to the future of jobs and economic growth in Europe.

If we want SMEs to succeed, we must ensure that funding can flow from investors to entrepreneurs and small business owners. That is why the European Commission launched the Capital Markets Union, our flagship project to develop and interconnect European capital markets, of which I am in charge. We also need to ensure that investors have clear and standardised information, while keeping the reporting burden for non-listed companies as low as possible. And also in this area there have been important developments, with the Accounting Directive entering into application in 2016. This volume by Eva Kaili, Dimitrios Psarrakis, and Raz van Hoinaru ties into the work we are doing, by exploring new models for SME funding and financial reporting from the perspective of experienced practitioners in the public, private and academic spheres.

The Capital Markets Union: Developing EU Capital Markets to Improve Access to Finance for SMEs

Access to finance is often mentioned in surveys as one of the major difficulties that SMEs face, despite a significant improvement in the availability of bank financing over the last years. Although the problem does not concern all SMEs, it is a highly significant issue in certain countries, such as Cyprus and Greece, where approximately a quarter of SMEs report this as their most pressing problem. But it is also a problem for more than 10% of SMEs in Ireland and Italy, according to the most recent SAFE survey[1] by the European Central Bank.

One of the aims of the Capital Markets Union is to improve and diversify access to finance for SMEs, by developing capital markets as a complement to Europe's dynamic banking sector. This is needed, because bank financing may not be suitable for certain start-ups and high-risk ventures, where past earnings and business operations cannot be used to forecast future cash flows. In contrast, capital markets can sometimes offer funding alternatives that are more flexible and long-term with regards to repayment schedules or the way future earnings are calculated.

European SMEs are very diverse, ranging from micro-enterprises through start-ups and fast-growing innovative firms to well-established companies. These companies all have different funding needs. Some types of SMEs, such as high-risk and innovative SMEs, can have relatively more difficulties accessing funding.

As part of the Capital Markets Union, we are working on various legislative and non-legislative actions to improve all steps of the funding ladder for SMEs. The goal is that European companies can easily access financing no matter their business model, country of origin, or size.

For example, venture capital can play an important part in funding high-growth businesses, but it is far less available in Europe than, for example, in the US. So we have taken action to boost European venture capital markets. In particular, new rules recently entered into application for the EU label for venture capital funds—EuVECA, to make it easier for fund managers of all sizes to run these funds, and for a greater range of companies to benefit from their investments. And we have just launched VentureEU, a pan-European

[1] Survey on the Access to Finance of Enterprises in the euro area—October 2017 to March 2018.

venture capital funds-of-funds programme, which is expected to trigger up to €6.5 billion of new investment in start-ups and scale ups across Europe.

Equity finance holds particular promise for firms seeking long-term investment to sustain innovation, value creation and growth. But today, out of 20 million SMEs in Europe, only about 3000 are listed on stock exchanges. So we have adopted a new Regulation on the prospectus, which is the "gateway" for issuers in need of equity or debt financing to gain access to European capital markets. It will enter into application in 2019 and will reduce the number of issuances subject to the European rules, facilitate secondary issuances, and simplify disclosures for smaller issuers with a dedicated SME Growth Prospectus. Recently the Commission has also proposed to simplify rules for SMEs listed on SME Growth Markets, which are a specific category of trading venue dedicated to small issuers. This should help SMEs to list and issue stocks and bonds on public markets, while safeguarding investor protection and market integrity.

As a final example of our actions to expand and diversify European capital markets, we have also presented a proposal to enable the growth of EU crowdfunding platforms, by allowing them to operate across the EU based on a single authorisation. This would help platforms scale up and offer more choice for investors, and more opportunities for entrepreneurs to attract funding from across the EU.

Of course, while developing capital markets, we also need to support banks, who are the main providers of financing to SMEs in Europe, to keep fulfilling this role. So we proposed in our Banking Reform Package to maintain the SME supporting factor and extend it to all loans to SMEs.

Information Barriers and Asymmetries

The second part of this volume deals with financial reporting for SMEs, which is an important part of the exchange of information between companies and investors. And it is also a piece of the puzzle for resolving the difficulties for SMEs to access finance.

For example, there is the issue of financial education and information barriers on the SME funding market. Securing finance is rarely a core strength of smaller businesses and entrepreneurs, which often lack the resources to employ a dedicated team for managing their finances. One SME out of three is not confident talking with banks, and only 20% are comfortable in negotiating with equity investors and venture capital firms.

The Commission has taken action to help small businesses navigate the complex financial landscape. For example, we have set up the Access2finance tool, which provides complete and up-to-date information on how businesses can access funding from various EU programmes—comprising over EUR 100 billion of finance in total—in each country and language. Every year, the EU supports more than 200,000 businesses through these programmes.

The problem of information barriers is compounded by the information asymmetries between investors and SMEs. SMEs often do not produce audited financial statements that yield credible financial information, but investors and lenders need verifiable information about a company before supporting it financially. Here, relationship banks benefit from a competitive advantage over other finance providers: their ongoing relationships with SME customers produce very valuable information for assessing their creditworthiness. This information is difficult to access for other finance providers.

Under CMU, the Commission has worked with EU banking federations and business associations to improve the feedback SMEs get from banks if their credit application is rejected. Small businesses need quick and constructive feedback to increase their chances of securing financing in the future. In 2017, the parties agreed on a voluntary code to ensure meaningful and helpful feedback to small businesses.

However, the most powerful tools for breaking down the information asymmetry can be found within the financial reporting of SMEs. And in this area, important changes have taken place in the last years. In particular, the Accounting Directive was thoroughly revised in 2013 with application in 2016. It harmonises the requirements applicable to small—non-listed—undertakings, with a view to avoiding disproportionate administrative burdens.

As this and other EU accounting rules have recently entered into application, we are currently in the stage of monitoring their implementation and functioning. Our overall aim is to keep making sure that EU accounting rules strike the balance between reducing the costs of those who prepare statements, and catering to the needs of end-users, such as investors or creditors. That is why we have, for example, commissioned a study on the accounting regime of micro-companies with limited liability. We are also collecting information from stakeholders through our fitness check on financial reporting, which also covers reporting for supervisory purposes.

Conclusion

SMEs are crucial to the future of Europe's economy. If we want our economy to keep growing and adding jobs, we need to support small businesses, and address their concerns by all means possible. So it is good that the various chapters in this volume capture issues that are on the minds of many small business owners and entrepreneurs across Europe, and are also of great importance for policymakers.

At times, building the new funding ecosystems and circuits that we need requires an updated legislative framework, and I have mentioned many projects where the Commission is working with the European Parliament and Member States on this, as part of our Capital Markets Union. But it is also important that other stakeholders get involved—market practitioners, academia and civil society, at European, national and local level. We cannot build the Capital Markets Union without their participation and support. So I hope the varied, relevant and interesting contributions in this volume can inspire further actions towards ensuring the vibrant capital markets that Europe's smaller businesses need to prosper and grow.

Valdis Dombrovskis
Euro and Social Dialogue, Financial Stability,
Financial Services, and the Capital Markets Union
European Commission, Brussels, Belgium

Acknowledgements

We express our sincere thanks to all the contributors from this book who have taken time from their busy schedules to write and provide insights to a professional world that would have been otherwise self-contained and unknown to most. Your original contribution is very much appreciated, especially as some of you had to go via an institutional process of approval.

We have to put forward special thanks to Dr. Konstantinos Sergakis from the University of Glasgow, UK, for his genuine help in getting this book published and his effort to understand a subject that is not necessarily his own cup of tea.

Special thanks to Professor Colin Haslam and Dr. Stella Ladi from the Queen Mary University of London who tolerated Raz's extra-curricular activities, together with MEP Theodor Stolojan, Chairman of the IFRS Permanent Team at the European Parliament, who also gave a great advice: 'focus'.

Many thanks to Alessandro de Luca from Deloitte, for his efforts and care for the subject.

Also we have to thanks to Tula Weiss from Palgrave Macmillan for keeping good contact and guiding us through the editorial challenges.

The editors

Brussels, 2018

Eva Kaili
Dimitrios Psarrakis
Raz van Hoinaru

Introduction

The key concept of this book is the European Small and Medium-Sized Enterprises (SMEs) and is looked at in two parts: financing and financial reporting. The editors decided on this perspective as money matters and a complete image, external and internal, is provided in such ways. Financing to SMEs is done from the external channels like investors or markets to the company, while financial reporting presents an inside-out perspective to investors and markets. Present practices of financial reporting, especially fair value, lead to a financialisation of accounting and in effect improved communication between the company, economic markets and financial markets. The framework of the European Union's Capital Markets Union is used to consider old and new methods of financing, public and private, understood via the new financial reporting methods: IFRS for SMEs. Before going into any details one has to understand what our key focus, the SME, is. This is important as 99% of the companies in the European Union are SMEs.

A World That Still Tries to Define SMEs

According to the European Commission's definition,[1] a medium-sized company can have up to 250 employees and can reach 'a maximum of 50 million euro turnover (or 43 million balance sheet)'. Even though different from SMEs, a micro company is normally mentioned aside due to a persisting common integrative perception. In some smaller economies such companies are regarded as SMEs. Accordingly, micro companies are defined by a ceiling of

[1] European Commission, *What is an SME?* Available at URL http://ec.europa.eu/growth/smes/business-friendly-environment/sme-definition_en

2 million euro maximum turnover and normally have different ways of getting financed and managed. In other geographical areas standards have been adapted to the local needs. For instance, in China an SME can reach up to 3000 employees, while in money terms criteria change in regard to industries, but from an interval of about 5 million euro to about 55 million euro.[2] Alternatively, Africa defines an SME as both profit and non-profit making entities with a maximum of 25 million euro in turnover and up to 300 human capital employed at work. The United States even has a governmental agency, dating back to 1953, called the Small Business Administration, which defines, regulates and has also the mission to provide support to such business entities in terms of capital, contracts and counselling. This approach is similar to that of the European Union. Even though similarities can be seen at global level, and SMEs tend to globalise, strangely enough there is no accepted global best practice guide to date. This shows a vast world, many typologies, a lack of founding fathers, lack of best practices, but a common global playground with space for competition and collaboration.[3]

There is a modern history of SME academic theory, which is rather left behind, creating confusions when applied today and generating the 'SME enigma'.[4] It is not only that SMEs are heterogeneous, generating confusion in many ways; it is also that SMEs tend to be defined rather legally, by the EU Commission and other governmental entities. This limits understanding, as such an optic implies size only, fit for employment policy and taxation purposes. Such political economy defined characteristics of SMEs are artificially created and may not necessarily defined the SMEs in its own terms. SMEs act on 'political markets' (Ramana's term) but more naturally in business markets.[5] The legal definition of SMEs may well address its business level; however, the business societies may have other values and references. A cliché in the literature on SMEs reads as follows: 'A small business is not a little big business'.[6] The oxymoronic term is half way right, as the SME concept is not

---

[2] African SME Organisation, *About African SME*. Available at https://africansme.org/index.php/about/about-african-sme

[3] Di Bitetto, M., Gilardoni, G., and D'Anselmi, P. (eds). (2013). *SMEs as the Unknown Stakeholder*, London: Palgrave Macmillan, 197p.

[4] Ifo Institute, Center of Economic Studies, Dannreuther, C., *EU SMEs Policy* (2007). Available at: https://www.cesifo-group.de/DocDL/forum2-07-focus2.pdf and Torres and Julien. (2005). *Specificity and denaturation of small business*, in International Small Business Journal, Vol. 23, pp. 355–377.

[5] US Small Business Administration, *About the SBA*. Available at https://www.sba.gov/about-sba

[6] Torres, O. (2006). *The proximity law of small business finance*, Communication présentée à l'International Council of Small Business, Melbourne, Australia, 2006. Available at http://oliviertorres.net/travaux/pdf/ICSB06.pdf

a one-size-fits-all umbrella. Contrary to what the term says, some SMEs are 'little big businesses' European companies representing rather big businesses, with capitalisation than can reach up to 200 million euro over a period of three years. This happens for the following two reasons: (1) the European market is very developed and professional, imposing somewhat high performance expectations at low-level benchmark in a more counter intuitive manner; (2) Scale: almost the entire European business market is made up of SMEs—98.8% of the EU companies. In this respect, small firms can have a large impact, as Kersten's title reads.[7] It seems that only the high end of SMEs are acting internationally and can be listed on MTFs, have business models and require special financial reporting standards.

From the business sector point of view there is no "official" definition but rather characteristics of SMEs. Torres, looking at SMEs' characteristics over time, presents unsophisticated management, lack of labour specialisation, informal procedures, and short term goals.[8] According to Mintzberg[9] and Shepherd & Wiklund,[10] SMEs are business entities where the key figure is the owner-manager. Most of the goals, vision and strategy, as well as business contacts often lead to one person or one family. Jocumsen[11] argues that SMEs are 'plagued by high failure rates and poor performance levels', which proves to be a rather unfortunate characteristic. As Storey[12] and Peacock[13] revealed, this happened due to the lack of proper planning and a local mentality of just surviving at a certain plateau level of profit. This conceptualisation, which translates in practice as a big effort in a small world, can still be relevant; however, a more sophisticated understanding came in time, as needs of business, human resources, and the relationship with authorities evolved. This gave way to better links in between business, policy and academic studies,

---

[7] Kersten, R., Harms, J., Liket, K., and Maas, K. (2017). *Small firms, large impact? A system review of the SME finance literature*, in World Development, Vol. 97, pp. 330–348.

[8] Torres, O. (2003). *A French perspective of research on small businesses: denaturation and proximity*. Available at http://oliviertorres.net/travaux/pdf/ECSBLodz.pdf

[9] Mintzberg, H. (1984). *Who Should Control the Corporation*, in California Management review, Vol. 27 (1), pp. 46–64.

[10] Shepherd, J., and Wiklund, D. (2005). *Entrepreneurial Orientation and Small Business Performance: A Configurational Approach*, in Journal of Business Venturing, Vol. 20 (1), pp. 71–91.

[11] Jocumsen, G. (2004). *How do small business managers make strategic marketing decisions? A model of process*, in European Journal of Marketing, Vol. 38 (5/6), pp. 659–674.

[12] Storey, D. J. (1994). *Understanding the Small Business Sector*. University of Illinois at Urbana-Champaign's Academy for Entrepreneurial Leadership Historical Research Reference in Entrepreneurship. Available at SSRN: https://ssrn.com/abstract=1496214

[13] Peacock, R. (2004). *Understanding small business: practice, theory and research*, Adelaide: Scarman Publishing.

which ultimately show an adaption, an evolution of the SME itself. This means that even some characteristics of the SMEs remained, nowadays an increased professionalisation and overall improvement in quality exists, despite the perception that remains. Perceptions are interesting to look at, and also practical, as Europe is not exactly unitary from one end to another in terms of economic capacity. A 50-million-euro business in the South-East of Europe is officially an SME accordingly to the EU definition; however, it is perceived as weighting more due to the market level of capitalisation and business mentality. From an outside perspective, even a small family business like a micro company (2 million euro revenues maximum), may not necessarily be named as such. Some scholars still perpetuate this image of small companies for SMEs. Why this happens and to what extent they are right or wrong will be analysed throughout the book.

Accounting and auditing are self-contained disciplines that developed somehow both in parallel, but part of economics. Accounting has its own ways of defining and characterising companies. IFRS for SMEs does not apply in a uniform manner to SMEs around the world. Strictly from an IFRS perspective, this book editors' opinion is that IFRS for SMEs does not aim at small companies. Better lenses to judge SMEs from an accounting perspective is to have a deeper understanding of what their business model is. In this context, size is an old fashioned variable that can be a puzzle to understand. Of course, for micro companies global standards will be too expensive and even useless. For a *sole proprietorship*, or family owned shares, there are more appropriate numbers and reports to be made use of, as well as intuition. Regulatory matter of accounting presented by the European Parliament and European Central Bank conclude that for the time being, IFRS for SMEs is presently too expensive a project for these types of companies. To what extent companies feel the same is arguable. Professional studies sampling SMEs and excluding public authorities from their survey showed exactly the opposite. To our minds the difference appears from the way business design of the SMEs and their needs are thought of from inside the company as opposed to authorities' sensitivity. Additionally, the economic environment has to be considered. Europe is good at setting trends at international levels, especially when it comes to IFRSs, but there is a Member State decision-making level, that has to be taken into consideration. National accounting standards have a history of being understood locally, being tailored to the local culture, and to some extent better known by SMEs' local managers and accountants. The other level, 'fully' international, also has to be considered where IFRS for SMEs interacts with full IFRS. Two of this book's chapters look at issues arising from these various interplays.

Accordingly, with regard to political, business and accounting perspectives, throughout the book the word SME is conceptualised slightly differently. Some authors seem indifferent to any definition. Others have used the official EU definition, though thinking more in terms of capitalisation, rather than annual revenues or number of employees. These authors had in mind new business types that do not only have distributive effects but also provide a new framework for risk diversification at the high end of SME world. The literature review revealed that some studies do not use the EU definition either, and use another approach, where size matters, but more important is the business model, management knowledge and skills in terms of financial markets (which are different form economic/capital markets). This happens as SMEs have recently experienced an unprecedented speed of change; it is a very heterogeneous world and scholars use the generic term, without specifically mentioning what segment from the SME concept they are referring to. In addition, old-fashioned perceptions still remain present. In the end, we want to underscore the importance for the SMEs world in terms of financing and financial reporting and the link between them, by presenting the two parts of the book.

The First Part of the Book: Financing

This volume opens with the new financing environment of the European SMEs. The contributors adopt an instrumental, policy-practical approach and bring to the readers the current discourse of the European policymakers and financing institutions. The fundamental changes in the financing of the European SMEs can be better examined in the light of the Capital Markets Union (CMU). CMU is a flagship initiative of the Juncker Presidency that was announced in July 2014. The aim is to introduce a more vibrant environment for market-based finance and improve the integration of the capital markets of the 28 Member States. The task was not only economically but also politically challenging, given Continental Europe's heavy reliance in bank-originated financing and the variegated capitalist traditions of the European countries.

The economic rationale behind the CMU initiative was that a coherent and functionally harmonised financial ecosystem like the one proposed, would (1) accelerate capital mobility from the EU and abroad as well as the intra-EU cross-border flows, (2) improve stability through dispersion of risk and minimisation of financial concentration to banking institutions, and (3) improve liquidity and the diversification of financing sources through deepening of the financial integration and increase of competition.

The European Commission's Action Plan on the Capital Markets Union (2015) addresses five priority areas, the first of which is the "provision of more funding choices for Europe's businesses and SMEs". In the mid-term review of the CMU Action Plan (2017), the Commission announced significant results in the areas of venture capital, the accessibility of the firms to public markets, the removing of national barriers to the free movement of capital, and in the area of preventive restructuring and second chance for entrepreneurs.

The CMU is one of the policy sectors of the EU that indicates significant "organic growth" with vast implications to the European SMEs landscape. As the CMU evolves, the policy priorities evolve drastically as well. The Commission announced in 2017 nine new priorities for the CMU among them: (1) the strengthening of the regulatory powers of the European Securities and Markets Authority (ESMA); (2) the increase of the support to initial offerings for investment firms through the creation of an agile regulatory framework that supports SMEs listing on public markets; (3) the drastic integration of financial innovations, including fintech, crowdfunding and ICOs; (4) the acceleration of cross-border investments through the improvement of the framework of the Alternative Investment Funds (AIFs) and the Undertakings for Collective Investment in Transferable Securities (UCITS); and (5) the strengthening of the local capital market ecosystems.

The CMU initiative employees a holistic view and the expectations are high. One of the problems of the pre-crisis financial environment was the limited consideration of the impact of financial frictions in the macroeconomic environment. The assumption of a "frictionless economy" is an academic simplification and does not reflect the real world, let alone the European economic ecosystem, where, in many cases, we can observe that Member States, even within the European Union framework, generate conditions that rather resemble closed economies' macroeconomics, especially in the behaviour of interest rates and the cash flows.

In a wider perspective, the CMU can be seen as step towards a democratised financial system, where the concentrations will be smaller, the investment barriers will be lower, and the access of the small players to capital will be greater. This reflects not only the demand of the European businesses for a real European economic union; it also reflects the significant technological developments that favour financial disintermediation. Crowdfunding and blockchain-empowered models of Initial Coin Offerings (ICOs) reflect these technological changes and the new regulatory challenges that nobody can ignore. The editors of this volume, are actively involved through their work in the Economic and Monetary Policy Committee of the European Parliament, in the transition to a new financial era where investment will not be a "job of specialists" but a function that blends "specialists' analysis and financial decision-making" with the dynamics of the "wisdom of crowds".

One key word of this transition is "harmonisation". EU, being a fragmented area of 28 Member States (soon 27), lacked the necessary conditions that would allow the optimal allocation of capital and risk throughout the Continent. Harmonising policies are now put in place to improve both the flows of capital and financial information. It is expected that European SMEs, will be the biggest beneficiary of this transition.

The contributors of this volume, despite their different professional origin, all converge to a set of very specific assumptions. First, they all agree that Europe needs to revisit its economic growth model. They believe that SMEs were, are and will be in the core of any future growth model, but the orientation of the SMEs should change and adopt a more innovative and technologically-savvy approach. Growth is a function of competition and competition is facilitated only by genuine and deep innovation. The question is who is going to finance this innovation effort? Second, all the contributors explicitly or implicitly highlight the problems that the post-crisis bank regulations imposed in the financing conditions of SMEs. Basel III and CRD IV increased the capital requirements of the banks and this affected disproportionally the SMEs in Europe that they were highly relied on traditional bank instruments.

The financing gap that the post-crisis macroeconomic environment created is the core concern of all the contributors. They all agree that EU should gradually move to sources of private and public equity as well as alternative financing vehicles. We can identify two major groups in this trend. There are authors who emphasise the shift from the global-banking-based financial intermediation to a more investment-banking-based financial intermediation approach. There is also another group of authors who believe that on top of that, it is also important SMEs to harness the new technological opportunities that allow us to move from financial intermediation to financial disintermediation. SMEs should not ignore these developments. In our view, a balanced approach that brings together traditional and innovative financial instruments is the most suitable. Fintech applications, based on cloud, machine learning and blockchain can be combined and build a significant financial infrastructure in Europe. This infrastructure will allow the emergence of synergies between SMEs, fintech firms and traditional financial institutions that will accelerate the mobilisation of capital to SMEs and the dispersion of risk among multiple actors, reducing, thus, the risk concentrations and the systemic financial dangers.

The Second Part of the Book: Financial Reporting

The second part of the book looks at the International Financial Reporting Standards (IFRS) for SMEs and challenges that both SMEs with their managers and IFRS/IASB face. Our approach is pro IFRS for SMEs as we believe that IASB provided a high quality set of financial reporting standards that are fit for purpose, improve transparency, and increase harmonisation and comparability. IASB acknowledged the need for a separate standard for SMEs derived from full IFRS, although differences could occur between the group's accounting practices and subsidiaries. This customised approach may look like a light version of the IFRS; however, it has its own inner complexities. This set of standards work for companies that do not have public accountability, but are developed in the public interest, to address real economic settings, like MTFs listing. SMEs should disclose information in such a way to ensure investor protection, which seems to be the purpose of IFRS, along with understandable, articulated and high quality accepted information disclosures for the use of the company itself. Therefore, a single set of accounting standards was developed for the backbone of the EU economy, providing not only understanding, but also simplification of costs, although some commenters called into question the price for trained professionals. Following the framework of the book, accounting solutions are considered in order to achieve the CMU's ambitions. According to the CMU Action Plan, accounting plays an important role in future growth. This was expected as markets are dynamic, new technologies and channels of business finance are invented and accounting has to keep up and play its role. It makes sense for companies to disclose information under one standard. The use of the IFRS for SMEs standard makes business environments more attractive to international investors. The use of IFRS globally by the EU companies, without the need for double reporting, is considered to have benefited companies with improved group reporting, and administrative savings, also improving decision-making and business efficiency.[14]

Currently, accounting has changed from a 'productionist' view to a 'financialisation' perspective.[15] Assets and liabilities of the company are no longer subject to internal control, but react to market value, and adjust themselves

---

[14] Bouvier, S. (2018). *Accounting roundup: IFRS questions EU plans to modify rules*. Available at https://www.ipe.com/pensions/pensions/pensions-accounting/accounting-roundup-ifrs-questions-eu-plans-to-modify-rules/10023979.article

[15] Zhang, E., and Andrew, J. (2014). *Financialisation and the Conceptual Framework*, in Critical Perspectives on Accounting, Vol. 25 (1), pp. 17–26.

according to future earnings perspectives and investments and investors' needs. It is interesting to see how there is an accounting logic, that is different from an economic one, but still part of it. It is true that preparers and investors have different perspectives, while management may or may not base their decisions on financial reporting numbers. Along with shareholders' needs, SME disclosures can quietly take into consideration stakeholders' basics. As standards are principles-based, there is a difference in between the standards as such and the interpretation and use of standards. As Professor Haslam argues in Chapter six, SMEs may therefore consider, for example, the nature of expense as different from the function of expenses. Next, the five chapters even though similarly titled, have different approaches, each chapter touching on different points. All of them are obviously centred on the IFRS, with the following perspectives: technical, or SMEs, or they consider the market as a whole. For a better understanding, also a parallel between full IFRS and IFRS for SMEs is provided. Some chapters are more informative in nature, while others are more critical, putting forward business and policy recommendations.

How to Read This Book

The book has a practitioners' perspective and is aimed at practitioners, professionals, policymakers and consultants, and is of an advanced academic level. Such a view is rare and stands isolated, as inside information is hard to obtain anyway, not to mention a proper inside perspective put in writing by the practitioner. Related approaches are applied research, empirical research, professional impact assessment or practical guides. Our research design has tried as much as possible to keep a unitary tone throughout the book, as in our case professional perspective sometimes means that educated opinions put in writing what practitioners do day by day, and their work varies. Accordingly, this book did not adopt such an approach where professionals were questioned, and authors translated their input in academic style. As our book can be used by academia as well, there was an academic touch on two chapters, authored by scholars. For example the literature review section provides further reading examples of articles and books, but also of professional studies and political reporting, having a balanced approach, and keeping this book's perspective. Each author was free to write on his and her subject matter and is responsible for the opinions and data presented. We, as editors, designed and structured the book, giving it direction, and we have put forward our own contributions. We tried as much as possible to provide the reader with "real life knowledge", timely information upon the new developments in the financial sector and financial reporting. Because this writing has a practitioners' view some chapters lack references as the knowledge provided is based on the work experience of the authors.

The chapters should be read in the order they are presented to get a complete picture. Chapters may look like stand-alone and make sense in themselves, but each chapter builds on from the previous one. Accordingly, chapter order was specifically chosen the way it is. The literature review chapter has an extra uniting role giving coherence to the book, and also positioning the current research among specialised studies. The key focus is the SMEs and the books start to present the framework in which SMEs act: the SMEs ecosystem, important SMEs drivers like innovation, models of finance for SMEs, finance of SMEs, and how finance is registered accordingly to IFRS for SMEs. Some chapters may look similar, but they argue from a different perspective: SMEs and respectively financial reporting. To have a broader picture, of course, cross-references do exist in both areas. More specifically, the book presents as follows:

Vladis Dombrovskis in his foreword note describes in a concise and straightforward way the state of play in the area of financing and financial reporting for SMEs in Europe. He depicts the vision, the strategy and the action of the Capital Markets Union, the flagship initiative of the Commission, that he leads, and provides a map of the policies that aim to the creation of a financial environment in EU where the SMEs have as frictionless as possible access to finance, no matter their size, their business model and their location.

Raz van Hoinaru and Georgiana Oana Stănilă authored a chapter that stands out as a literature review for both parts of the book: financing and financial reporting for SMEs. The aim of the chapter is to act like a uniting reading framework providing coherent understanding not only to the present book but to give a greater sense of the SME literature in general. Positioning the present book into the literature is also among the goals of the chapter. The literature was sectioned in three parts: academic, professional and political. Research showed that the present publication has a unique perspective and is the most complex study of its kind.

Peteris Zilgalvis opens the first part of this book by making a clear and straightforward statement: we need to adopt an economic policy framework that takes into account the dynamics of change of the economy and puts the entrepreneur in the centre of those dynamics. Competition and innovation walk hand in hand. Firms that know how to innovate also know how to compete. Unfortunately, short-termism, suboptimal policies and adverse financial realities had led innovation in Europe, and in the West in general, to a stalemate. Governments can play significant and pivotal role in boosting innovation through strong government-market synergies and the adoption of an innovation encouraging policy, which is reflected in a regulatory framework that is innovation-supportive.

Luca Payrano delves into the structural problem that the European economy faces in funding innovative SMEs and projects. He stresses that traditional firms no longer play the role they used to have in creating jobs and growth. Innovative SMEs have a strong potential to bridge the gap. He emphasises the inadequacy of the traditional banking channels to provide the necessary capital to those innovative firms and underscores the significant role of the CMU in addressing this problem. Luca describes the role of the ELITE initiative of the London Stock Exchange in addressing the four major challenges that European SMEs face today, namely, the lack of access to information and external advice, cultural barriers, insufficient networks and low access to international liquidity, and underscores the role of financial innovation in alleviating the structural problems that SMEs face in financing their scale up and operations.

Horst Heitz builds on his experience as director of "SMEs Europe" to underscore the fundamental problems of the traditional sources of funding for SMEs. He begins by stressing the systematic consequences of the banking regulations that followed the financial crisis and the Capital Requirements Directive (CRD) that led to the reduction of available lending and increased the cost of lending for SMEs. He stresses that the Basel III regime puts SMEs in a disadvantaged position compared to bigger corporations. Alternative sources of funding, thus, are of paramount importance, Horst Heitz notes. He highlights the importance of, supportive structural programs and instruments that the EU deploys to strengthen the SMEs ecosystem.

Ruth Wandhöfer goes deeper in the problem caused by the regulatory constraints in the banks due to the increase of regulatory capital requirements. She stresses the increased role of the emergence of fintech and the strong potential of synergies between SMEs, banks and fintech firms in the "open banking" ecosystem. She highlights that the gradual digitisation of the economy also accelerates the digital transformation of the financial environment for SMEs. Ruth agrees with the other contributors that equity investment schemes are crucial for the funding of SMEs and stresses the significant role the CMU can play towards this direction. She underscores alternative financing paths that an SME can follow to finance its growth, such as the "mini-bonds". But the availability of good quality financing for the SMEs operations is always critical. For that reason, Ruth places considerable emphasis on the growing significance of supply chain finance (SCF) products as an efficient and cheap alternative and the capacity of blockchain technology in improving the quality and efficiency of processing the financing requirements of the SMEs.

Dimitrios Psarrakis and Eva Kaili conclude the first part of the book, expanding the scope of financing for SMEs by moving from the traditional financial intermediation to a brand new model, the financial disintermediation. The significance of peer-to-peer lending, crowdfunding and the Initial Coin Offerings (ICOs) are detailed, explaining why they comprise a dynamic set of financial instruments. These instruments can mobilise idle capital in cutting edge new technologies, usually considered as "un-bankable" due to their high risk and the uncertainty of their free cash flows. Investing in emerging technologies like blockchain, AI, machine learning, IoT and biotechnology, will guarantee the leading role of EU in the new global competitive environment of the Fourth Industrial Revolution. Eva and Dimitrios propose a set of characteristics that is necessary for EU to adopt in order to create an innovation-friendly regulatory framework that will boost both equity- and lending-based crowdfunding as well as a policy approach that will allow ICOs to become a distinct asset class, with the opportunity to be blended with traditional financial instruments. This chapter reflects the regulatory approach adopted by Eva, who was the European Parliament's rapporteur and co-rapporteur of regulations and resolutions related to blockchain and crowdfunding, as well as of Dimitrios who was the draftsperson of those regulatory texts.

Colin Haslam underscores the importance of SMEs in a vibrant international economy, where investors need to compare companies' performance. The financial results translated into IFRS increase (market) efficiency and achieves a reduction in the cost of raising capital for companies, which ultimately helps to boost growth. Financialising SME Financial Reporting reveals how market conditions impact upon the financial performance and sustainability of SMEs and also generates innovative policy interventions and financing strategies for SME integrity and efficiency.

Olivier Boutellis-Taft presents the European SMEs as a heterogeneous group, accounting for 99% of the enterprises in the EU. His contribution looks at present challenges like new technologies, cloud and Big Data. Non-financial reporting is also taken into consideration due to its increased importance. All these points help to better present challenges for the accounting profession. He concludes that human judgement and emotional intelligence and moral values of trained professionals are still needed in business. At the end a set of recommendations to policymakers are provided.

Andrew Watchman's chapter considers whether a new accounting solution is needed to help achieve the CMU's ambitions for the successful development of the quoted SME sector. It is important to know the present state of play and of some of the various options in order to move forward. The angle is IFRS-based and shall firstly consider if IFRS is sufficiently scalable, and secondly whether the core information objective on which IFRS is founded is optimised for quoted SMEs.

Darrel Scott focuses on the standards as such and presents the use of IFRS globally by EU companies. The global reach of the IFRS Foundation and the positive effects that they have brought in terms of quality, transparency and comparability of financial reporting stands at the core of its promotion and acceptance. The main objective of the IFRS Foundation and the Board is to take into consideration the needs of entities in diverse economic approaches and prepare financial reporting standards also for small listed companies. This helps to consolidate sets of high quality, understandable, enforceable and globally accepted financial reporting standards based upon clearly articulated values for regulated markets and also for MTFs.

Jens Berger, Veronica Poole and Laurence Rivat provide an overview of the IFRS for SMEs to enable users that have already adopted IFRSs to understand the key differences between the IFRS for SMEs and full IFRSs. The differences between the IFRS for SMEs and full IFRSs are those that are unavoidable, so they cannot be eliminated by judicious selection of accounting policies. Differences may arise between the group's accounting policies and the subsidiary's accounting policies because it will not always be practical, or desirable, for the group to choose accounting policies that are in compliance with the IFRS for SMEs.

Raz van Hoinaru concludes the book, which provided a twofold research—financing and financial reporting united in one single dimension: the SMEs in the new business environment of the Capital Market Union. The concluding remarks include a recapitulation of all the contributions, limits of our research and further comments. In this way our readers can better understand new ways of obtaining finance, 'if IFRS for SMEs is good for SMEs?' and how IFRS increases market efficiency, which later on influences performance and funding of SMEs in a financing and financial reporting business circle. 'Takeaway' bullet points are provided for simplification of knowledge and understanding.

Finally, we have to acknowledge the limits of our research and mention that we realise this book is not perfect in general. It is perfect, however, considering the time we had to do it and the resources and networking we had access to. We are aware of some of the critics, some of them being mentioned to us from early drafting stage. A frequent comment was that the practitioners' perspective is not "academic" enough and this would not be right for the book. Also, it is hard for the market to digest such a research, as in the business practice there is no minimum quality. This point is that we did not consider weak points but rather the advantages that made us differentiate. There is no institution to award a chartered businessman title. Therefore, practitioners in business may be a very wild category, totally uncontrollable. We did our best to select the good contributors whose opinions follow the same direction. It was hard enough for us as editors to unite the two constituent parts of the book. Therefore, we did not introduce any counter argument or debate chapter, as we preferred a unitary approach. Other critics relate to the general framework of the book, which is CMU and carries a heavy political economy dimension or at least policy one. All the editors have a greater EU institutional perspective of business then a proper private one, even though this latter perspective is not completely foreign to some of us. Therefore, for credibility reasons we decided to go this way, but we understood that the perspective could have been a business for business perspective. The second part of the book touched on IFRS for proper business purposes, providing an accounting method for business perspectives, at least.

All in all, our book, *New Models for Financing and Financial Reporting for European SMEs: A Practitioner's View*, is one of the most consistent studies on the market connecting financing with financial reporting, with a rare perspective providing insights from industries. Even though the connection between the two may look obvious, research in this area is not very common. The little that exists is done from academic and professional perspectives, and starts to become old. Moreover, one study in particular deplores the lack of structured data. Accordingly, we hope the readers will enjoy this book, that it will be useful to them, and that they will appreciate the way we designed and framed our research.

Raz van Hoinaru
Eva Kaili
Dimitrios Psarrakis

Contents

1 The SMEs Literature Review: Perspective of Studies 1
Raz van Hoinaru and Georgiana Oana Stănilă

Part I Financing 21

2 The Role of the State in the Innovation Triangle: Law and Policy Fostering the Optimal Regulatory, Business and Innovation Policy Environment 23
Pēteris Zilgalvis

3 Catalysing the SME Growth Ecosystem in the New Information Age 39
Luca Peyrano

4 Financing SMEs in the EU: Challenges and Opportunities 55
Horst Heitz

5 Financing Models for SMEs in the Age of Disintermediation 63
Ruth Wandhöfer

6 Funding Innovation in the Era of Weak Financial Intermediation: Crowdfunding and ICOs for SMEs in the Context of the Capital Markets Union 71
Dimitrios Psarrakis and Eva Kaili

Part II Financial Reporting 83

7 **Towards Business Model Reporting for SMEs** 85
Colin Haslam

8 **New Relevance of Accounting and Reporting: SMEs, Ethics and Sustainability** 95
Olivier Boutellis-Taft

9 **Financial Reporting for Small Listed Companies** 107
Darrel Scott

10 **Financial Reporting by Quoted SMEs** 117
Andrew Watchman

11 **The IFRS for Small and Medium-Sized Entities** 133
Veronica Poole, Laurence Rivat, and Jens Berger

12 **Conclusion: Closing the Circle of Financing and Financial Reporting for SMEs. Our Formula** 161
Raz van Hoinaru

Bibliography 167

Index 177

Notes on Contributors

Jens Berger is the Professional Practice Director IFRS of Deloitte Germany and leader of the German IFRS Centre of Excellence. He is a member of Deloitte's Global IFRS Leadership Team. He is responsible for all member firm consultations under IFRS and is also working together with the relevant market partners in developing new service propositions with regard to IFRS. Between 2007 and 2008 he was seconded to the IFRS Global Office which coordinates the IFRS activities of Deloitte. From 2008–2009 he was seconded to the IASB to work on the projects on financial instruments and fair value measurement, while he is currently a member of the Financial Instruments Working Group of EFRAG. He is also a member of the Deloitte expert advisory panel on financial instruments and is liaising with the relevant German standard-setting bodies—DRSC and IDW. Jens is author and contributor of several articles and monographs on IFRS, including Deloitte's iGAAP, as well as a frequent speaker at conferences. He is a Certified Public Accountant in the USA with expertise in developing and implementing IFRS strategies, and quality assurance reviews on IFRS implementation projects.

Olivier Boutellis-Taft has been Accountancy Europe's CEO since 2006. He benefits from a diverse professional experience, having been a public prosecutor in France, a director with PricewaterhouseCoopers, a board member of the European Policy Centre, a director of XBRL international and a business and policy consultant. He regularly speaks on issues related to European affairs and the impact of technology on accountancy. A lawyer and economist by training, Olivier started his professional career in equestrian sports (show jumping).

Valdis Dombrovskis is the Vice-President of the European Commission responsible for the Euro and Social Dialogue, also in charge of Financial Stability, Financial Services and the Capital Markets Union. Prior to that, he served three consecutive terms as Prime Minister of Latvia, becoming the longest serving elected head of government in Latvia's history. Before becoming European Commission Vice-

President, Valdis Dombrovskis was elected for the second time as a Member of the European Parliament (first, 2004–2009) and Head of the Latvian Delegation in the EPP Group. He served as a Member of the Saeima (Parliament) of Latvia (March 2004–June 2004; January 2014–June 2014) and was Latvia's Minister of Finance from 2002 to 2004. He graduated with a degree in physics from the University of Latvia (1993) and economics from Riga University of Technology (1995). He received his master's degree in physics in 1995 from the University of Latvia. Prior to joining politics, he worked as a senior economist and Chief Economist at the Bank of Latvia (1998–2002). Together with Anders Aslund, he co-authored the book *How Latvia Came Through the Financial Crisis*, which was published in 2011.

Colin Haslam is Professor of Accounting and Finance at Queen Mary University of London. He has been an adviser to the European Financial Reporting Advisory Group (EFRAG) from 2012 to 2015. His research on Business Models reporting was noted in the EFRAG 2014 report. In 2016 he was appointed as a Fellow to European Institute for Law (ELI) and was involved with the Special Interest Group (SIG) for Accounting and Business Law, where he participated in the policy report 'Which Accounting Regulation for Europe's Economy and Society?' He has also acted as a technical adviser to the United Nations Environment Program (UNEP)/World Resources Institute (WRI) report on carbon-asset risk (UNEP 2015). He has presented a number of times to the European Parliament on stress testing financial reporting standards and reporting on carbon-asset risk to meet the Paris 2050 decarbonisation objectives.

Horst Heitz is the CEO of the business representation platform SME Connect and the Executive Director of SME Europe. After his military service he studied political science, history, communication science and international law in Munich and Salzburg. After successfully completing his master's degree, Horst completed a doctoral degree in Vienna with a dissertation on "Lobbyism in the European Union." In addition to his many years of membership and activities in various divisions, including the current Bavarian ruling party, CSU, Horst has been involved in various European networks, such as the Paneuropa Union and the European Economic Senate, for more than 15 years. His professional focus has been on promoting SMEs' interests in various associations at European level for more than 10 years. His professional focus has now been on promoting SME interests at the European level for more than a decade. Dr. Heitz is known as a profound expert in the EU political system with a large network. Born in Basel (Switzerland) he lives and works in Brussels and Munich.

Raz van Hoinaru Business minded, policy consultant by vocation, economist by education, and historian by heart, all together and all separately recommend Raz as a 'man of social sciences and society'. Raz translates technical economic language into policy and vice versa to allow for better public policy and business results and understanding for all. His work has spanned across public affairs agencies, government bodies, private companies, lobby and Parliament in-house policy development and advocacy. In his job, he meets with representatives from both public and private sectors to discuss how to find winning solutions, especially in financial reporting. As an academic Raz taught two modules of accounting at Queen Mary University of London, organised conferences on the IASB's work, sustainability, and contributed to two Financial Reporting Council (FRC) UK studies, among other publications. Educated at Sheffield and KU Leuven, for the time being, he works for MEP Theodor Stolojan, Chairman of the IFRS Permanent Team of the European Parliament and researches at Queen Mary University of London.

Eva Kaili is a Member of the European Parliament, elected in 2014. In her capacity as the Chair of the European Parliament's Science and Technology Options Assessment body (STOA) she has been working intensively on promoting innovation as a driving force of the establishment of the European Digital Single Market. She has been particularly active in the fields of blockchain technology, m/eHealth, big data, fintech, AI and cybersecurity. Since her election, she has also been very active in the field of taxation, where she has been the Rapporteur of the ECON committee's annual tax report. As a member of the ECON committee, she has been focusing on EU's financial integration and the management of the financial crisis in the Eurozone. She was the European Parliament's Rapporteur and Shadow Rapporteur of critical files, including the Extension of the European Fund of Strategic Investments, the Family Business Report, the Blockchain Resolution, the Crowdfunding Regulation, and the Digital Platforms Report. Prior to her position in the European Parliament, she has been elected two times in the Greek Parliament (serving between 2007 and 2012), with the PanHellenic Socialist Movement (PASOK). She holds a bachelor's degree in Architecture and Civil Engineering, and a master's degree in European Politics. Currently, she is conducting her PhD in International Political Economy.

Luca Peyrano is CEO of ELITE, a company of the London Stock Exchange Group whose mission is to support private and public companies connecting with capital using the digital technology. With over 15 years of experience in the industry, Luca started with Borsa Italiana in 1999 with responsibility for companies admission to listing and then moved on to manage the SMEs markets offering until 2007. Following the merger with the London Stock Exchange he was appointed Head of Continental Europe for Primary Markets, until he took on his present position as CEO of ELITE in 2016. Prior to the London Stock Exchange, he worked in the consumer goods sector and in the automotive industry. He holds a degree in Business Administration from Bocconi University and received an MBA from IMD. Luca serves as member of the Board of the Scale-up Institute in the UK and the Board of Trustees of OIV, the Valuation Standard setter in Italy.

Veronica Poole is a Senior Accounting Technical Partner at Deloitte. She chairs the Deloitte Global IFRS Leadership Team, which provides Deloitte member firms around the world with guidance and support they need over to deliver best-in-class

IFRS services to their clients, both from a technical and practical perceptive. She joined Deloitte in 1996 and became Partner in 2002. In the initial days of implementation of IFRS in Europe, she was part of the triumvirate that led the Deloitte UK IFRS Implementation Services. In parallel, she established and led the UK IFRS Centre of Excellence responsible for Deloitte UK IFRS policy. In her current role as the UK National Head of Accounting and Corporate Reporting, Veronica leads a team of partners, directors and senior managers who are responsible for Deloitte UK policy, views and positioning on all UK accounting matters and acts as the National Professional Practice Director on accounting matters. She has expertise in developing and implementing IFRS strategies and holds a Diploma and an MSc in Higher Mathematics from Moscow State University.

Dimitrios Psarrakis is Advisor of Economic and Monetary Policy at the European Parliament. He works mainly on files related to the Capital Markets Union, fintech, and financial innovation. Prior to his work in the European Parliament he worked as credit risk specialist in the banking sector and he was also economic policy advisor at the Parliament of Greece during the years of the Greek debt crisis. His research interests are related to financial industry transformation, banking innovation, digitalisation of financial services and crypto-crowdfunding. He was the European Parliament's draftsperson of the Blockchain Resolution, the Legislative Opinion of the ITRE Committee of the European Fund for Strategic Investments, and the Crowdfunding Regulation. He is affiliated with universities in Europe, USA and Asia, and he studied Finance at Harvard University and has executive management education from MIT, Sloan Business School, the Wharton Business School and Stanford Business School.

Laurence Rivat is a partner of the National Office of Deloitte France that combines a double expertise in auditing and IFRS. She heads the French firm's IFRS Centre of Excellence and she is also a member of the Deloitte Global IFRS Leadership Team, the global technical body in charge of setting the Deloitte policy on IFRS matters. After 7 years (1988–1995) practising auditing at Deloitte (in France and in the USA), she specialised in IFRS, working 3 years (1995–1998) at the IASC (the IASB's predecessor) as a Research Manager. Back at Deloitte France in 1998, and as leader (since 2001) of one the nine Deloitte Global IFRS Centres of Excellence, she has dedicated herself to the development and running of the Deloitte support structures on IFRS at a French, European and global level, which are active in the fields of IFRS consultations, learning, communications and standard-setting. She was appointed to the newly created European Financial Reporting Advisory Group (EFRAG) Board on 31 October 2014. She is also the President of the Accounting Committee of the Public Interest Entities (PIEs) Department of the Compagnie Nationale des Commissaires aux Comptes (CNCC—French statutory auditors institute) since January 2017 (Vice-President from January 2015). Her expertise is in regulatory and policymaking on IFRS and holds DESCAF Diploma (MBA equivalent), major in Finance/Accounting from Grenoble École de Management (Business School).

Darrel Scott is Chair of SMEs Implementation Group to the IASB. He became a member of the International Accounting Standards Board (Board) in October 2010, having previously been a member of the IFRS Interpretations Committee and a member of what is now called the IFRS Advisory Council. He was reappointed to the Board to serve a second term in 2015. Prior to joining the Board, Mr. Scott was chief financial officer of FirstRand Banking Group, one of the largest financial institutions in South Africa. He was responsible for both financial reporting under IFRS Standards and regulatory reporting under the Basel II Accords. He is chairman of the Board's SME Implementation Group. Mr. Scott studied accounting at the University of the Witwatersrand, South Africa.

Georgiana Oana Stănilă is Associate Professor at the Bucharest University of Economic Studies, Department of Accounting and Auditing and Vice Dean of the Faculty of Business Administration, in Foreign Languages. She has authored several books, articles and scientific materials (as the sole author or as co-author), is a member of research teams, and teaches Accounting, Financial Accounting and Managerial Accounting. She holds a bachelor's degree in Economics, from the Bucharest University of Economic Studies, the Faculty of Accounting and Management Information Systems, a Bachelor of Laws, a master's degree in English Language Education and Research Communication for Business and Economics from the Faculty of International Business and Economics, a postgraduate specialisation in Company Accounting based on International Accounting Standards, and a PhD in Accounting. Her field of research interests are mainly Business Accounting, International Financial Reporting Standards, Financial Analysis and Reporting, and Performance Management.

Ruth Wandhöfer is an expert in the field of banking and one of the foremost authorities on transaction banking regulation and innovation in financial technology matters. With over 11 years at Citi, where she drove regulatory and industry dialogue and developed product and market strategy in line with the evolving regulatory and innovation landscape, she has recently left in order to embrace a more independent career. Ruth is an independent NED on the boards of the London Stock Exchange Group, Permanent TSB, and Pendo Systems, Inc. She is also Head of Regulatory and Industry Affairs at Coinfirm, a senior adviser at KPMG, and Chair of the European Payments Council Payment Security Group. She continues to focus on her passion for bringing the financial industry and the emerging financial digital ecosystem together, in particular across the blockchain/distributed ledger space, an area which she recently researched for her PhD. She also mentors fintechs and works closely with the venture capital and private equity community to help identify and support firms with true potential. Ruth was named as one of 2010s 'Rising Stars' by *Financial News*, and she was named in *Management Today*'s 2011 '35 Women under 35' list of women to watch (*Sunday Times*), and one of the 100 Most Influential People in Finance 2012 by *Treasury & Risk* magazine. In 2015 she was the recipient of the 'Women in Banking and Finance Award for Achievement' and in 2016 and 2017 she was named on the global 'Women in Fintech Powerlist' of Innovate Finance. In 2018 she became one of the Top 10 Global Fintech Influencers (Fintech Power 50). She speaks five languages (English, German, French, Spanish, and Italian) and has completed studies in various countries, including an MA in Financial Economics (UK), an MA in International Politics (France), and an LLM in International Economic Law (UK). She has published two books: *EU Payments Integration: The Tale of SEPA, PSD and Other Milestones Along the Road* (2010) and *Transaction Banking and the Impact of Regulatory Change: Basel III and Other Challenges for the Global Economy* (2014), both with Palgrave Macmillan. She is a visiting professor at the London Institute of Banking and Finance and also lectures at Queen Mary London School of Law.

Andrew Watchman is CEO of EFRAG and TEG Chairman. Prior to joining EFRAG Andrew was the Global Head of IFRS for Grant Thornton, leading a team supporting the application of IFRS across the international network and chairing the firm's global IFRS expert group. Responsibilities included consulting on technical issues, developing publications, delivering training and responding to IASB proposals. Between July 2013 and joining EFRAG, Andrew also served as a member of the IFRS Interpretations Committee. Prior to joining Grant Thornton, Andrew served as Accountancy Adviser to the UK's Department of Trade and Industry (DTI), providing expert advice on public policy in financial reporting and the transition to IFRSs in the UK. Prior to that Andrew spent 14 years in the audit practice of an international accounting firm, up to partner level.

Pēteris Zilgalvis is the Head of Unit for Startups and Innovation in the Digital Single Market Directorate in DG CONNECT of the European Commission. He was a Visiting EU Fellow at St. Antony's College, University of Oxford for 2013–14, where he was a Senior Member and Associate of the Political Economy of Financial Markets Programme. From 1997 to 2005, he was Deputy Head of the Bioethics Department of the Council of Europe, in its Directorate General of Legal Affairs. In addition, he has held various positions in the Latvian civil service (Ministry of Foreign Affairs, Ministry of Environment). He was Senior Environmental Law Advisor to the World Bank/Russian Federation Environmental Management Project and was Regional Environmental Specialist for the Baltic Countries at the World Bank. He has been a member of the California State Bar since 1991, completed his J.D. at the University of Southern California, his B.A. in Political Science Cum Laude at UCLA, and the High Potentials Leadership Program at Harvard Business School. A recent publication is 'The Need for an Innovation Principle in Regulatory Impact Assessment: The Case of Finance and Innovation in Europe' in *Policy & Internet*.

Abbreviations

ABS	Asset-Backed Security
ACCA	Association of Chartered Certified Accountants
AI	Artificial Intelligence
AIM	Alternative Investment Market
AMLD	Anti-money Laundering Directive
ANC	L'Autorité des Normes Comptables (Accounting Standards Body in France)
CBCR	Country by Country Reporting
CMU	Capital Market Union
COSME	EU Programme for the Competitiveness of Enterprises and Small and Medium-Sized Enterprises (SMEs)
CRD	(III and IV) Capital Requirements Directive
DG FISMA	Directorate-General for Financial Stability, Financial Services and Capital Markets Union
DLT	Distributed Ledger Technologies
DP	Discussion Paper
EBRD	European Bank for Reconstruction and Development
EC	European Commission
EFRAG	European Financial Reporting Advisory Group
EFSI	European Fund for Strategic Investments
EGC	Emerging Growth Company
EIB	European Investment Bank
EP	European Parliament
ERP	Enterprise Resource Planning
ESAs	European Supervisory Authorities
ESMA	European Security Markets Authority
EU	European Union
EY	Ernst & Young

FRC	Financial Reporting Council
FV(A)	Fair Value (Accounting)
GDP	Gross Domestic Product
GDPR	General Data Protection Regulation
HCA	Historical Cost Accounting
IAS	International Accounting Standards
IASB	International Accounting Standards Board
ICAEW	Institute of Chartered Accountants in England and Wales
ICOs	Initial Coin Offerings
IFAC	International Federation of Accountants
IFRS	International Financial Reporting Standards
IFVS	Integrated Financial Viability Statement
IPOs	Initial Public Offerings
IR	Integrated Reporting
JEREMIE	Joint European Resources for Micro to Medium Enterprises
KPIs	Key Performance Indicators
LSEG	London Stock Exchange Group
MEP	Member of the European Parliament
NFI	Non-financial Information
NPLs	Non-performing Loans
OECD	Organisation for Economic Co-operation and Development
ORB	Order Book for Retail Bonds
PIEs	Public Interest Entities
PP&E	Property, Plan, and Equipment
PSD	Payment Services Directive
SCF	Supply Chain Finance
SMEs	Small and Medium-Sized Enterprises
SNS	Startup Nations Summit
SPAC	Special Purpose Acquisition Company
UEAPME	The European Association of Crafts, Small and Medium-Size Enterprises
VAT	Value Added Tax

1

The SMEs Literature Review: Perspective of Studies

Raz van Hoinaru and Georgiana Oana Stănilă

Introduction and Purpose of the Chapter

The purpose of this chapter is (1) to unite the two parts of the book, (2) provide a further reading insight into the subject area, and (3) position the book in the literature. The first point (1) is important as generally the literature treats SMEs financing and financial reporting independently one from the other. There is a small amount of research, not necessarily binding them together but touching upon the two subjects, casting analysis in a different light compared to our study. In this sense, specialised literature presents research similar to ours, but their direction is slightly different. It is, of course, important to understand certain aspects, like, for instance, correlations between growth accounting, economic growth and healthy businesses in regard to a new world of SMEs and a new accounting system,[1] among other things. Accounting is still considered the

[1] Brem, A., Kreusel, N., and Neusseu, C. (2008). *Performance Measurement in SMEs: Literature Review and Results from a German Case Study*, in International Journal of Globalisation and Small Business,

R. van Hoinaru (✉)
European Parliament, Brussels, Belgium

Queen Mary University of London, London, UK
e-mail: razvan.hoinaru@europarl.europa.eu

G. O. Stănilă
The Bucharest University of Economic Studies, Bucharest, Romania
e-mail: oana.stanila@ase.ro

E. Kaili et al. (eds.), *New Models of Financing and Financial Reporting for European SMEs*,
https://doi.org/10.1007/978-3-030-02831-2_1

language of business and any access to finance can be understood at the very beginning via accounting numbers, unless other resources and reports are being used. Considering the first part of the book, some of our research is new and developed in parallel with certain EU legislation dealing with FinTech and related technologies like blockchain, giving original input. It is important to understand how the International Financial Reporting Standards (IFRS) addresses these. The literature review chapter will show many interesting connections and conclusions resulting from other publications, looking in fact for second opinions, when they exist. As we are performing an up-to-date literature review, we only took into consideration recent publications in connection with point (2).

On the third point (3), this book can be positioned in the literature considering its informational perspective, but also its analysis angle. Worth mentioning is that none of the studies known by the authors of this chapter are as consistent as the present book or have a similar practical perspective in uniting financing and financial reporting. The present book comes with new knowledge on funding SMEs, and the IFRS for SMEs, as well as with a new perspective: that of the practitioners. Such a view is new and stands rather isolated in the discipline, as inside information is hard to get, not to mention a proper inside perspective. Nearby approaches are applied research, empirical research, professional impact assessment or practical guides. For example, some researchers interviewed practitioners or asked them to provide input which was later on translated into academic language. Generally, these studies argue in a broader sense about funding, decision usefulness and utility of the IFRS, financing and business management.[2] It is important to understand how new ways of funding and the IFRS for SMEs interact, if and how they properly influence one another. Whether the IFRS for SMEs, as not 'full IFRS', is (not) good enough and appropriate for the new ways of funding may lead to some different conclusions from author to author and institution to institution. A replication of the present study would be interesting. Up to now, some of the commenters have been more reserved, such as in the position papers published by the European Commission and EIB, while others take a more daring and business oriented approach. In effect, this chapter scans through the literature for a better understanding of the positioning and integration of the present book in the specialised literature. Next, the IFRS for SMEs type of literature will be presented, as it has some special characteristics. By this it is meant that even

---

Vol. 2(4); Garengo, P., Biazzo, S., and Umit, S.B. (2005). *Performance measurement systems in SMEs: A review for a research agenda*, in International Journal of Management Review, Vol. 7(1), pp. 25–47.

[2] Carraher, S., and van Auken, H. (2013). *The use of financial statements for decision making by small firms.* Available at https://www.researchgate.net/publication/272532573_The_use_of_financial_statements_for_decision_making_by_small_firms

academic studies on this subject matter carry a big touch of professional dimension to them. This chapter has no conclusion, but only a sum up at the end, as we have saved our comments for the concluding chapter of the book.

Part I

Financing

This section looks at various perspectives: academic, professional and political, for a complete understanding. In the SME world, specialisation is usually not very high, sometimes forcing a general perspective. Studies look at both government financing and private sector variants, including new ones such as shadow banking and initial coin offerings (ICOs). Certain publications that may not necessarily be considered dealing with SMEs are included.

Access to finance by SMEs has always been treated in the literature due to its capital importance. There are a few literature reviews on this subject matter. Abdulsaleh and Worthington present financial behaviour of SMEs,[3] Roman shows country by country comparisons,[4] and Kersten et al. look at low income countries and policies towards SMEs[5], while Zabri et al. reference sustainability and owners/managers preferences,[6] and Macado focuses on growth of SMEs.[7] Some of the research taken into consideration considers both government-owned firms and private funding as well as behaviour of SMEs in the market. Sources of financing presented are among the most varied: from personal loans and friends' money, to venture capitalists and sales self-support. It can be argued that an SME can use all of them during its various development phases; shareholders' own money or business angels are

[3] Abdulsaleh, A.M., and Worthington, A.C. (2013). *Small and Medium-Sized Enterprises Financing: A Review of Literature*, in International Journal of Business and Management, Vol. 8, pp. 36–54.

[4] https://www.researchgate.net/publication/227462778_SMES'_SECTOR_ACCESS_TO_FINANCE_AN_OVERVIEW

[5] Kersten, R., Harms, J., Liket, K., and Maas, K. (2017). *Small firms, large impact? A system review of the SME finance literature*, in World Development, Vol. 97, pp. 330–348.

[6] Zabri, S., Yusoff, W., Ahmad, K., and Lean, J. (2017). *Literature Review on Financing Preferences among Small and Medium Enterprises*, Conference: The 29th International Business Information Management Association Conference. Sustainable Economic Growth, Education Excellence, and Innovation Management through Vision 2020. Available at https://www.researchgate.net/publication/318315680_Literature_Review_on_Financing_Preferences_among_Small_And_Medium_Enterprises

[7] Machado, H. (2016). *Growth of small businesses: A literature review and perspectives of studies*. Available at http://www.scielo.br/pdf/gp/v23n2/en_0104-530X-gp-0104-530X1759-14.pdf

typical to the start-up phase, progressing to more complicated financing schemes later on when the SME can be internationalised. Some authors counted sources and possibilities, while others even establish patterns of financing.[8] It looks like there are 13 ways of financing SMEs around the world, some of them typical to some communities only (even in Europe), like Islamic banking. Research discovered that financing is influenced by location of the firm, age, industry sector and legal structure. It is interesting that even where money and solutions do exist, between 70% and 90% of SMEs fail, and the most common among surviving ones are micro companies, under a million dollar equivalent capitalisation.[9]

Books on financing of SMEs are subject to many designs, as sometimes the situation in Europe is not properly considered, but rather regarded in comparison, Europe being a good model to be judged against and compared to. This may give the impression that EU SME titles are rarer to encounter; an opinion which is not necessarily true when reviewing contents of the books. On the economic and political situation of SMEs financing in Europe there are more general and more specific works, which in our case can be divided into three categories: books on (1) framing the EU economy for SMEs, (2) EU SMEs, and (3) EU SME financing. One general title simply reads as *Change in SMEs: Towards European Capitalism* by Bluhn and Smith. This book provides general understanding of varieties of capitalism in Europe and entrepreneurship in various Member States, presenting organisational cultures and corporate finance. For the second category of books, those framing the SME world, some representative titles are: *SME Performance: Separating Myth from Reality* by John Watson, or *SMEs, Unknown Stakeholder: Entrepreneurship in the political area* by Massimiliano Di Bitetto. Some critics may argue that books on SMEs are too narrow, generally considering and analysing only the smaller companies, including start-ups and sole-proprietor companies. In this way, the old fashioned perception still persists, contrary to the EU definition, which presents an SME of a certain economic standard. Considering the third category,

[8] Masiak, C., Moritz, A., and Lang, F. (2017). *Financing Patterns of European SMEs Revisited: An Updated Empirical Taxonomy and Determinants of SME Financing Clusters*, EIF Working Paper, No. 2017/40, European Investment Fund (EIF), Luxembourg. Available at http://www.eif.org/news_centre/publications/EIF_Working_Paper_2017_40.htm and Helwege, J., and Liang, N. (1996). *Is there a pecking order? Evidence from a panel of IPO firms*, in Journal of Financial Economics, Vol. 40(3), pp. 429–458.

[9] Nicole, T. (2016). *9 Different Kinds of SMEs Funding*, in the Entrepreneur. Available at https://www.entrepreneurmag.co.za/advice/funding/attracting-investors/sme-funding/, and UOB. (2018). *7 Ways SMEs can level up with budget. 2018 measures*. Available at https://www.uobgroup.com/business/inbusiness/article.html?id=7-ways-smes-can-level-up-with-budget-2018-measures and Kaminskaite, J. (2017). *Reducing the Failure Rate of SMEs*. Available at https://www.theseus.fi/bitstream/handle/10024/129581/Reducing-the-failure-rate-of-SMEs-Julija-Kaminskaite-thesis.pdf?sequence=1

books on access to finance by SMEs, one great title is The Customer-Funded Business: Start, Finance or Grow Your Business with Your Customers' Cash by John Mullins. This book is great when considering an organic way to grow your company from within the market, getting self-financed by a good sales strategy and more. Great case studies and even examples of day-to-day running of SMEs are provided. Other authors, including some contributors of this present book, would disagree with such an approach, favouring MTFs, or the more traditional bank-centred approach.

Before presenting some relevant books which primarily discuss our subject, it is worth mentioning that there is a special category of relevant books, practical but not that obvious, dealing with leadership, planning, self-development, and so on. A good publication is *Who Moved My Cheese?* by Spencer Johnson, which is a very good allegory of how business can be done, businesses 'sniffed for', and what sort of skills and mindset a businessman needs. From the same category: *The 4-Hour Workweek* by Timothy Ferriss and the 'oldies but goodies' Ricardo Semler's *Maverik and The Seven Day Weekend*. Extrapolating other classical titles, like *The Prince* by Niccolò Machiavelli, can be considered. Far too many academic business books present business as an easy-to-play game, creating the impression that anyone can do it. Business is something you can 'try at home' up to a certain level. However, at its heart, business takes place in a risk-taking environment, where scarcity exists, markets are not that rational, and even though win-win situations are the norm, overall the 'business industry' tends to be a zero-sum game that never ends. It is for this Machiavellian reason, *The Prince*, an old European classical, fits in. After all, when financing an SME, skilful managers, owners' credibility, and image-capital and networking may prove to be decisive, more than numbers shown in the balance sheet. Profit must be seen, whatever the means.[10]

An excellent contribution to the study of SMEs can be found in David Munro's *A guide to SME financing*, which in many ways has closed the gap between theory and practice. Munro's research is very consistent. The book has a holistic approach and concentrates not only on the entity of the SME as such, but also on the market, government funding and incubators. It also touches upon very important aspects inside SMEs: staff and staff training, how SMEs are being monitored by banks for repayments, customer issues and so on. It seems that there is a 'general' SME approach, as similar problems are noticed everywhere, but sometimes specific geographical places like North America, or the developing world: Nigeria and Malaysia are mentioned. The key issues SMEs face are bureaucratic, and bank processes that are the same ones applied

---

[10] Bogner, E. (2011). *Machiavelli: 16 lessons from the master manipulator*, in Business Insider, June 20. Available at https://www.businessinsider.com/machiavelli-the-prince-2011-5

to the big companies, leading to high transaction costs without sufficient collateral. Some chapters look like practical business guides, especially Chapter 4: 'An Outline of the Credit applications, Analysis and Approval Process' and Chapter 7: 'Documentation Loan Agreements and Documentary Requirements', as well as the appendix. These chapters are useful as general practical guides, providing an understanding of accounting notions, although the book does not have an IFRS or accounting perspective in general.

There are some 'solution' books that present and argue for various ways of getting financed, like alternative banking or crowdfunding, or others that look at inconsistences in the market and propose solutions. The book *SME Funding: The role of Shadow Banking and Alternative Funding Options by Oricchio et al.* presents SMEs and new credit risk models as viable channels. On this subject matter there are other great titles like *Bank 4.0* by Brett King, the *FINTECH book* by Susanne Chishti and Janos Barberis, as well as a variety on blockchain and ICOs.[11] *Crowdfunding for SMEs: A European Perspective* by Roberto Bottiglia and Flavio Pichler (eds.) presents the perspective of both funders and funded companies, and includes business context, how crowdfunding works, platforms, return associated with crowdfunding debt or equity, as well as business risks and legislation. Interestingly enough is that the author considers that legislation should protect the investor, which is the general view of scholars favouring IFRS. Other books look at the present situation and imagine improvements. *A Road Map to the Development of European SME Networks* by Agostino Villa and Dario Antonelli (eds.) discovered that there is not enough correlation and coordination among EU SMEs, among other problems, and how low wages may look like an advantage, but come at the cost of not very skilled labour.[12]

Many academic books address only 'beginner level'; complicated schemes of financing, buy-out strategies and hard knowledge tend to exist only outside academia, in the professional studies. Whether the academic world is proactive, while businesses and policymakers are reactive, or the other way around, is hard to assess. This happens because it is unsure if theory or practice came first, but the way it looks like is that it varies from case to case. For sure, nowadays it is hard to draw a clear-cut distinction between what is purely academic and what is professional, as the topics are closely related and often overlap. Policy is more

---

[11] FinTech Switzerland, *Top FinTech Books you must read.* Available at http://fintechnews.ch/top-fintech-books/

[12] Boreiko, D., *Alternative Finance: ICOs as new financing mechanism.* Available at URL https://www.researchgate.net/project/Alternative-Finance-ICOs-as-new-financing-mechanism

recognisable when it appears in official journals, but interpretations are provided by the other categories. To what extent literature goes in parallel with economic reality is hard to say, as in the first year of the global financial crisis of 2008, scholars concentrated on their established research, with a few reactions put in the context of the crises, risk management and so on. Interestingly enough, it seems that people who consider financing do not really use accounting reports, but reply on other sources, some of them being consultants' analyses of the accounts or even media reports, among other sources. Up to this point, academic literature and general entrepreneurial publications have been presented. The next section will show another dimension.

Professional Studies

Professional studies are bespoken studies made by certain organisations and associations. They are not always available to the public at large but rather limited to members of certain clubs, except the ones produced by think tanks, and companies on behalf of authorities. There are professional studies put forward by lobby organisations with particular methodologies and research undertaken to prove arguments, help clients, or exercise pressure. This last category was not taken into consideration in this literature review.

Professional studies are very interesting as they address professionals, politicians and advanced level of academia. First of all, the nature of information is different from the academic standard. Secondly, the information provided is very precise and tends to be timely, as data is collected from clients, providing a general picture of the industry overall and in effect pulling alarm signals, informing policymakers, and telling customers how well certain products or industries are doing. There is not too many publications generally available, as guild membership is required, or some sort of paid access. Thirdly, there is a difference between a professional study as such, and the use made of professional information. An SME annual report with numbers and portfolios of clients and any other information can serve professionals in very particular ways.

The European Association of Crafts, Small and Medium-Size Enterprises (UEAPME) is an example of an issuer of professional studies on SMEs and micro companies. They issue various papers, as there is no 'official' professional type of study. Even a press release done in accordance to the industry standards can be considered a professional communication. Otherwise, they have publications and position papers on horizontal policies and sectorial policies having joint positions with other organisations, or just comment letters from the perspective of their members to various EU policies. A great input provided is when educated opinions are launched to consultations, like comments to the European Commission's open consultation. In such a way professional studies have a say and potentially an influence on policies. It can be noticed among UEAPME publications, which are free access type, that they are a mix of reactive with proactive perspectives. Their comments relate to many issues concerning SMEs acting in certain industries like the food industry, chemical waste, or digital transformation, to aspects that affect all companies, like VAT, GDPR and working conditions. Statements on financial aspects of, for example, the Multiannual Financial Framework of the European Union are also provided. The role of such position papers is multiple. On the one hand, they give the professional association bargaining power in negotiating certain legal and economic positions for their members. On the other, professional studies can also present the best practices in the industry helping certain businesses to do better in their practice, possibly saving them time and money. When studies are well done, this gives more credibility and capital image via reports to outsiders. In comparison, the present book, is written from the practitioner's view, and therefore most of the chapters are professional writings. For instance, Horst Heitz in Chapter 3, representing the European SME Business Club (Member of SME Connect) looks specifically at how SMEs can obtain finance and the problems they encounter. It is very interesting to study the publications of the two organisations, European SME Business Club (Member of SME Connect) and The European Association of Crafts, Small and Medium Size Enterprises (UEAPME) in parallel, for a better insight into the world of SMEs.

Political Reports

Political reports are official reports presenting aggregated data, normally old, according to present time characteristics, featuring speedy development and continuous new information hungriness. It takes time for national governments and supranational institutions to check, gather, cumulate and present data. One characteristic of it is that official reports from the EU, OECD, and so forth are unbiased and cannot be suspected of vested interest or a certain intended business perspective.

Since 2000, the OECD has produced specific reports on SMEs, finance and entrepreneurship. Some of the earlier studies, for example the 2004 study, presented data collection only as an introduction.[13] Eventually, the situation

[13] OECD. (2004). *OECD Compendium on International and regional Bodies: Activities and initiatives related to small and medium-sized enterprises (SMEs)*. Available at https://www.oecd.org/cfe/smes/

was corrected as huge interest surrounded SMEs started to develop, with even the G20 issuing a report on SME funding where problems were identified, and guidance for solutions was provided, along with sound financing principles.[14] The 2018 OECD report (considering 2016 data) presents good statistics and an industry scoreboard. In the 240 page-page report, 43 countries are analysed. The EU structures have the upper special place as EIB, EBRD and EC programmes are specifically mentioned and taken into consideration. This shows that SMEs nowadays act in a global world and the EU is having the lead. The OECD's 2018 SME scoreboard mentions Australia, for example, where the situation has improved: bankruptcy at SME level has recently dropped by one third. Part of the private oriented useful global information on crowdfunding includes, of course, government perspective on credit guarantee schemes. One leading example is China, where in 2016 a total of $240 billion was provided by venture capitalists in their extended forms to SMEs. One interesting aspect discovered by a performed survey analysis is that credit conditions are better, and SMEs are traditionally considering this option; however, demand is diminishing as other options are available.

The European Commission is a lawmaking body, creating policies for easing access to funding, but it also provides certain funding opportunities in specific forms like loans, equity funding, and so on, via the so called EU funds—about 55 of them, one example being Horizon 2020. A number of the funding programmes are connected with the EIB and EIF and also with private banks. Some of the programmes are mentioned in the present book as well, specifically in Heitz's chapter and Psarrakis and Kaili's. Notable programmes include: (1) COSME is a more general programme aimed to finance SMEs at various stages of existence, connecting the EU level with local level, as local financial institutions are responsible for the programme. (2) The European Fund for Strategic Investments has a 5.5 billion euro budget for SMEs with a risker profile, aiming at innovation, and has two types of financing: funding or guarantee provided. (3) InnovFin is for innovators, but this programme scales up and connects to EIB and EIF, where advisory services are also provided. (4) EU Programmes for Employment and Social innovation (EaSI) aims at sustainability in employment for vulnerable groups, and has a budget of 919,469,000 euros for the period 2014–2020. The social dimension of this programme is important, as on one hand it fights poverty, and on the other addresses some

2090691.pdf and OECD. (2004). *Promoting entrepreneurship and innovative SMEs in global economy*. Available at https://www.oecd.org/cfe/smes/31919278.pdf

[14] OECD/G20. (2015). *High Level principles on SMEs financing*. Available at http://www.oecd.org/finance/G20-OECD-High-Level-Principles-on-SME-Financing.pdf

of the labour problems mentioned in some articles. (5) The Cultural and Creative Sector Guarantee Facility offers loans for cultural heritage, film production, libraries and more. Similarly to the rest of the programmes, it runs up until 2020.[15] Sometimes official information does not directly reach citizens, as channels are not in place, or the citizen himself is not very interested in accessing institutional information. Elected politicians, like Members of the European Parliament in their capacity and work have better contact with people, professional associations, and companies via meetings or information sessions. Three MEPs spread knowledge, providing guidance and better understanding on the EU funding. MEP Dan Buda's activity guide for the years 2014–2016 promoted a European Commission Guide for EU funding opportunities tailored on farmers' needs, SMEs, NGOs and public authorities.[16] Similarly, MEPs Cristian Buşoi and Mihai Ţurcanu created a guide addressing larger and multiple domains. One specific chapter is on SMEs and further guidance to online application to finance is provided.[17]

Part II

Financial Reporting

The IFRS for SMEs literature is more recent than SMEs funding one, as IFRS for SMEs was publically realised as of 2009, after five years of conception (draft presented in 2007). The IFRS for SMEs standards were amended in 2015 generating fresh information and literature. To date, studies show that there are mixed feelings on the use of IFRS for SMEs in both professional and academic literature. This happens due to the heterogeneous world of SMEs encompassing both small and larger type of companies. It is worth mentioning that some studies do not criticise IFRS for technical reasons (some studies do), but rather for the governance arrangements surrounding it, or political (in the large sense) motives.

The financial reporting standards issued by the IASB are of greater interest to practitioners like chartered accountants, financial analysts, CFOs, and pos-

[15] European Commission. *Overview of funding programmes*. Available at https://ec.europa.eu/info/funding-tenders/funding-opportunities/funding-programmes/overview-funding-programmes_en

[16] Dan Buda, MEP. (2016). Raport de Activitate si Ghid de Finanțare UE. Available at http://www.danielbuda.ro/ro/raport-de-activitate-2014-2016/ [Romanian Language].

[17] Cristian Buşoi, MEP. (2016). *Ghid pentru accesarea fondurilor europene*. Available at http://www.cristianbusoi.eu/publicatii/

sibly managers for obvious money reasons, and to academics for educational, technical and even moral matters. Recent financial reporting theory mentions that accounting can be of interest even to society at large, borrowing from the stakeholder theory perspective. Some studies even look at moral hazard and impacts of IFRS over stability,[18] a large number of studies analyse harmonization[19] with local GAAP, cost of debt before and after,[20] and regulation of IFRS.[21] Some scholars and professionals criticise IFRS for SMEs for technical reasons, other for its systemic approach, while others for the political arrangements surrounding the IASB. It is worth mentioning that all the studies on IFRS including the academic ones, due to the nature of IFRS, are first of all technical and empirical, with the possibility to be driven into more theoretical approaches.[22]

Books on IFRS for SMEs

Considering the nature, novelty, technicality and niche of IFRS for SMEs, the academic books are rather limited. Before we mention some books of interest, one book in particular needs to be mentioned at least due to the information offered and perspective: *Financial Statement Analysis: A practitioner's guide* by Martin Fridson.[23] Otherwise, *Full IFRS and IFRS for SMEs Adoption by Private Firms: Empirical Evidence on Country Level* by Maximilian Saucke is among the available titles. This book was originally Saucke's PhD thesis and therefore follows strict academic criteria with hypothesis development, clearly delimiting the field of research and providing research design, methodology, discussions and empirical results. As mentioned in the title, the focus is not solely IFRS for SMEs but also full IFRS. Also, the book surpasses the boundaries of

---

[18] Andersson, T., Haslam, C., Tsitsianis, N., Katechos, G., and Hoinaru, R. (2016). *Stress testing International Financial Reporting Standards (IFRSs): Accounting for stability and the public good in a financialized world*, in Accounting, Economics and Law – a Convivium, Vol. 6(2), pp. 93–118.

[19] Baldarelli, M. (2012). *Accounting harmonization for SMEs in Europe: Some remarks on IFRS for SMEs and empirical evidences*, Economic Research – Ekonomska Istrazivanja, Vol. 25(1), pp. 1–26.

[20] Bauwhede, H., and Cauwenberge, P. (2015). *Financial reporting quality and the cost of debt of SMEs.* Small Business Economics, Vol. 45(1), pp. 149–164.

[21] Di Pietra, R., McLeay S., and Ronen, J. (Eds.) (2014). *Accounting and Regulation. New Insights on Governance, Markets and Institutions.* New York, London: Springer, 412pp.

[22] Devrimi, K., and Koch, M. (2015). *Countries' Adoption of the International Financial Reporting Standard for Small and Medium-Sized Entities (IFRS for SMEs) – Early Empirical Evidence*, Accounting and Business Research, Vol. 45(1), pp. 93–120. Quagli, A., et al. (2010). *How is the IFRS for SME Accepted in the European Context? An Analysis of the Homogeneity Among European Countries, Users and Preparers in the European Commission Questionnaire*, in Advances in Accounting, Vol. 28(1).

[23] Alvarez, F., and Fridson, M. (2011). *Financial Statement Analysis: A Practitioner's Guide.* New Jersey: John Wiley & Sons, 378pp.

the EU, touching upon the USA,[24] Canada, South Africa and other IFRS jurisdictions, at times drawing parallels with what the author calls Big GAAP and Little GAAP, harmonisation and cost of compliance. The book starts by looking at the history of IFRS for SMEs, why it appeared and how it developed, and continues with key drivers for its adoption and private sector acceptance. The public sector is considered to some extent, as with the existence of the IASB there has been a loss of legislative sovereignty. In this sense, the economic networks and relationship among companies from different countries seemed to have improved due to IFRS. Considering the use of IFRS for SMEs, five type of users are identified: banks, vendors, credit rating agencies, customers and SME shareholders (that are not managers of the company) and this constitutes a large part of the argument. Towards the end, some of the classical accounting debates are considered, like the classical stewardship vs. decision usefulness in regard to IFRS use. Arguments lean more towards the stewardship side in the specific case of IFRS for SMEs, even though the IASB does not necessarily have a tendency to see the two concepts as conflicting, but rather complementary.[25]

A book properly concentrating on IFRS for SMEs with EU country by country is *Harmonization of SME's Financial Reporting in emerging CEE countries*, edited by Jiri Strouhal. The book looks at seven countries which are not among the commonly researched ones, like Estonia, Latvia, Lithuania, Czech Republic, Poland, Slovakia and Romania, plus an extra dimension of worldwide globalisation process. The book has a very practical approach with quotes from national legislations, and pictures of how actual balance sheets look. The driving force of analysis is the shift of paradigm between HCA and FVA as well as parallels between national and international legislation; the two chapters at the beginning and the end giving a complete understanding.[26] Somehow similar, an interesting piece of writing is the book *Applying IFRS for SMEs* by Bruce Macenzi et al. The book is authored mainly by professionals that are consultants, directors and partners at various companies in the world. One of the authors, Danie Coetsee, is Professor of accounting at the University of Johannesburg. In the general description of the book it can be read that 'this important book includes comprehensive coverage of this

[24] Similarly to full IFRS in the US IFRS for SMEs is permitted to be used by non-domestic companies, though rarely opted for.

[25] Gassen, J. (2007). Are stewardship and decision usefulness complementary of conflicting objectives of financial accounting? Available at http://sfb649.wiwi.hu-berlin.de/fedc/events/Motzen07/gassen.pdf

[26] Strouhal, J. (2011). Harmonization of SME's Financial Reporting in Emerging CEE Countries, WSEAS Press. Available at http://www.wseas.us/e-library/conferences/2011/Strouhal/Strouhal.pdf

recently issued standard aimed at small and medium-sized business', being most probably the first book in the market on applied IFRS for SMEs standard. In effect, the book has 30 chapters and an index and looks at all the standards. Accordingly, the book can be considered professional, but technical would be a more appropriate word.

A notable study for two reasons is *IFRS for European Small and Medium-sized Entities? A Theoretical and Empirical Analysis* by two Professors: Rolf Uwe Fülbier and Joachim Gassen. This study was commissioned from outside academia and has both perspectives. An academic overview as well as quantitative research on the usefulness of IFRS for SMEs, takes into account two layer of analysis: firms' needs and country-by-country organisational infrastructure. This happens because SMEs are individual companies with different management styles and behaviours, very heterogeneous as a whole, acting in regulated capital markets. This double perspective is important especially as IASB is a private body setting financial reporting standards for companies in various states. The study has two main parts: characteristics of SMEs and their needs, followed by objectives of financial reporting: contracting (stewardship) vs. valuation. The research results are interesting as they show a tendency of IFRS standards to incline to a valuation perspective, contrary to Saucke's research results. The other conclusion mentions that mandatory IFRS for SMEs seems impossible for now and the standards as such are only good when the cost of harmonisation is smaller than the benefits. In this sense, harmonisation is a process and a result, not the beginning point as some may think. In the end, country to country governance, legislation, SMEs' needs and business infrastructure are different one from the other.[27]

Professional Studies

Professional studies on IFRS can be divided into four categories; namely, publications by (1) the issuers: the IASB and IFRS Foundation, (2) publications by accounting professional organisations like the IFAC, ICAEW, ANC, (3) publications by the Big 4 and other similar firms; and (4) publications by other professional associations. As a general characteristic, professional studies with few exceptions are very concise and up to the point in plain technical language. Next, we look at exemplifications of all of these categories.

Any professional study on IFRS for SMEs starts with the standard as such. The IASB is an industry self-regulator setter that issues and amends the

[27] Gassen, J., and Fülbier, R. (2010). *IFRS for European Small and Medium-Sized Entities? A Theoretical and Empirical Analysis.* Available at https://dgrv.de/webde.nsf/272e312c8017e736c1256e31005cedff/df403f6ea057d8dac12577c800441300/$FILE/DGRV_IFRS_fuer_KMU.pdf

standard as well as providing derived publications such as fact sheets, newsletters and so forth. In the same categories, EFRAG issues studies on IFRSs. According to this institution, good practices consultations were done at various stages, discussions, exposure drafts and so on. EFRAG has some studies of its own, while others are in partnerships, like the one with Mazars.[28] EFRAG's studies have a double role, that of consulting the private sector, and providing advice to the European Parliament. This literature review will not look in detail at these studies as two prominent members, Darrel Scott, Board Member to IASB and Andrew Watchman, EFRAG's CEO have contributed a chapter to the present book. Interesting research from a professional perspective is that of ANC's,[29] a couple of studies by ACCA articles, meant to help practitioners in their work, but also ICAEW's studies and Talk Accountancy debates.[30]

An important category of studies on IFRS are those done by Big 4. Scanning through the literature, two common types can be identified: either presenting IFRS for SMEs by itself, of in comparison with full IFRS. Certain similarities in the information presented can be tracked, as the originating source is the same. IFRSs being principle-based, certain interpretations are allowed which account for some differences, as well as structure and presentation design. Also, the perspective is different and some studies mention where the standards apply, while others take the opposite approach, listing some situations where the standards do not apply. One way or another, high clarity and quality information is being provided. One such study issued by Deloitte can be found in this book. The purpose of the chapter is to provide an overview of the IFRS for SMEs to enable users that have already adopted IFRSs to understand the key differences between the IFRS for SMEs and full IFRSs. PricewaterhouseCoopers has an alternative one. One very important mention about the study and their image of SMEs can be read at the beginning of the paper: '…is therefore based on the nature of an entity rather than on its size'. Their perspective is similar to IASB's, that the standard was needed for costs reasons for disclosure, as non-listed companies are different from larger firms. Their perspective is one of preparers and apart from the technicalities which

[28] Mazars. (2005). *The IFRS for SMEs accounting standard: Perceptions and expectations across Europe*. Available at https://www.mazars.co.th/Home/News/Our-publications/Publications/Surveys/The-IFRS-for-SMEs-accounting-standard

[29] ANC. (2007). *ED IFRS for SMEs*. Available at http://www.anc.gouv.fr/files/live/sites/anc/files/contributed/ANC/2.%20Normes%20internationales/NI%202007/IASB_2007ED_ifrs_sme.pdf

[30] Deloitte. (2007). *ACCA detailed summary of proposed IFRS for SMEs*. Available at https://www.iasplus.com/en/news/2007/August/news3157

are taken from the standard, this study gives a hint that it is a political matter if IFRSs for SMEs are allowed to be used in certain jurisdictions.[31] Other examples are BDO's publication, which issued a straight-to-the-point study named *IFRS for SMEs at a Glance* as of 1 July 2015 showing new developments, slightly differentiating from other studies,[32] or EY's.[33]

Among the great firm networks, Grant Thornton issued a special edition on IFRS for SMEs in 2015 due to the IASB review, commenting on amendments on taxation and the bridge done with IAS 12 on Income Tax, the time taken to make the changes, and being appreciative as more guidance is being provided for preparation.[34] More extended studies were done by Mazars (with EFRAG) and respectively PKF. *The IFRS for SMEs Accounting Standard: Perception and Expectations across Europe* surveyed 1500 SMEs from France, Germany, Italy, the Netherlands, Spain and the UK to reveal some interesting aspects:

- Banks are this the biggest finance provider to SMEs: 92% In Italy, 86% in Germany, 71% in the UK.
- Companies favour the adoption of IFRS for SMEs, though certain countries prefer their own ways.
- Companies favour IFRS for SMEs for transparency and comparability.
- IFRS for SMEs provides a reduction in costs.
- IFRS for SMEs may improve their relations with board business partners, as one account language is being used.
- National standard-setter plan to converge with IFRS for SMEs.
- SMEs are the most concerned with (1) impairments and (2) various tax legislation in different countries.

PKF present their study from a totally different perspective. They do not even try to look at the market, or aggregate data and analysis, but invent a company and show practical accounting with imagined business, presenting complementary notes and source references. Useful information on accounting policies,

[31] PwC. (2009). *IFRS for small and medium-sized entities Pocket guide 2009*. Available at https://www.pwc.com/gx/en/ifrs-reporting/pdf/ifrssme09.pdf

[32] BDO. (2015). *IFRS for Smes at a glance at 1 July 2015*. Available at https://www.bdo.global/getmedia/8760a193-5417-4497-84c7-a77d412d1006/IFRS-for-SMEs-at-a-Glance_July2015.pdf.aspx

[33] EY. (2010). *IFRS for small and medium-sized entities A comparison with IFRS—the basics*. Available at https://www.ey.com/Publication/vwLUAssets/IFRS_for_SMEs_Comparison/%24FILE/IFRS_for_SMEs_Comparison.pdf

[34] Grant Thornton. (2015). The IFRS for SMEs. Available at https://www.grantthornton.global/en/insights/articles/the-ifrs-for-smes/

estimation uncertainty and judgements is also provided. In addition to the 'hands-on' business guide, finance cost, profit before tax, income tax, inventories, provisioning, disposal of assets, etc. are presented individually.[35]

Political Literature

This section could have been integrated into the professional literature part; however, due to the slightly different nature of political thinking and political decision-making it was kept separate. Politics, after all, is defined by its coercive force, and even law and impact study assessments created by professionals are somewhat different. Later on, EU institutions papers will be looked at.

The European Commission launched a four-month consultation on IFRS for SMEs in 2009. More than 200 responses were achieved, from four categories: users, preparers, public authorities and accountants. The vast majority of them showed 'linkage between taxation and capital maintenance rules' creating problems of double reporting and increased costs as well as some potential difficulties with the Accounting Directive. Also, commenters that did not favour IFRS for SMEs considered the size of most of SMEs and feared not only high costs, but also the complexity of the reports. Companies that were acting internationally and seeking international finance had a different approach favouring the standard for its benefits in terms of transparency and comparability. Interestingly, there were divergent opinions not only among companies, but also among public authorities from the same country and other EU ones. Some Member States were thinking along the same lines as their SMEs.[36]

A second one was done in 2015, when desk research was combined with surveys. This time the study was conducted by EY for the European Commission. It was acknowledged that SMEs accounting practices have to be addressed and red tape cut, while retaining high quality information. Not surprisingly, the study revealed that small SMEs were not in favour considering administrative burden for nothing. They did not see any need for producing more information; however, for micro entities a need for better reporting on profit and loss was discovered.[37] Overall, even though not explicitly stated

[35] PKF. (2015). *IFRS for SMEs illustrative consolidated financial statements*. Available at http://www.pkf.com/media/10031232/ifrs-for-smes-illustrative-financial-statements-standard-eff-1-january-2017.pdf

[36] European Commission. (2010). *Summary Report of the responses received to the Commission's Consultations on the international financial reporting for small and medium-sized entities*. Available at https://www.iasplus.com/en/binary/europe/1005smeconsultationsummary.pdf

[37] European Commission. (2015). *Accounting guide for SMEs – SME Accounting in Europe: Insights provided by a desk research and a survey*. Available at https://ec.europa.eu/growth/content/accounting-guide-smes-sme-accounting-europe-insights-provided-desk-research-and-survey-0_en

as such in the two studies, suggestions lean towards a 'no' approach of the Commission to IFRS for SMEs, the same opinion being shared by the European Central Bank.[38]

The European Parliament issued its own studies, similarly to the European Commission and European Central Bank. MEP Radwan in 2009 considered that IFRS for SMEs is 'far too complicated for most of them'; however, he recognised the need for such a standard for larger companies, calling on the Commission to conduct research on it.[39] In 2015, the option of IFRS for SMEs to be used by such entities quoted on MTFs was considered realistically, but on a voluntary basis and to be explored further by the Commission and the IASB.[40]

Similar Publications to Our Research

One article similar in research to this book is 'Private Company Finance and Financial Reporting' by Ole-Kristian Hope and Dushyantkumar Vyas. The article succeeds in connecting the two parts, looking at debt financing and especially bank financing, equity financing, family ownership and private equity, as well as trade credit and IFRS. Data was not easily available as aggregated information for non-listed companies required a lot of work. There are multiple conclusions attached to this article. The most general one is that the SME world is very heterogeneous world where SMEs go their own way in terms of management of capital, financing and financial reporting needs. Of benefit for research and knowledge is that the minority shareholders situation is also addressed. From an IFRS perspective, the obvious was finally stated: preparers and investors think differently in terms of financial reporting needs.

The IFAC has one study on the *Relationship between Accountancy Expertise and Business Performance.* It is interesting that the study mentions non-financial performance as well as financial performance and considers accountants as part of a company's success and that good accounting practices may lead to higher accomplishments. The study conducted by researchers at the Bucharest

[38] European Central Bank. (2015). *Building a Capital Markets Union – Eurosystem contribution to the European Commission's Green Paper.* Available at https://www.ecb.europa.eu/pub/pdf/other/150521_eurosystem_contribution_to_green_paper_-_building_a_cmuen.pdf

[39] European Parliament. (2008). *Strong criticism of the International Accounting Standards Board's governance.* Available at http://www.europarl.europa.eu/sides/getDoc.do?pubRef=-//EP//TEXT+IM-PRESS+20080410BRI26349+ITEM-024-EN+DOC+XML+V0//EN&language=SK

[40] Ibid.

University of Economic Studies (ASE) looked at 90 studies, surveys and other data. The IFAC study starts by doing a differentiation, mentioning large SMEs as a special category. Findings show that companies using proper accounts in a proper way are performing better. It concludes that 'specifically organizational development and performance lead to an increase utilization of accountancy expertise, and accountancy expertise leads to superior performance development'.[41]

Instead of a Conclusion: Recapitulation

This chapter looked at access to funding for SMEs and IFRSs for SMEs, in order not only to provide further reading titles and to provide a unitary understanding of the two subjects and interactions, but also to position our book in the literature. It proved that, to date, not many studies are similar to ours, the authors of this chapter being capable of identifying only two of them: one academic article and one professional study conducted by academics. Some other studies looked at growth accounting and how manipulation of earnings connects with business economics, a perspective which is interesting, but different to ours. In this sense, our practitioners' approach on financing and financial reporting is rather unique in the literature.

Among the interesting aspects of conducting this literature review was to see the multitude of approaches of thinking and research designs. Not all the articles read were mentioned, but among the good reads scholars were connecting financing with marketing,[42] while others with innovation[43] or policy.[44] Considering IFRSs, various practitioners and academics went from highly technical design and empirical studies to scanning thought literature and establishing connections, fostering debate. Challenges existed as many

---

[41] IFAC. (2016). *Research Insights—Accountancy Expertise and Business Performance*. Available at URL https://www.ifac.org/global-knowledge-gateway/performance-financial-management/discussion/research-insights-accountancy

[42] Hogarth-Scott, S., et al. (1996). *Do small businesses have to practice marketing to survive and grow?* in Marketing Intelligence & Planning, Vol. 14(1), pp. 6–18. And in Parry, S. (2012). *Marketing for survival: A comparative case study of SME software firms*, in Journal of Small Business and Enterprise Development, Vol. 19(4). Available at https://www.researchgate.net/publication/262966360_Marketing_for_survival_A_comparative_case_study_of_SME_software_firms

[43] Hausman, A. (2005). *Innovativeness Among Small Businesses: Theory and Propositions for Future Research*, in Industrial Marketing Management, Vol. 34(8), pp. 773–782. And in O'Dwyer et al. (2009). *Innovative marketing in SMEs: An empirical study*, in Journal of Strategic Marketing, Vol. 17(5), pp. 383–396.

[44] Eshima, Y. (2003). *Impact of Public Policy on Innovative SMEs in Japan*, in Journal of Small Business Management, Vol. 41(1), pp. 85–93.

professional studies are limited to members only. Also, it was a challenge to decide where to place some articles as, for instance, EY conducted researched ordered by the European Commission, or some publications could have passed as academic but also as professional, due to their high degree of technical and somewhat similar users such students of accounting practice and young professionals.

All in all, this chapter provided a fresh literature review, as the literatures we identified were at least three years old, and so we brought this up to date. This chapter does not provide a conclusion as such, because our thoughts have been saved for the concluding chapter of the entire book, where the question stated by ICAEW: 'Is IFRS for SMEs, good for SMEs?' will be answered.

Part I

Financing

2

The Role of the State in the Innovation Triangle: Law and Policy Fostering the Optimal Regulatory, Business and Innovation Policy Environment

Pēteris Zilgalvis

This chapter will address the role of the state in the "Innovation Triangle" of regulatory, business and innovation policy; for example, in the area of fintech and related technologies that stretch beyond finance, such as blockchain/distributed ledger technologies (DLT). The economic competitiveness of the European Union and its Member States, and their ability to further develop and maintain a 'good society' that creates possibilities for citizens to thrive depend on a conducive environment for all types of innovation.

Joseph Schumpeter's theory of "creative destruction" describes how in capitalist economies, innovations provide new and often unforeseen sources of economic growth, while displacing existing companies and industries.[1] Professor Schumpeter wrote, "This process of Creative Destruction is the essential fact about capitalism. It is what capitalism consists in and what every capitalist concern has got to live in.[2]" In a dynamic economy, poorly managed companies with a lack of something new to offer should see their places taken by more innovative and productive competitors.

[1] Schumpeter, J. (2009). *Can Capitalism Survive? Creative Destruction and the Future of the Global Economy*, New York: Harper Collins Publishers, originally published as *Capitalism, Socialism, and Democracy* by Harper & Row, New York, 1942.

[2] Ibid., pp. 42–43.

P. Zilgalvis (✉)
European Commission, Brussels, Belgium
e-mail: Peteris.ZILGALVIS@ec.europa.eu

E. Kaili et al. (eds.), *New Models of Financing and Financial Reporting for European SMEs*,
https://doi.org/10.1007/978-3-030-02831-2_2

While manufacturing and the jobs it provides are an important part of an innovation ecosystem, policymakers should not try to preserve or subsidise all existing companies, industries or jobs at any cost, but to forge an economic and social environment conducive to innovation. As André Sapir and Reinhilde Veugelers of the Bruegel Think Tank have written, "Europe needs innovative firms that operate in activities with a high value-added and participate in European and global value chains."[3]

Many commentators and economists have stated that the rate of innovation in the "West" has fallen over recent years. For example, Professor Edmund Phelps, winner of the 2006 Nobel Memorial Prize in Economic Sciences, argued in his recent book that "Mass Flourishing"[4]—noting the financing being provided to new and innovative enterprises—is insufficient. Both Professor Phelps and Professor Mariana Mazzucato have noted the rise of short-termism in business and finance, with the result that private "patient capital" with a long-term view in finance has become increasingly rare.[5] Further, one can observe that many of innovation's "low-hanging fruits" in areas like ICT and transport, for instance, have already been plucked. Investor Peter Thiel has also argued that technological progress halted at the end of the 1960s,[6] saying "We wanted flying cars, instead we got 140 characters," speaking of the incremental nature and lower ambition of most recent innovations.

The areas that are most ripe for innovation today are those like finance, education, health and climate change/energy, which are often characterised by high levels of regulation, and in some cases by state provision, procurement (including public procurement of innovation—PPI, and pre-commercial procurement—PCP), the need for long-term planning and programmes. Therefore, in these areas, which are so promising for future innovation, substantial state involvement is inevitable and it is important that it be mobilised as a positive factor, supporting innovation.

---

[3] Sapir, A., and Veugelers, R. (2013). *Manufacturing Europe's Growth*, in European Voice, 31 October 2013, p. 13.

[4] Phelps, E. (2013). *Mass Flourishing*, Princeton and Woodstock: Princeton University Press; and the Distinguished Lecture at the Sheldonian Theatre, University of Oxford on 17 October 2013. Politicians have also sounded this alarm; see George Osborne quoted as saying, "Look at innovation, where Europe's share of world patent applications nearly halved in the last decade", *The Guardian*, politics, "Reform EU or Britain quits - George Osborne lays down ultimatum", 15 January 2014.

[5] Mazzucato, M. (2013). *The Entrepreneurial State*, London: Anthem Press, pp. 26–27; and the Economics Department lecture at the London School of Economics on 8 October 2013, accessed at www.richmedia.lse.ac.uk

[6] Financial Times, *Lunch with the FT: Peter Thiel*, December 21/December 22, p. 3, Life & Arts.

Meanwhile the rate of innovation and related manufacturing is rising in the "development states" of Asia. Writing about competitors to the United States, Robert D. Atkinson and Stephen J. Ezell stated, "Other nations have put in place the tax, trade, talent and technology policies both to draw in and to grow innovation and productivity-enhancing investment.[7]"

From the 1940s to the 1960s, economists such as Friedrich Hayek and Joseph Schumpeter had to expend much energy and many pages of their tomes such as *The Road to Serfdom*, *The Constitution of Liberty*, and *Can Capitalism Survive?* to answer the claims made for the superiority of statist domination of the economy and to defend the vital role of the entrepreneur in a dynamic economy. It is indicative that even on the right of the centre of the political spectrum at that time, British Prime Minister Edward Heath stated, "I fear that to place one's faith in some invisible hand, rather than to grapple with problems with determination, is a failure of the human spirit. What distinguishes man from animals is his desire and his ability to control and to shape his environment.[8]" However, it is a vast oversimplification to say that Adam Smith himself believed only in an "invisible hand" regulating all. He said that according to the system of natural liberty, one of the duties of the sovereign was that of "erecting and maintaining certain public works, and certain public institutions, which it can never be for the interest of any individual, or small number of individuals to erect and maintain."[9] Regarding the topical issue of inequality, which is also of more than minor relevance to innovation policy, Adam Smith wrote, "No society can surely be flourishing and happy, of which the far greater part of the members are poor and miserable."[10]

Today the ideological pendulum often seems to have swung in the other direction to the extent that a discourse on the subject may start with the premise that the only role for the state in the economy of innovation is at the most in funding basic research, addressing "market failures" and lowering corporate taxes. It can be questioned whether the experience with innovation in

---

[7] Atkinson, R., and Ezell, S. (2012). *Innovation Economics: The Race for Global Advantage*, New Haven and London: Yale University Press, p. 31.

[8] Ziegler, P. (2010). *Edward Heath*, London: Harper Press, p. 71.

[9] Smith, A. (2010). *The Wealth of Nations: The Economics Classic*, UK: Capstone, p. 298.

[10] Ibid., p. 88. Nobel Prize laureate in Economic Sciences, Amartya Sen, wrote in his introduction to the 250th Anniversary Edition of Adam Smith's "The Theory of Moral Sentiments", Smith "rejected *market-excluding* interventions but not *market-including* interventions aimed at doing those important things that the market may leave undone." Penguin Books, New York, 2009, p. xiii.

Europe and the United States in the past and today, and in Asia recently, would justify such a premise. It is important that policy rest on a foundation of evidence and facts, and not simply ideology.

Taking the example of the once fabulously innovative and now defunct AT&T's Bell Labs from the United States, often presented as a free market citadel state in the past and today, it is "the received wisdom that innovation and competitiveness are closely linked. Companies that are good at innovating are good at competing in the market; the uncompromising nature of the market, in turn, is a powerful force on companies to innovate. But Bell Labs' history demonstrates that the truth is actually far more complicated. It also suggests that we tend to misinterpret the role of markets."[11] To justify an ambitious state role in innovation, the examples of the government-developed technologies that make the iPhone "smart", namely, the Internet, GPS, SIRI and the touch screen,[12] the track record of the Pentagon's Defense Advanced Research Projects Agency (DARPA) in general,[13] and the funding of the Google algorithm by the National Science Foundation in the United States[14] can be cited.

Therefore, the role of the state in either fostering or hampering innovation is an important and timely subject in need of analysis, reflection and discussion. This chapter will focus on two aspects of state and private sector interaction: firstly, that of public/private collaboration in fostering innovation and, secondly, drawing out ways in which an innovation-friendly policy stance can be taken by regulatory bodies in regard to new initiatives being developed by private actors, such as in the area of fintech and blockchain/distributed ledger technologies. A sub-theme will be how the Internet has changed the context and framework of innovation policy in the public and private sectors and in the networks where they both are present.

[11] Gertner, J. (2012). *The Idea Factory: Bell Labs and the Great Age of American Innovation*, New York: Penguin Books, p. 352.

[12] Mazzucato, M. (2013). The Entrepreneurial State in Chapter 5 – The State behind the iPhone, pp. 87–112.

[13] Dugan, R., and Gabriel, K. (2013). *Special Forces Innovation: How DARPA Attacks Problems*, in Harvard Business Review, October, pp. 74–76.

[14] National Science Foundation, *On the Origins of Google*. Available at http://www.nsf.gov/discoveries/disc_summ.jsp?cntn_id=100660, accessed on 27/12/2013.

What Is Innovation?

A definition of innovation and the type(s) of innovation under discussion is a good starting point; otherwise, the term can easily become a catch-all signifying everything and at the same time, little of practical applicability. Firstly, innovation discussed in this chapter is more than science or the production of new commercially marketed products.[15] Research is an input of innovation. The OECD defines innovation as "the implementation of a new or significantly improved product (good or service), process, a new marketing method, or a new organizational method in business practices, workplace organisation or external relations."[16] The observation of Eugene Gordon, Bell Labs development scientist, can supplement this definition: "If you have not manufactured the new thing in substantial quantities, you have not innovated; the second is that if you haven't found a market, you have not innovated."[17]

The scope of this analysis encompasses public sector and social innovation, so consequently if the "new thing" or new process cannot actually be implemented in a societal context or in public services then one has not innovated; if it cannot be replicated in other similar societal contexts or public services, then one has not innovated. This can be considered especially relevant in assessing the utilisation of the concept of "smart failure" in a public sector innovation context. If this approach is to be rolled out widely in order to endorse experimentation for better performance of public services it is essential that the freedom to act of the civil servants concerned is not simply at the whim of a benevolent superior but is structurally part of the system and is included in standard operating procedures.

There are problems faced by countries and their citizens that because of their size and complexity require a mobilisation of societal and economic actors beyond solely the state or the market and both a long-term strategy and long-term risky financing. They can be labelled societal challenges and include climate change/movement to a clean and green economy, financial inclusion, education and addressing the demographic changes that are putting the sustainability of health and social care in Europe into question.

---

[15] Fagerberg, J., Mowery, D., and Verspagen, B. (2009). *The focus on the economic exploitation of knowledge. Innovation, Path Dependency, and Policy: The Norwegian Case*, Oxford University Press, p. 3.

[16] The OECD Innovation Strategy (Paris, 2010), Oslo Guidelines for Collecting and Interpreting Innovation Data (2005), accessed at www.oecd.org on 15/12/2013.

[17] Gertner, J. (2012). *The Idea Factory: Bell Labs and the Great Age of American Innovation*, New York: Penguin Books, pp. 18–19.

The State Leading Innovation

There are multiple examples where the public sector can take an active role in funding and supporting innovation. The EU multi-annual research and innovation programme Horizon 2020[18] has introduced instruments taking novel approaches to close the "innovation gap" such as inducement prizes, support to innovative procurement, the Fast Track to Innovation scheme, access to finance and the Open Disruptive Innovation Scheme. The European Commission supports the Startup Europe partnership to network Europe's leading innovation ecosystems, and links them to other markets such as Silicon Valley, and India, Latin America and Africa.

Business Policy

Additionally, business policy at the regional, national and European levels should foster innovation as part of a dynamic economy. Removing barriers to setting up startups, bankruptcy procedures to allow entrepreneurs to risk again, and initiatives like the Startup Europe programme and the European Commission's Communication on a Startup and Scale-up Initiative in 2016 serve to support a conducive business environment. The Communication underlines the role that instruments like regulatory sandboxes can play in ensuring that innovators can test new solutions while other public policy goals are achieved. This is discussed below in the section on the state as a regulator.

The network of law incubators to assist startups with the legal advice that they need to get their venture off the ground that was initiated and funded by the European Commission is another example of ways in which an innovation-friendly business environment can be encouraged and sustained.

This type of environment should be welcoming to SMEs and to larger industry as well as to consumer-innovators. Barriers should not be placed in the path of consumers creating in the new consumer-innovator paradigm, and the use of the Internet to harness this power should be actively encouraged.[19] The state can also best support worthy businesses directly using tools

[18] Europe Commission, *Horizon 2020*, Available at URL ec.europa.eu/research/horizon2020/, accessed on 17/12/2013.

[19] Hippel, E., Ogawa, S., and De Jong, J. (2001). *The Age of the Consumer-Innovator: Why It's Time to Rethink Product Development*, in MIT Sloan Management Review, Fall 2011, Vol. 53(1), p. 29. Their

like pre-commercial procurement and public procurement of innovation, rewarding those able to offer innovative solutions rather than simply supporting a class of businesses.

Innovating in the Public Sector

The state can foster innovation in the public sector itself, enabled by the possibilities of the Internet. An example is the proposal that was made by then Estonian Prime Minister, now European Commission Vice President, Minister Andrus Ansip to the European Council of October 2013 in his letter, "Sign up to a digital revolution".[20] He emphasised that the adoption of an EU regulation on digital signatures during the current mandate of the European Parliament was essential, underlining the importance of implementation by the STORK project. Further, the Prime Minister called for the creation of a framework for reusing and sharing data collected by EU public authorities. He cited the Estonian law, adopted in 2007, requiring citizens to submit their data to public authorities just once, after which, if the citizen has given consent, Estonian public authorities must share and reuse the data if they need it to deliver other public services.

Prime Minister Ansip proposed enshrining a similar right across the European Union starting in 2016, allowing European citizens and companies not to have to resubmit data to any public sector agency in the whole of the EU. He proposed "common EU-wide data exchange platforms—or at least administration-to-administration links—so that we can reuse the data." The aim is to "bring about the essence of the digital economy and the digital single market: seamless cross-border services in the whole of the European Union." This was already taking place in Estonia and Finland's collaboration on automated exchange of data in the cross-border version of Estonia's X-road.[21]

Such an initiative could serve to reduce the burden on small and medium enterprises (SMEs) and industry, and promote innovation utilising public sector data, with suitable privacy safeguards built-in, as well as simplifying the lives of EU citizens. If the tasks involved were in relation to institutions, offices, agencies or bodies of the European Union,[22] such an initiative could also be seen as

research also highlights a link with education policy and the importance of STEM fields of study. People with a higher educational background and a technical one are more likely to be consumer-innovators.

[20] European Voice, 24 October 2013, p. 14.

[21] Republic of Estonia, Information System Authority, www.x-road.eu, accessed on 25/12/2013.

[22] Though the ruling of the Court of Justice in *AMS* (15 January 2014) on whether the Charter of Fundamental Rights applies in a dispute between private parties is of relevance to whether such a distinc-

part of the implementation of Article 41 of the European Union's Charter of Fundamental Rights guaranteeing a right to good administration in relation to having "affairs handled impartially, fairly and within a reasonable time". It is worthwhile emphasising the wording on "reasonable time". When digital tools and platforms become available that can provide greater efficiency, time-savings and simplicity in providing public services, I would venture to say that the concept of "reasonable time" should evolve to take into account the availability of these technologies and their potential for efficiency gains and reducing administrative burden. Wasting citizens' time in asking them to repeatedly provide the same information to public authorities can be seen as bad administration and as a tax on their time, one which does not benefit state revenues either and if anything takes citizens away from more productive and interesting tasks.

The Internet and social media are enabling the public sector to maximise efficiency while actually increasing access to services and the possibilities for citizens to provide their inputs on policy and administration matters. Helen Margetts and Patrick Dunleavy observed in their influential article, "The second wave of digital-era governance: a quasi-paradigm for governance on the Web",[23] that three themes stand out already in the first wave of digital era governance: (1) reintegration; (2) needs-based holism; and (3) digitalisation. Reintegration amalgamates and "de-silos" public-sector processes, needs-based holism tries to design services around the citizen's needs and perspectives, not those of the administration, and digitalisation is the movement to a "digital by default" assumption.

The proposal by Prime Minister Ansip can be seen as taking this reintegration, needs-based holism and digitalization to the next, European, level of governance. The second wave of digital era governance, based on the power of social media, will continue the transformation of government.[24] This should be the point at which citizens do not simply provide inputs but are empowered to manage processes themselves (the eHealth example) and are given the possibility to socially or commercially innovate utilising open government data and social media networks.

The Ansip proposal, especially if related to efforts to move public services at the national or European levels, does presuppose attention being given to

tion is relevant. The CJEU held that the Charter is applicable "in all situations governed by European Union law". Oxford Human Rights Hub, "The CJEU's Ruling in AMS and the Horizontal Effect of the Charter", www.ohrh.law.ox.ac.uk, accessed on 21/01/2014.

[23] Published on 18 February 2013 in Philosophical Transactions of the Royal Society, March 2013, Vol. 371, no. 1987 20120382.

[24] Ibid., p. 7.

digital literacy and digital access by policymakers and by those implementing policy. Without the tools of digital literacy and actual accessibility of the Internet to all, especially in vital areas like retail finance or digital health, there is a risk that some citizens will be disadvantaged rather than empowered by the introduction or wholesale move of public or private services to the digital sphere. As part of moving to its model of eGovernment on the national and local levels, Estonia invested in digital literacy and eInclusion.

The State as Regulator: An Innovation-Friendly Policy Stance

Turning to the second aspect of the state's role in innovation: where the state is not necessarily leading development itself, it can take an innovation-friendly policy stance in regard to a sector, technology, technological application or platform where the regulatory framework may be revised or adapted, therefore not hampering new products or approaches. John Pierce of Bell Labs stated that "Everyone faces the future with their eyes firmly on the past and they don't see what's going to happen next."[25] While the state can play an essential role in enunciating missions endorsed by the democratic process and in providing a long-term view in finance and development, it should not pretend to omniscience. It must allow space for the creativity of private enterprise and civil society to be released. Examples of some pertinent sectors that may be addressed in regulatory policy in the fintech and Digital Single Market space are blockchain, crypto currencies and Initial Coin Offerings (ICOs).

It is clear that the financial sector is vital as a motor for innovation across the economy and that fintech, being digital innovation in finance, is important in achieving this goal. While networks, legal frameworks and the dissemination of knowledge are essential, as the physicist, Phil Anderson, stated, "Never underestimate the importance of money".[26] Economic competitiveness and the prosperity of a nation or group of nations, namely the European Union, depend on the flow of loans, especially "patient" long-term finance from a banking sector possessing a sufficient industry and sector-specific skills base, depth and a plurality of views. Professor Edmund Phelps, wrote, "A country's dynamism also depends on the pluralism of views among financiers."[27]

---

[25] Ibid., p. 201.

[26] *The Idea Factory*, p. 154.

[27] *Mass Flourishing*, Edmund Phelps, p. 38.

Along with deepening the banks' industry-specific skills base and improving their credit evaluation mechanisms to better analyse enterprises' innovation potential, fintech, including crowdfunding and blockchain applications, could conceivably provide depth and a plurality of views supporting innovation in financial services and ideally in the broader economy. Mariana Mazzucato observed, "From a policy-making point of view, it is crucial to consider how the 'eco-system' of financial institutions can 'broaden out' the innovation landscape rather than close it down, as is currently the case in many sectors."[28] The European financial system is bank-dominated and characterised by lending a majority of its funds to households as well as by a depleted industry and sector-specific skills base in lending and risk management. Professor Mazzucato made the general observation: "As traditional profit maximizing banks fear the kind of fundamental uncertainty underlying innovation, innovation has often had to be funded by alternative sources, such as venture capital, business angels or public funding bodies, including state investment banks."[29] Concurrently, Professor Mazzucato noted the tendency of "financialisation"[30] of large private companies on both sides of the Atlantic, cutting investments in productivity and innovation while concentrating on raising their stock prices through buybacks of their shares.[31]

While there is, and was, a need for lending to finance the real economy and innovation in particular, the funds that flowed from north to south in the early years of the Eurozone were going primarily for real estate and consumption. Overall, the "boom" years saw a huge over investment in property, construction, financial services and consumption. This was not, and cannot be, the basis for sustainable growth in European economies. However, especially now, as a reaction to the markets having priced risk too low, risk is being priced too high in Europe and this is starving innovation efforts of private financing at a time when much public funding has been cut due to austerity efforts.

Professor Mazzucato has opined that "regulation of financial markets must go hand in hand with policies that are aimed at innovation and industrial policy."[32] That is to be considered when policy decisions are to be taken in this sector.

---

[28] Mazzucato, M. (2013). *Financing innovation: Creative destruction* vs. *destructive creation*, in Industrial and Corporate Change, Oxford Journals, Oxford, Vol. 22(4), August, p. 856.

[29] Ibid., p. 852.

[30] Ibid., p. 853.

[31] "During the past decade, Fortune 500 companies have spent $3 trillion on share buybacks … such spending has occurred at the expense of innovation". Ibid., p. 856.

[32] Ibid., p. 863.

In general, SMEs in Europe go much less to the markets but to the banks, making classic banks much more important to financing the real economy in the EU[33] while venture capital investment is more prominent in the United States, for example. The *Financial Times* has stated, "The willingness to bet a lot on an untested venture is deeply rooted in the US business culture and start-ups in Europe often face a more sceptical investor climate."[34]

It is important that any legal frameworks developed and implemented aiming to prevent systemic risks and regulatory arbitrage do not serve inadvertently to cut off financing for innovative enterprises, especially new high-tech startups. It should additionally not magnify the retreat of capital behind national borders, one of the consequences of the financial crisis.

Considering crypto currencies, a monetary innovation made possible by the Internet and gaining in popularity because of it, there is much ongoing discussion whether Bitcoin,[35] for example, is truly becoming a viable alternative (fiduciary) currency or whether it is just a speculative bet.[36] If the answer is that it or one of its alternatives is a viable currency not issued by a central bank, then there are implications for the central banks, the sovereign model of finance, macroeconomic stability and the regulation of financial markets. Current regulatory guidance on crypto currencies is rudimentary and its actual implementation even where existing is no simple matter.

Money can be seen as a measure of value, a medium of exchange and a unit of account. Adam Smith wrote that, "every prudent man in every period of society, after the first establishment of the division of labour, must naturally have endeavoured to manage his affairs in such a manner, as to have at all times by him, besides the peculiar produce of his own industry, a certain quantity of some one commodity or other, such as he imagined few people would be likely to refuse in exchange for the produce of their industry."[37] After the choice of metals as the commodity that best served as a means of

[33] For instance, in the area of green technologies, global venture capital investment in 2011 went 76% to the U.S. while only 14% went to the EU. "Europe seeks to close funding gap with US," European Voice, 19 September, p. 16.

[34] Financial Times. (2014). *The long strive to reach Silicon Valley – other tech hubs will struggle to copy California's success*, January 4, January 5 2014 U.S. edition, p. 6.

[35] Started in 2008 with a pseudonymised white paper, published under the name of Satoshi Nakamoto, which can be found at http://bitcoin.org/bitcoin.pdf. The identity of its creators is still unknown. The first known purchase with Bitcoins took place on 21 May 2010.

[36] As written in FT Money, the question is 'whether the digital currency is an asset class, a means of trade or just an online pump-and-dump operation', FT Weekend, Saturday January 11/Sunday January 12 2014, p. 1.

[37] The Wealth of Nations, p. 39.

exchange, public stamps gained favour as an alternative to weighing and testing metals for their content, thereby facilitating seamless exchange. It can be deduced that the cryptocurrencies[38] are a step towards an even more seamless, common medium of exchange in the digital era, but may also introduce instability into the monetary system.

A pertinent point for our discussion is that Bitcoin's open source approach to its protocol has allowed for innovation on top of the existing project, now sometimes called the "blockchain revolution" across sectors, something that is also hoped for in relation to the cross-border eHealth data exchange infrastructure that epSOS prepared and that is being implemented in the Connecting Europe Facility.

Cryptocurrencies can be seen as a way to get around bad governance in many parts of the world, as a disruptive threat to debit and credit cards, as a mode to decouple the economy from politics or as an enabler for money laundering and other types of criminality. The ramifications can be negative as well as positive: creating new opportunities for innovation, creativity, and efficiency in transferring funds or destabilising currently beneficial arrangements for economic governance. In the EU for the time being, regulators are following developments and not moving to regulate yet.

If in the future, EU specific legislation in these three areas was to be considered because self-regulation and other alternatives had proven insufficient or because the current regulations were to be revised, it would be subject to the European Commission's impact assessment procedure. Impact assessment was introduced by the European Commission in 2003 to assess the potential consequences of an economic, environmental and social nature of initiatives it aims to propose. The impact assessment process collects evidence on the pros and cons of policy options under consideration on the basis of their potential impact.

Any legislation that might eventually be proposed should be "future proofed" and technology-neutral in that it should not lock in, or be predicated on, today's existing technologies, business models or processes.[39] Not only should room be left for change, in the form of innovation it should be encouraged by policy and legislative frameworks. In this context, the recent proposal of an "innovation principle" in a letter from 12 of the largest inves-

[38] 'Bitcoin is both a computer protocol and a digital asset or unit of account', Jonathan Levin, University of Oxford, Department of Economics, note prepared for the Cryptocurrency seminar at the Oxford Internet Institute, 21 November 2013.

[39] As the European Risk Forum notes in its Background Note 14, "Regulation of risk can also affect the creation and diffusion of ideas", p. 3, which is the main subject of this chapter.

tors in innovation in the EU to the Presidents of the Commission, Parliament and European Council under the auspices of the European Risk Forum[40] is pertinent. They proposed revising the European Commission's Impact Assessment Guidelines (2009) "to require formal evaluation of the impact on innovation and new technology development of new or amended legislation or administrative decisions".[41] The introduction of such a principle into impact assessment procedures could be evaluated as a part of European Union innovation policy as well as considered at national and regional levels.

The European Risk Forum noted that the European Union has concentrated more on funding than on the regulatory environment. While it can be conceded that a great deal of attention and resources were devoted to the programming and management of the Framework programmes, it cannot be denied that efforts to set up impact assessment and to institute better regulation procedures have aimed to improve the business environment in Europe, comprising that of the innovation-driven economy. However, in an activist role, using legislation and standards as enablers of innovation, as well as in a role aiming not to hinder developments utilising innovation-friendly policy stances and explicitly considering innovation impact during the impact assessment procedure, the European institutions could forge a more holistic innovation policy, comprising the aspects of regulation, business policy and promotion of innovation. If Europe wants to take the innovation-driven economy seriously, innovation needs to be consistently considered in the framework of other policies and initiatives, to evaluate the influence that policies have on the innovation potential of companies, social actors and the public sector.

Regulatory and Supervisory Innovation

An initiative to support innovation in regulated areas that was put forward in the European Commission Communication on Startups and Scaleups is that of regulatory sandboxes, with the Communication proposing exploring an enabling framework for them. A regulatory sandbox creates a "safe space" in which businesses can test innovative products, services, business models and delivery mechanisms in the context of regulation, with regulators. The sand-

[40] European Risk Forum Communication 12, The Innovation Principle – Letter to the Presidents of the European Commission, the European Council and the European Parliament, October 2013.

[41] European Risk Forum, Background Note 14, p. 4.

box framework enables firms to manage regulatory risks during the testing stage. The sandbox is intended for testing new solutions, in real-life situations, where a potential consumer or user needs to be demonstrated, as well as the need to manage potential risks and to respect binding legal rules. Regulatory sandboxes are not about "de-regulation", but rather an approach based on a *two-way regulatory dialogue* between an entrepreneur and an approachable regulator.

From a regulator's perspective, the largest advantage of a sandbox will be that anyone applying for a license will understand exactly what the process is before attempting to launch. This also allows regulators to guide the innovative company through the process, enabling (and accelerating) the speed of launching the new product or service.

Another advantage is the possibility of real-time impact analysis, which ensures that the innovation is not going to undermine the safety and robustness of a sensitive sector (e.g. financial services ecosystem, connected transport), as envisaged by the regulatory bodies. This is a feature that adds value from the regulator's perspective, as the process mitigates the overall risk.

Innovative firms, both startups and incumbents, often face disproportionate, inconsistent or over-cautious application of regulatory requirements. In the case of startups, their smaller teams may lack the experience to deal with regulatory compliance. Among established firms, current structures may be unable to efficiently respond to new developments emerging from their innovation teams or take an overly risk averse approach due to broad regulatory concerns.

Regulatory sandboxes are already considered to be a useful tool for areas such as fintech, blockchain, data, municipal services, automated transport and drones. It is in the financial sector—due to its intrinsic highly regulated nature—where sandboxes have primarily been tested.

Some European sandbox supervisors set up dedicated teams and departments to support fintech developments, via the so-called "innovation hubs" that aim to provide guidance to innovative firms (regardless of their size) and help them understand regulatory requirements. Other sandbox supervisors also started a more systematic monitoring of innovation by establishing a regular forum with relevant stakeholders.

Finally, some are setting up regulatory sandboxes to work with preselected firms in testing innovative technologies. Sandboxes are mainly supervisory tools for firms and supervisors to explore how regulation should be interpreted and applied in light of a firm's new solution, by running live tests. The sandbox framework enables ventures to manage regulatory risks during the testing stage, even though more solutions may be trialled later and potentially introduced to the market.

Existing examples of regulatory sandboxes in the EU are in the Netherlands, Lithuania and the UK, where the Financial Conduct Authority in the UK has designed a regulatory sandbox program. Similar steps are being considered in Sweden and in Portugal (in other sectors). Another case is that of the Monetary Authority of Singapore, who have a dedicated page and materials.

The public consultation on *FinTech: A More Completive and Innovative European Financial Sector*, published on March 23 2017, asked stakeholders: "Are guidelines or regulation needed at the European level to harmonize regulatory sandbox approaches in the Member States? Would you see merits in developing a European regulatory sandbox targeted specifically at FinTechs wanting to operate cross-border? If so, who should run the sandbox and what should be its main objective?"

The Startup Nations Summit (SNS) in Tallinn has proposed that policymakers from outside Europe will test the approach hands-on via the SNS Policy Hack in order to provide feedback and adapt the process to their own ecosystems. This is an initiative of the Estonian Presidency of the EU and the European Commission.

Conclusion

As Jon Gertner wrote in *The Idea Factory*, in regard to innovation, "capitalism is more deeply intertwined with government than many of us realise."[42] This is certainly true in regard to the "development states" like South Korea, China and Singapore, Europe's competitors on the global stage, and as Mariana Mazzucato and Jon Gertner have shown, this is also true for the development of the innovation-driven economy in the United States.

An active and farsighted role of state institutions in shaping, regulating and financing innovation can benefit the whole of society both in allowing individual initiative to flourish and by strengthening the knowledge and innovation-driven economy. Public sector engagement alone is not sufficient but neither is leaving everything to the market. Mutually beneficial cooperation of the public and private sectors on the basis of holistic innovation strategies coordinated by competent and sufficiently resourced civil services taking full advantage of the game-changing possibilities offered by the Internet for

[42] *The Idea Factory*, p. 352.

enabling the digital economy and digitally transforming public services is necessary. Europe needs to be in the forefront of adopting and adapting to new approaches such as fintech and blockchain. Only such a shift in thinking and action can ensure the future competitiveness of European economies as a basis for fair and sustainable societies and the maintenance of our global role.

3

Catalysing the SME Growth Ecosystem in the New Information Age

Luca Peyrano

Part 1: Why the SME Ecosystem Is the Key to Growth

Introduction

While EU GDP has rebounded recently, moving back towards pre-crisis levels, and many of the economic forecasts have shifted upwards, showing regained confidence in European economy, there remain some serious underlying structural problems in European economies. The cautiously positive current economic conditions should give Europe the chance to address burning societal issues such as youth unemployment, which remains at around 20 per cent, as traditional sources of European job creation have dried up. Public sector monoliths can no longer be relied on to create jobs, while big blue-chips have not directly created net new jobs for a decade.

The world has always been undergoing change, but the pace of that change is accelerating. We are faced with a world full of disruption and challenges, ranging from climate change to resource scarcity, from increasing digitalisation to rapid population growth.

To fully deliver on the fact that Europe has some of the most educated population, and relative economic mobility, we need bright individuals getting together and founding companies that take up those challenges and come up

L. Peyrano (✉)
ELITE – London Stock Exchange Group, London, UK
e-mail: elite@lseg.com

E. Kaili et al. (eds.), *New Models of Financing and Financial Reporting for European SMEs*,
https://doi.org/10.1007/978-3-030-02831-2_3

with solutions that help providing human beings with equal or better standards of living, safe yet diversified consumer choices and experiences—while using only a fraction of current resources. We need highly innovative people, solutions and companies that can think out of the box and who—once they get from idea to product—are able to secure financing for those products.

Europe has this potential. However, there remain some missing pieces which hinder these good ideas and the companies behind them grow and prosper. Equally, they hinder investors and thereby savers and the wider population from investing in these companies and benefitting from this growth and prosperity.

In support of the European Commission's Capital Markets Union (CMU), our common goal should be to diversify the financing of these companies, promote and simplify the cross-border distribution of the financing. Bank financing is not enough—and often not a suitable source of support—for these highly innovative and new companies. The gap in funding for small and growing businesses within the EU is still an obstacle that needs addressing.

Overview of EU SME Landscape as Seen by Markets Infrastructures

The SME sector is not homogeneous. It encompasses enterprises with different ownership structures and varying numbers of employees and sectors of economic activity, which translate into different levels of access to financing alternatives, administrative and regulatory burden and information and financial literacy. The 'SME' term masks a wide variety of companies, from sole traders to substantial firms employing hundreds of people. Most of these would not require the sizeable injection of growth capital that would justify an approach to the capital markets. Yet, as we will demonstrate, SMEs in general, and those with high growth potential in particular, make a crucial contribution to the economy and particularly to job creation.

High growth companies (such as those profiled in the London Stock Exchange Group's (LSEG) '1000 Companies to Inspire Europe' 2018 report—see map below) boast a two-year job creation rate of 37 per cent and an incredibly impressive three-year average annual compound growth rate of over 100 per cent for the top performing 100 companies. The largest sector represented in the report is Manufacturing and Engineering (at 20 per cent) followed by Food and Drink (at 13 per cent), pointing to a rich and varied community of SMEs throughout Europe. Because these companies are highly innovative (the companies in our report lay claim to nearly 10000 patents and trademarks between them—a 20 per cent increase compared to the previous year's edition) the jobs they create tend to be high quality and well paid, helping to boost productivity.

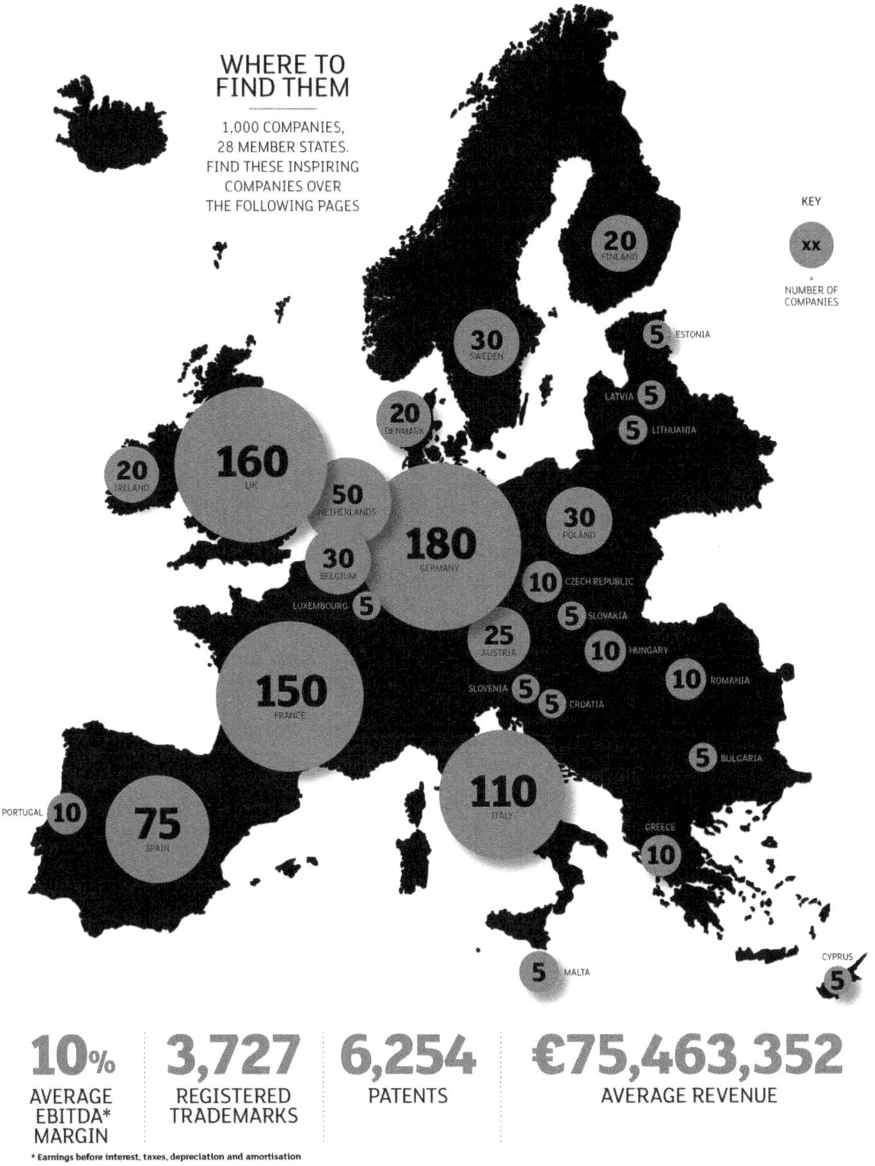

LSEG's '1000 Companies to Inspire Europe', 2017 report, Europe's map distribution

These companies clearly highlight the potential of European SMEs to drive European economic recovery. With around 23 million SMEs—and around 19 million people unemployed—in Europe, if we were to realise the potential of high growth SMEs like these to create real jobs, the effect would be transformational. Yet this vast potential is not being fully realised because too few companies are accessing the capital they need to grow. In particular, there is enormous scope for greater use of equity capital. Too few companies go public in Europe; too many either settle for a steady-as-she-goes approach to growth or are sold to established industry rivals—often based outside Europe. Of the total number of existing 'unicorn' companies (commonly understood as a privately held company with a valuation over 1 million USD), 77 per cent are located in the US and China, compared with only 10 per cent in the EU's 28 member states.[1]

The Commission has noted that 'a key objective of the Capital Markets Union is notably to facilitate raising on capital markets. Capital markets offer access to a wide set of funding providers and provide an exit opportunity for private equity and business angels, which invest in companies at an earlier stage of their development.'[2] In Europe, 80 per cent of business financing is currently conducted through bank financing and only 20 per cent through capital markets (the exact opposite of the situation in the United States). This needs to change and therefore achieving a Capital Markets Union (CMU) throughout Europe is vital. Fragmentation of capital markets means less liquidity, not only making it harder for companies to scale up, but also making the wider European economy less globally competitive. CMU should break down the barriers and simplify access to multiple sources of finance throughout the EU, including making it easier to access finance from other countries both within and outside the EU. As access to finance becomes more diverse, it will drive competition and reduce the cost of finance for growing companies. By encouraging more investment through equity, the CMU will also make the European economy more resilient by being less reliant on debt, and giving people more of a share in that economy. If Europe is to have a sustainable economic future as a key goal of CMU, it must support new companies, new ideas, new jobs and a new funding model.

What Do EU SMEs Need?

The Commission has identified the importance of Europe's 'funding escalator': 'The number one priority identified by respondents to the consultation on CMU is how to fix Europe's "funding escalator". How can we build a financial system that is better able to meet the financing needs of all our businesses—from the smallest micro-firm to the largest listed companies—at the different stages in their development?'[3] Europe has an excellent record for

[1] London Stock Exchange Group, *1000 Companies to Inspire Europe*. Available at https://www.lseg.com/resources/1000-companies-inspire

[2] European Commission, *Securities Market*, Explanatory Memorandum, page 2. Available at https://ec.europa.eu/info/business-economy-euro/banking-and-finance/financial-markets/securities-markets_en

[3] European Commission, *Q&A accompanying CMU action plan*. Available at http://europa.eu/rapid/press-release_MEMO-15-5732_en.htm

building and incubating new, dynamic, market-changing businesses. From software to biotechnology, and from business services to innovations spun out of Europe's world-class universities, there is enormous potential to create market-leading businesses. If this potential is to be realised, and those firms are to continue as European-based, independent companies, it is essential that they are able to access support and financing. Fixing the funding escalator in order to unlock the potential of capital markets is key to achieving growth, innovation and job creation in the economy.

External finance is an important part of the market mechanism for allocating resources within the economy by facilitating economic churn. External finance enables new businesses with innovative products or more efficient production processes to displace older less efficient businesses. This will contribute to improvements in productivity and initiates usage of underutilised resources within the economy. Capital is necessary for business investment, to finance new equipment, recruit and train new staff, and so improve productivity and output. It is also essential when ambitious firms seek to acquire a rival company or one that offers valuable business synergies. Conversely, a lack of capital can hinder cash flow and put the very survival of the company at risk. This limits the ability of firms to survive, to grow, finance new equipment, recruit and train new staff, merge with other firms where potential synergies exist, and so boost productivity and output. On top of this, companies not only need financing but also support in form of know-how, investor relations, networking, and cross-border guidance (see section below on challenges for SME financing today).

A company's financing needs evolve with its growth in size and specialisation over time. Its stage of development, growth objectives, innovativeness, operations, and credit profile determine its financing needs. This is generally defined in corporate finance as the 'funding escalator' (see diagram below). The funding ladder stages should not be see in isolation. Those institutions—and indeed firms—'further up' the ladder clearly could not exist without the investors needed to get companies to that stage. Similarly, investors at a lower stage ideally need a clear exit strategy, such as initial public offering (IPO), before they can commit to providing funding, and the less certainty there is surrounding that exit, the more expensive equity finance will be to the affected firms. Strengthening one part of the funding ladder can therefore have a positive impact upon others, ultimately meaning lower costs of capital and faster growth.

Both private and public markets parts of the founding escalator offer advantages and disadvantages. Although playing a role, private markets today are inherently opaque and relatively inefficient. Companies are faced with higher cost of capital due to information asymmetry and due to the cost of agency in the private market (private equity, private placement). On the other hand, public markets are symbols of transparency and overall efficiency. Public markets in particular have a role to play in 'dragging' companies if those in venture capital see public offerings as a likely outcome of their investment. However, the significant changes these markets experienced over the last 10 years, mainly due to regulation, have brought additional costs and complexity. New technologies, and initiatives like ELITE, are contributing to companies being able reap the benefits of both—the flexibility of the private market with efficiency of the public market.

An increasing number of innovative SMEs, for whom equity financing is often the best option, are using crowdfunding for early funding rounds before advancing to the public markets at a later stage of growth. The average number of investors in projects financed by the top four equity crowdfunding platforms[4] in the EU is around 700. There is also strong growth in business angel investing, particularly in syndicates, resulting in private companies being backed by a wider range of founding investors than has historically been the case.

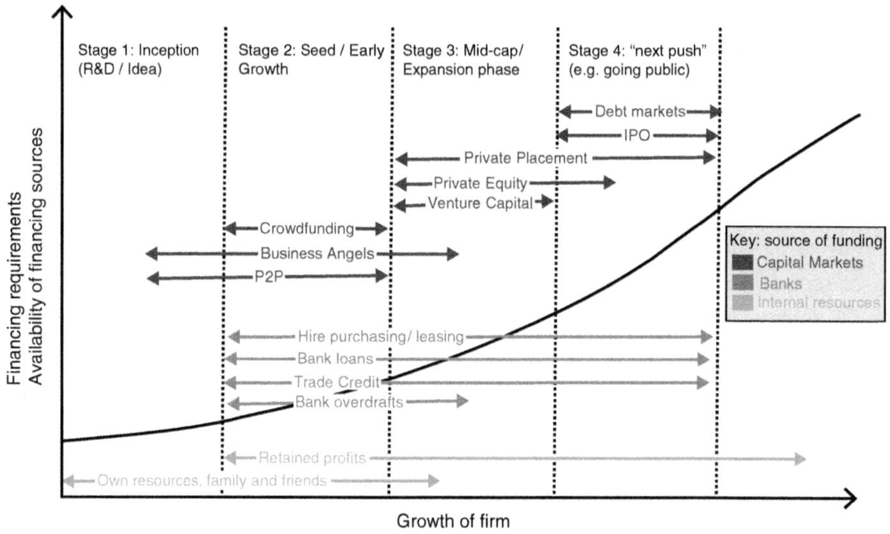

European Commission, funding escalator. Source: Commission services

Existing Channels for SME Financing

So why are there not more European growth companies that scale up to fulfil their full potential? Why do 60 per cent of the world's most valuable companies come from America and less than 15 per cent from Europe (down from over 30 per cent a decade ago)? How can we take these dynamic companies

[4] Investiere, *Europe's Top 5 Crowdinvesting Platforms*. Available at https://www.investiere.ch/sites/default/files/Top5platformsinEurope_PressRelease.pdf

from 'start up to stardom' and address the fact that—even among these 1000 stand-out firms—the majority have revenues of less than €50 million, while less than 1 per cent have revenues of over €250 million.

Debt Financing

The answer is recognising that the funding system is biased against these companies towards big established companies. Large companies mainly rely on debt to manage and refinance their obligations. In 2016, European Government spent €570 billion of taxpayers' money subsidising this corporate debt through tax deductibility. But while debt may be a suitable funding tool for big established firms, it is ill-suited to help SMEs and high-growth potential companies. Small companies in receipt of a bank loan must prioritise managing that debt or risk default, instead of using all their financial and human capital to innovate and grow. Debt finance creates "a mismatch" between the level of risk that entrepreneurs take and that which is shouldered by banks; put simply, the entrepreneur has to extend the mortgage on their house, while the bank gets a fixed rate of return. By comparison, an equity investor may want 30 per cent of your business, but they won't want you to pay for a mortgage. There is no immediate cost to the business and there is less personal risk to the entrepreneur. Therefore, it is important to recognise that debt has pros and cons.

Public Equity

SMEs need long-term patient capital, like equity, where companies at different stages of development seek investment to grow their business either through individual investors and capital markets, or through crowdfunding and peer-to-peer platforms. They need capital to flow directly from investors to entrepreneurs and small business owners, in addition to the efficient bank lending engine already supporting larger companies. Finance must come from the bottom up, not the top down. But this bias persists because while debt remains tax deductible, equity is often, and punitively, taxed—in some cases up to four times.

The ability to issue share options (not only to management but also to all employees) is also cited as a significant reason for a company to go public, to reward employees and to ensure that their incentives are aligned to the growth of the company. This is vital for "new economy" companies in the high tech and medical tech sectors that are increasingly important for the EU innovation, growth and employment. These companies must compete for increasingly scarce talent, often against a US incentivisation model. However, whilst equity offers these advantages, a company must feel comfortable with the downside of giving away a share of control of their business.

Private Equity

Private equity and venture capital can be a critical source of funding and a key part of the funding escalator. In 2016, according to Invest Europe's research, European private equity invested €53.7 billion into almost 6000 companies, 83 per cent of which were SMEs. Since 2008, private equity has invested €400 billion into 35,000 European companies. As companies have faced challenges securing finance, private equity has been part of the solution, connecting large institutional investors with capital to deploy and SMEs that need investment. One reason private equity is so important—and differentiated from other forms of finance—is that investment managers provide much more than just funding to companies. Private equity firms provide business expertise, market insight, established professional networks, ideas and practical know-how that results in businesses being better equipped for global success, whatever the political or macroeconomic backdrop. However, this can also be a downside of private equity in that the investor will expect to have a considerable degree of control over the company.

These existing channels have also been impacted by the technology innovations, as we address in the second part of this article.

Challenges for SME Financing Today

Access to financing is a key part of the puzzle; however, the challenge faced by SMEs who wish to grow is wider than that. The entire ecosystem of players that support them was largely destroyed by the financing crisis and it takes time and determination to rebuild this. The ecosystem must be restored to help SMEs to tackle the common challenges that they share across Europe. There is an education as well as a financing gap that SMEs across Europe are facing. These companies share the same challenges:

- *Cultural barriers* such as a lack of aspiration and confidence (too few high profile positive case studies) or a willingness to give up control of a company
- Lack of information or skills or access to external advice
- Insufficient networks
- Challenges in accessing international liquidity—including private equity and debt

On top of these challenges, there is an overarching need to allow SMEs to access the financing and advice that they need in an environment of *trust*, so that they have confidence in reaching out and having ambitions without the fear that they are going to be taken advantage of or misadvised by the large range of other stakeholders with whom they need to work if they are to fulfil their potential. Therefore, creating an effective ecosystem of entrepreneurs, business leaders, advisors and investors, can transform the European economy and the success of European entrepreneurs for the long term.

It is with this in mind that LSEG launched the ELITE programme, designed to support exciting and ambitious companies towards future growth and investment by offering a unique opportunity to unlock their potential, developing long-term strategic thinking and giving them structured access to the international financial community (see box below).

The ELITE Programme: Re-catalysing the High-Growth SME Ecosystem

ELITE was initially developed in Italy in 2012 and launched in the UK in 2014. In 2015, the programme was extended and opened to European ambitious companies willing to raise their profile within the business and financial community and accessing to business matching and financing opportunities. ELITE is growing as a Pan European community.

Today ELITE operates across the funding ladder, following its clients along their entire life cycle, from early stage businesses to long-term successful corporations, providing easier access to global capital. As of December 2018, it features:

- 1050+ companies from 40 different countries
- 200+ advisors
- 200+ investors

ELITE has been designed to cater only for companies with a sound business model and clear growth strategy. It offers an innovative approach, including a training programme, a working zone supported by a tutorship model and direct access to the financial community through dedicated digital community facilities. ELITE is a programme that helps fast-growing private companies prepare and structure for further growth through sharing experiences, access to financing opportunities and education.

The benefits to companies that join ELITE include: becoming part of vibrant ecosystem that supports and promotes innovation, entrepreneurialism and growth; accessing a platform to enhance the business profile of the company with stakeholders, supported by an extensive media campaign and web portal; bespoke access to a network of leading local and international advisers, investors, experts, entrepreneurs and public companies; earlier engagement with the investor community helping to access capital from a range of sources as and when appropriate for the company; developing the expertise to help make informed business and funding decisions for the company.

There are a few requirements for companies interested in joining ELITE. They should be willing to commit at the highest level (CEO/CFO) for the three phases, generating >£5m revenue and be able to demonstrate progress to date and growth potential.

ELITE is a community of excellence, benefiting not only companies but also investors by providing access to investment and exit opportunities at local and European level; benefiting policymakers by providing a practical platform for delivering innovation, growth and cross-border investment; benefiting advisors by allowing them a new channel to support clients to generate opportunities on a national and cross-border basis and also benefiting university research through offering a clear route to commercialise scientific breakthroughs.

There is a huge opportunity here to be seized. For European companies ELITE can unlock a vast amount of growth capital, enabling innovative and dynamic firms to grow at a rapid rate, to remain independent and to continue to operate from, and be based in, Europe. At the same time, ELITE can make Europe the international marketplace for fast-growing companies and ambitious entrepreneurs. Europe can become the incubator for the world's disruptive industries and host to a new class of strong, thriving companies. Technology has a key role to play in facilitating efforts to rekindle the high-growth SME ecosystem and bringing companies, investors and advisors into more valuable and action-orientated connections although it cannot act in isolation as a transformational change agent.

Part 2: The Role of Technological Innovation as Part of the Solution to SME Financing

Technological development has been continuously enabling innovative approaches that are transforming SME financing and alleviating conventional challenges in areas such as:

- Information asymmetry
- Lack of standardisation to allow viability and comparison
- Access to financial and broader ecosystem
- Lack of financial knowledge
- Geographic limitation

Technology does not mean only innovation for SMEs, but sometimes the sheer foundation—a core—of the company, as they shift from traditional resource and supply chain heavy models.

How Technological Developments Alleviate Challenges in SME Financing

Data Analytics

One of the main challenges of SME financing for investors is information asymmetry. The relative lack of visibility on corporate and financial data observed in many SMEs raises the costs and risks for investors and leads to higher cost of capital. However, in an ever-increasingly digitalised world, new SME digital data supply continues to be more dynamic and accessible. Furthermore, the current wave information revolution, with development in areas such as the 'big data' analytics, utilises expanding sets of data as alternative metrics (e.g. online reputation and social media analytics) of researching SMEs' status, improving SME data availability and mitigating the transparency challenge presenting in SME financing. With technology facilitating greater data sharing for SME financing, we expect continuous innovations in the space with new services and products that leverage the data to extract value-added intelligence in order to meet different investors' appetites. ELITE has signed an agreement with Zirra, an Israeli start-up, to offer AI-led solutions for company analysis. The partnership will provide ELITE with an additional set of unique tools powered by automated signals, artificial intelligence and big data to support ELITE company on-boarding and growth. Zirra provides automated smart analysis tools that enhance and support existing manual verification processes. These will be used by ELITE to enrich its integrated service offering for ELITE customers and partners.

Innovations in data analytics also allow further standardisation of data that provides consistency for faster and simpler cross-border searching and comparison. The landmark annual 1000 Companies to Inspire Europe Report, which identifies Europe's most inspiring and fast-growing SMEs and highlights how uniquely critical they are to future economic growth and job creation, would not been made possible without these innovations.

Emerging Technology

Various institutions in the industry, including LSEG, are looking into utilising emerging technologies, including blockchain, to improve the current state of SME financing. Borsa Italiana, part of LSEG, has teamed up with IBM to build a blockchain solution digitising the issuance of securities for SMEs in Europe. Designed to simplify the tracking and management of shareholding information, the new system is focused on creating a distributed, shared registry containing a record of all shareholder transactions, helping to open up new opportunities for trading and investing. Instead of having to deal with the paper trading certificates commonly issued to private companies today, unlisted European SMEs can look forward to enjoying a more digitised, streamlined and transparent process—giving issuers, regulators, investors and others increased insight into company information. This blockchain solution is aimed at giving SMEs better access to credit and linking them into a broader and more mature ecosystem, so that they can set up new trading networks and obtain funding by sharing financial data in a security-rich and transparent public arena.

Online Platforms

Technology-enabled online financing platforms, for such as crowd funding or peer-to-peer lending, can also ease access to finance constraints for SMEs, by providing extra channels of direct and efficient access to funding. They offer big potential to improve the funding of SMEs, with institutional capital readily available and retail investors who seek higher yields eager to participate. Such platforms, if appropriately organised, could provide SMEs with cheaper financing and investors with easier access to wider range of investment opportunities. With higher retail participation, efforts need to be made to ensure that investors are aware of risks and provided with a standardised level of public disclosure but are still given the choice to invest when they deemed it as appropriate. The demand for such services is evidently high with a surge in supply of such platforms and services observed across EU and the globe. If appropriately regulated, crowdfunding has an important role to play as part of a diverse financing environment for growing companies.

As highlighted earlier, the current challenge presented in the SME financing space is not only the relatively limited access to capital available to SMEs but also a common lack of sufficient financial knowledge by SMEs. Improving SMEs' financial skills and capability is another area where digitalisation can improve the current state by allowing easy access to online financial training and education to equip SMEs with sufficient knowledge to fully explore the available channels of funding to them and to face the potential funding challenges through their next stage of growth. We are encouraged to see a growing number of such initiatives in EU. LSEG'S own ELITE programme offers an innovative approach, including a training programme, a working zone supported by a tutorship model and direct access to the financial community through dedicated digital community facilities.

Another key benefit that technology brings to the space is removing geographic limitation and enabling access cross border, expanding and linking various networks of expertise and capital for SMEs. With a larger liquidity and expertise pool within reach for SMEs, this global connectivity allows for a more active ecosystem and more synergy creations for stakeholders.

As an example, LSEG's ELITE programme is a cross-border success story, supporting the Capital Markets Union project in its ambition to unlock EU growth and jobs. Its most recent innovation, ELITE Club Deal, aims to further streamline the capital raising process and channel growth capital to Europe's businesses, thanks to technology advancement, as an online platform.

ELITE Club Deal (ECD) is an online private placement platform for ELITE companies and professional investors. The initiative aims to help bridging a funding gap by bringing together professional investors with high growth companies in a secure and efficient environment through an online platform. ECD provides ELITE companies, which are typically high-growth businesses, with access to a broad group of international investors. ECD bridges the gap between the supply and demand of capital in a new way, allowing professional investors to have a stake in some of Europe's fastest growing private businesses. For companies, ECD is a 'one-stop shop', giving them access to a host of institutions in a secure environment, ultimately allowing them to finance their growth and in turn drive job creation and innovation across Europe and beyond. ELITE has partnered with THE HUB, a fintech scale-up, in order to refine its bespoke technology solutions to power ELITE Club Deal.

To access new private growth capital using the platform, be that equity or debt funding, ELITE companies are supported by "ELITE Partners," such as banks, financial advisors, lawyers and auditors to help them prepare and upload required corporate documentation to the platform. All company documentation is presented in a standardised format, further streamlining the investment process for participants.

Cornerstone Investors, including institutional investors, private equity and venture capital firms, are given the opportunity to access company data in advance and negotiate deal terms as "Cornerstone Investors" on the platform in a fully compliant environment. These financings are later be made available to "Follow-on Investors." "Agents"—typically corporate brokers and banks—facilitate introductions between companies and investors.

Case study: ELITE Basket Bond (EBB) As part of the initiative, ELITE has also launched the ELITE Basket Bond (EBB), offering a unique way of providing debt financing to high growth companies participating in ELITE. This innovative tool aims to contribute to reducing a structural gap between demand and supply in access to the capital markets. Its unique features not only substantially enhance SME creditworthiness but also facilitate the efficient direct involvement of the European Investment Bank in using EBB as a vehicle to directly invest in the real economy of Europe, supporting economic growth and the job creation.

The innovative key benefit of the EBB is credit quality enhancement achieved by two means. First, default risk mitigation through diversification of sector, size and geography of aggregated SME bonds and second, the unique high quality filter of ELITE company status—indicating that a firm has already been identified and selected as an excellent prospect for strong growth. Strict screening means that ELITE serves the most exciting and ambitious businesses with a strong business model, clear growth strategy and the commitment to implement useful changes for development.

The "ELITE Basket Bond" is represented by an asset-backed security collateralised by a basket of bonds issued by the ELITE Companies. A group of ELITE companies each issue a bond with the same characteristics, except for the amounts and covenants. These individual bonds are then grouped under a securitisation transaction carried out by a Special Purpose Vehicle (SPV). The SPV then issues an asset-backed security (ABS) then made available to professional investors through the ELITE Club Deal private placement platform. In the EBB process, bonds are used as collateral under a securitisation transaction and relocated as ABS notes through the ELITE Club Deal platform to professional investors. The cash flows deriving from the repayment of principal and interest under the bonds are used by the SPV as remuneration and redemption of the ABS, with ELITE issuer credit quality supporting the creditworthiness of the ABS notes. EBB has been designed by ELITE together with a lead arranger bank handing the issuance, structuring and placing.

ELITE has launched the first ELITE Basket Bond in December 2017. The €122 million 10-year bond is made up of 10 well performing and innovative Italian ELITE companies with European Investment Bank (EIB) and Cassa Depositi e Prestiti (CDP) being the lead investors.

Structural Challenges Remain

Technology as an enabler will continue to bring more benefits to the world of SME financing, by alleviating some of the existing challenges, such as transparency of SME data, geographic fragmentation of liquidity pool, barriers for retail investors, financial literacy of SMEs. It offers SMEs more possibilities to finance their projects and companies on top of the traditional approaches. However, it is important to note that technology is only one of the channels to address the challenges identified, and does not change the underlying principal of SME financing. There still lay more structural challenges faced by SMEs in EU nowadays, as we identified earlier.

The unchanged fundamentals of SME financing also mean that the identified risks still lies with new approaches, and they still need to be addressed by the relevant regulatory frameworks. We believe in the technology neutral principle that, regardless of the underlying technology, any provider who is in effect performing a regulated activity must be authorised and the service must comply with existing relevant regulation, according to a functional approach, to ensure financial stability and customer protection. If appropriately regulated and managed, these innovative solutions, alongside traditional channels of financing, can unleash great potential to provide the financing needed by the SMEs in the EU to build global champions, create jobs, deliver economic growth and support EU's global competitiveness.

Conclusion and Recommendations

To delivering a thriving SME all actors have a clear role to play.

- *Policymakers* like the European Commission should be congratulated on their vision for CMU and the granular actions being taken forward (e.g. SME Growth Markets). However, national governments need to address the fiscal bias against equity, and policymakers in general need to recognise that policy has focussed too much on macro-prudential regulation and investor protection at the expense of growth. Risk cannot be eliminated entirely and even if it could that would not be conducive to high growth. Individual investors should be responsible for risk-taking and government should not seek to prevent them from doing so or cushion them when things go wrong. We urge an approach that balances financial stability and investor protection with a drive for growth. Furthermore, we support the policymakers' tech neutrality principal because the unchanged fundamentals of SME financing also mean that the identified risks still lies with new approaches utilising new technologies, and they still need to be addressed by the relevant regulatory frameworks.

- *Financial market infrastructure*, regardless as to whether a fintech start-up or an existing service provider, must leverage the unique role it has to play at the centre of capital markets to help to foster programmes and initiatives to contribute to both cultural renaissance of entrepreneurialism and practical means to overcome challenges like SME access to finance (e.g. ELITE). Innovative solutions should continue to be explored to improve customer value creation in terms of efficiency, broader choice, transparency and investor protection, while maintaining resiliency in the market.
- *Investors* should commit to opening their mandates also to include high-growth companies. In some cases, even where the regulation permits, the investment mandates remain too rigid and SMEs' shares are considered illiquid assets by default. Institutional investors' asset allocation varies widely, but is on average overexposed to bonds. Households should be stimulated to have a more balanced asset allocation, away from the predominance of deposits in Europe. An example of successful diversion of households' money from less productive allocations (government bond, real estate, deposits, etc.) into productive ones (SMEs both private and public) is the Italian PIR fiscal incentive system. Finally, the creation of a fund of funds (as foreseen in the Commission's Working Document on CMU) is another mechanism which could foster an SME dedicated investor. Such a diversity of (20–40) funds would help stimulate the ecosystem (it's not just about the amount of financing, but the specialities, competition, innovations).
- *Entrepreneurs* themselves should have the greatest ambition for their companies and be less willing to see their company sold to a corporate, providing them with an exit and enabling them to retire. As part of this, they may have to give away part ownership of their businesses and be open to external advice.

4

Financing SMEs in the EU: Challenges and Opportunities

Horst Heitz

For over 10 years I have been dedicated to promoting a better environment for SMEs in Europe. Among many topics, one issue never changes, and that is how SMEs can have better access to finance. A lot has been done in Europe so far; however, the financial crisis proved that SMEs, and with them over 65 per cent of employees in Europe, are the first victims of wrong developments in finance sectors. SMEs are the power cells of Europe, but they need access to finance for their energy to create innovation, investments and jobs.

In the course of the financial crisis, major international banks went bankrupt or had to be saved by government funds because they were "too big to fail"; that is, they were systemically relevant. A similar crisis had to be prevented just recently. The decisions of the Basel Committee of the Bank for International Settlements (BIS), called Basel III, aimed to ensure the banks to become more crisis-resistant. The key measure to achieve this goal is an increase in the capital cover of the banks, which will inevitably lead to a shortage of credit supply. At the same time, banks have learned from the financial crisis and have become more reluctant to lend.

For SMEs, this results in increasing difficulty for debt financing their business, even though it is a particularly important structural tool of many European SMEs. Therefore, they have to look more and more to alternative financing options—for which there are different possibilities, like the subsi-

H. Heitz (✉)
SMEs Europe, Brussels, Belgium
e-mail: h.heitz@eupag.eu

E. Kaili et al. (eds.), *New Models of Financing and Financial Reporting for European SMEs*,
https://doi.org/10.1007/978-3-030-02831-2_4

dies offered by the European Union. Meanwhile, ensuring funding across the board is a key challenge for Europe's prosperity, since companies will only remain internationally competitive if they can invest in sustainable technologies. Since SMEs make up the majority of businesses in Europe and are also of enormous importance as an economic factor, they play a special role in this respect. At the same time, their financing options differ from those of large corporations. This text is intended to provide an overview of the current situation and the existing challenges and opportunities.

The European Commission defines SMEs as enterprises with a maximum of 249 employees and an annual turnover of a maximum of 50 million euros or a balance sheet total of 43 million euros. National definitions may differ; in particular, when it comes to funding or competition or law issues, the exact demarcation line between SMEs and large corporations plays a role. Overall, the share of SMEs in enterprises in the EU is 99 per cent. Two-thirds of private-sector employees are employed in SMEs.

While large companies had an equity ratio of 29.8 per cent in Germany in 2012, the value was only 24 per cent for SMEs. Although SMEs have more than tripled their equity from 7.3 per cent in the previous 15 years, the value continues to show how heavily companies rely on borrowed funds. In international comparison, the quota is still relatively low.

> Traditionally, Germany is bank-financed—unlike, for example, the USA, where capital market financing plays a major role. Thus, in the euro area, the share of bank loans in the debt of non-financial corporations amounts to 88.3 per cent, while in the US, the share of corporate bonds in debt amounts to 86.4 per cent. While US corporations use the capital market more for debt financing, the differences in equity financing are marginal. (09052016, Daniel BENDEL, GVB: ".IW über Unternehmensfinanzierung Banken spielen die Hauptrolle", https://www.gv-bayern.de/standard/artikel/iw-ueber-unternehmensfinanzierung-6370)

As a result of the financial crisis, companies in Europe have strongly and repeatedly complained about more restrictive lending policies of the banks. In the two peak years of the crisis alone, lending to companies in Germany fell by 34 per cent. Since the end of 2016, however, new lending has now risen again, in 2017 even by 3.1 per cent. Despite the growing economy, the level of new lending is thus not significantly higher than before the crisis.

In individual European countries, the specific situation of lending may vary. In Austria, for example, just under two-thirds of companies expect financing costs to continue to rise. And not quite 50 per cent complain that access to credit has become more difficult over the past three years. In a sense, this creates a dilemma: while companies that are currently in trouble need loans, access to them is particularly difficult. According to a study by the consulting firm Ernst & Young in 2017, companies' assessments of access to lending differ depending on the sector. According to the study, companies from the fields of agriculture and forestry, energy and water supply as well as transport and traffic complain most strongly about a more restrictive credit policy of the banks. Electrical engineering, automobile industry and the chemical-pharmaceutical industry for instance complain less than the average. Interestingly, the assessment also differs by revenue size. Companies with an annual turnover of more than 100 million euros assess the situation most critically. Understandably, top performers do not see the situation as negative as low performers.

Most SMEs depend on external financing. As a result of the more restrictive lending by banks, creditworthiness is becoming increasingly important, which can also be improved by a higher equity ratio. Basically, many companies focus on long-term financing options. Classically, this would include bonds or loans. In Germany, until a few years ago, financing needs were covered mainly by bank loans and long-term loans. Various coincidental events now lead to financing and liquidity bottlenecks for SMEs. This is not least the result of the decisions of Basel III.

Basel III: The Measures and Their Consequences

The reform package of the Basel Committee, known as Basel III, can be described above all as a consequence of the financial crisis of 2008. These provisions on banking regulation are among the most important and recent financial reforms of the past. The European Union Implemented Basel III through the Capital Requirements Directive (CRD). The CRD replaced the Banking Directive and the Capital Adequacy Directive.

The most significant results are as follows. The banks must gradually increase their core capital by 2019 in order to avoid the need for public injections of funds in a new crisis. Thus, the Basel II resolutions were significantly tightened again. With the increase in capital requirements for banks, it should in the future prevent governments from having to step in to save banks. Particularly in the heyday of the crisis, tax revenues were spent on saving systemically important banks from bankruptcy. As the case of the two Italian banks Banca Popolare di Vicenza and Veneto Banca from 2017 shows, incidences of bank bailouts are not over. In addition to the increased capital requirements, the Financial Regulator was also awarded harsher sanction possibilities in case of non-compliance. In addition, there will be greater scrutiny of whether the rules are actually being complied with. In extreme cases, banks may even lose their approval if they violate the rules. In addition, banks now have a debt ceiling. The bank supervisory insolvency takes place with an 8 per cent equity ratio.

By lending and reinvesting savings, banks actively contribute to the creation of bankroll money. The higher the banks' withheld capital, the lower the amount of money in circulation. In concrete terms, this means that loans are more difficult to obtain. In Germany, there were talks that banks would have to build up equity of about 100 billion euros. That would correspond to a loan reduction of about 1000 billion—money that is no longer available for investment and financing. In addition to the risk aversion of post-crisis banks, higher capping in particular is affecting banks' lending, which is generally seen as more restrictive than before the crisis. In addition to changing financing practices for SMEs, this also has economic implications. The more restrictive lending by banks can also have an impact on economic growth, not least because the missing funds could deny the companies investments in their technical equipment, but also companies will remain competitive only if Europe as a business location is at least on par with its international competitors.

In professional circles, however, raising the equity base is certainly viewed critically in terms of impact. Better risk management and more effective banking supervision could achieve significantly better results here.

Basel III affects SMEs in particular. Large corporations are usually incorporated companies. These can procure new money by the issue of further shares. Depending on the legal form, this is not possible for SMEs. As a result of the current lending practice, SMEs need to think about other ways of obtaining liquidity, in addition to traditional bank loans. Capital requirements could be reduced through efficiency measures, for example, through better receivables management. Additionally, many alternative forms of financing have developed in recent years. From crowd investing and SME bonds to profit participation rights and microloans from private individuals, medium-sized companies have plenty of options at their disposal. Overall, according to a representative study, 67 per cent of the surveyed decision-makers estimate the situation in such a way that questions of financing will continue to gain importance in the future.

Funding Opportunities

There is a whole range of alternative financing options for SMEs, some of which have only developed or established in recent years. Not all are suitable for any size of company and some are associated with enormous effort.

A listing on the open market of a stock exchange is indeed an opportunity to generate debt. This so-called small initial public offering (IPO) is also open to companies that cannot yet be traded on the regulated market. Due to lower requirements and follow-up obligations, the effort is also significantly lower. However, there are considerable risks for investors in particular. Other trading venues are setting higher hurdles. The number of companies taking this route is rather low.

Crowdfunding and crowd investing models are becoming increasingly popular. Crowdfunding is a kind of a donation. It's about putting a project into action. For example, this model is quite popular with publishers who use it to leverage financing for books. Crowdfunding is also popular with start-ups. After completion of the project, the participants receive perks or other benefits, for example, a copy of the published book. In crowd investing, investors expect participation in the company's success. As a rule, they receive the capital back after a set period. Banks usually fall away as financial intermediaries. Instead, private agents appear. There have been numerous online platforms that serve this purpose. For companies, this form of debt financing involves a great deal of effort, not only because the financing requirement as well as the planned distribution and so on must be calculated, but above all, because it is about selling investors an attractive project. Therefore, the crowd has to be brought on board. To achieve this, first-class promotional materials must be created. For example, short films that can be viewed online. Special Purpose Acquisition Companies (SPACs) are a quite young financing possibility. These are specifically acquisition-purpose companies that collect capital from typically institutional investors, prepare their own IPO, then merge with a target company to provide capital to the target company. Compared to the US, the SPAC market in Europe is still relatively small.

SME bonds have also become increasingly popular in recent times. The issuance of corporate bonds is subject to lower legal thresholds than the going public of stocks. This makes bonds attractive as an alternative financing option. Above all, large projects such as takeover or massive technical investments can often no longer be financed by a bank loan. Bonds can come into play here, especially because they improve the financial base of a company and do not burden a credit line. SME bonds are particularly interesting for smaller institutional investors and private investors. Therefore, the denomination should not exceed 1000 euros. Although there have always been failures of SME bonds in the past, some experts still do not see the bond market as being exhausted.

Insight into the Role of the European Union

Since at least the Lisbon Strategy of 2005, the promotion of SMEs has been one of the EU's priority areas of action. It is a matter of promoting entrepreneurial potential in order to be able to stand up to international competition. Among other things, the focus was on reducing bureaucracy hurdles. The Commission and the Parliament have taken up the issue of SMEs time and time again, demonstrating that these companies play a special role in the European economic system. For example, in January 2014, the European Parliament adopted a resolution highlighting the importance of SMEs for the economy in the European Union. Or, in September 2016, for example, the European Parliament adopted a resolution on improving access to finance for SMEs and diversifying funding opportunities.

SMEs can also benefit from numerous support programmes. The Competitiveness and Innovation Framework Programme (CIP) has provided over €30 billion to help SMEs with the participation of private investors. Since 2014, CIP has been replaced by the EU Programme for the Competitiveness of Enterprises and Small and Medium-sized Enterprises (COSME). Initiatives such as Joint European Resources for Micro to Medium Enterprises (JEREMIE) also allow Member States to use structural funds to finance SMEs. The programme will take place under the collaboration of the European Commission, the European Investment Bank and other institutions, and will run until 2020.

There are various types of funding available to companies. The classic ones include investment loans, guarantees, risk capital or equity funding. As a rule, the companies have to go through their house bank or one of the cooperation institutions of the European Investment Bank (EIB). More detailed information can be found on the websites of the EIB, the European Investment Fund or the official promotional bank.

Conclusion

SMEs have been in the focus of the European institutions for quite some time. The European Parliament and the European Commission regularly comment on the importance of SMEs in Europe. To tackle the specific funding challenges faced by SMEs, the EU has launched strong programmes. The main challenge for SMEs is the fact that the offers are often confusing, although access to COSME has already been simplified. Entrepreneurs still have to find the right funding, which means that the opportunities for funding should be even more transparent. All in all, many SMEs see funding as an increasing challenge. The capital increase measures under Basel III had a decisive influence on this assessment. Failure to provide the backbone of the European economy, the SMEs, with realistic and easy access to business finance will undermine Europe's competitiveness in the foreseeable future, because with the European structure of the SMEs, these are dependent on possibilities of debt financing to make promising investments.

While debating access to finance for SMEs, we must not forget other important issues here: fair and lower taxation, less bureaucracy and the cessation of late payments by the governments. SMEs can help themselves, if one lets them. I am trusting in our SMEs and that is why our legislation in the European Union should become a showcase of trust in the "Freedom for Entrepreneurship"—often more valuable than any programs or grants.

5

Financing Models for SMEs in the Age of Disintermediation

Ruth Wandhöfer

Introduction

Europe's economy continues to be dominated by small and medium-sized enterprises (SMEs). Financing of these SMEs has traditionally been a space for banks. Over the last decades and in particular in the aftermath of the global financial crisis, which was followed by a string of sovereign crises in Europe, that source of financing has significantly dried up.

At the core of the financing question is the objective of unlocking the ability of those that want to provide funding to match them with the relevant SMEs that require financing.

Over the last decade, technology innovation as well as the arrival of new types of providers in the financial ecosystem has led to alternative financing opportunities for SMEs. In addition, the example set by the US market, where capital raising through financial markets is not limited to large companies, serves as an inspiration for Europe to broaden the opportunities for SMEs' access to financing.

In this chapter we will provide an overview of the state of SME financing and various existing and emerging solutions that can contribute to supporting the backbone of the European economy. In addition to the role played by the

R. Wandhöfer (✉)
I-NED for LSEG, Permanent TSB and Pendo Systems, London, UK

Senior adviser KPMG, London, UK

Head of Regulatory & Industry Affairs, Coinfirm, London, UK

E. Kaili et al. (eds.), *New Models of Financing and Financial Reporting for European SMEs*,
https://doi.org/10.1007/978-3-030-02831-2_5

European Commission's Capital Markets Union (CMU) initiative, we will highlight alternative solutions that support the objective of easier, faster and cheaper access to quality financing for SMEs.

Europe's SME Financing Models: State of Play

SMEs represent approximately 99 per cent of all businesses in Europe, according to the European Commission. This makes it absolutely critical to help these firms on their growth and innovation path. At the same time one of the biggest challenges of this sector is access to finance.

As a consequence of the financial crisis, new banking regulations, such as the Basel III Accord, made it more complex and expensive for banks to lend to SMEs. Prudential rules of the Basel framework meant that risk capital had to be significantly increased when lending to SMEs, translating into an uncomfortable shortfall of SME funding by banks. Yet small businesses still needed funding. They are the lifeblood of the economy, and the past, present and future of Europe.

After complaints from SMEs some European governments initiated financing programmes for SMEs but a real long-term solution to the financing needs of SMEs was provided again by the banking sector. Investments bankers realised that they could help companies to issue bonds on the financial markets without impacting their balance sheet and capital ratios. At the same time national regulators created the frameworks to allow simple, fast and cheap issuance of SME bonds. The so-called "mini-bond" market was born.

These bonds are a means for companies to tap into new sources of funding across a value range of €20 to 300 million per issue. At the same time private retail investors gain greater access to fixed income securities. The London Stock Exchange Group created a dedicated platform in the UK and Italy to trade these bonds, called respectively ORB (Order Book for Retail Bonds) and ExtraMOT PRO. These bonds can also be traded on other exchanges. Similar mini-bond markets exist in Germany, Spain and France. In addition, the French government passed a new ruling in 2016 authorising the use of distributed ledger technology—a form of distributed data base technology—for the issuance of mini-bonds and recording of trades, enabling the latest technology to make this market more efficient and transparent.

Even though mini-bonds are starting to be an established and fast-growing asset class with hundreds of bonds listed, reaching an aggregate value of tens of billions of euros, the fragmentation of capital markets along national borders diminishes their value to the SME community. It is thus imperative to move away from domestic fragmentation of trading and instead develop a pan-European approach to access and trading of SME mini-bonds at a low cost. At the same time only the largest SMEs tend to access this type of funding model, which calls for identifying whether more incentives can be developed for smaller SMEs to leverage this financing approach.

Aside from risk capital/Basel III considerations, one of the greatest challenges for financiers (such as larger banks, corporates and EU and Member State institutions) in providing financing for the SME sector is the sheer number of engagements necessary to invest comparatively small amounts of capital. Structures that rely on the financier resourcing a bilateral engagement and negotiation with the SME are inevitably challenging to scale on any commercial basis. In recent years, technology has facilitated the development of two-sided marketplaces that allow for 'self-service' commercial structures which can be scaled far more efficiently than traditional structures.

Financial technology firms, or fintechs, have been at the forefront of the development of many of these marketplaces, with one illustrative example being C2FO's Dynamic Discounting solution, which has been widely adopted by many of the world's leading corporates. The solution leverages a marketplace through which suppliers can offer discounts for early settlement of receivables (at a rate they elect). The efficient marketplace then automatically matches the demand (supplier offers) against the supply (available liquidity from their buyer). The technology allows the market to scale with no corresponding increase in resourcing, or need to introduce minimum size SME or transaction size.

A further example of technology driven innovation in financing has been the arrival of peer-to-peer (P2P) lenders that appeared across various countries in Europe, Zopa being the first one that launched its services in 2005. Whilst the P2P lending market in the UK still dominates in size over the continental European markets, valued at $4.9 billion in 2015, the largest P2P lending market is in China, valued at $101.69 billion, followed by the United States with $36.17 billion in the same year.[1]

As the digital economy grows, additional forms of digitised finance are entering the market. These typically make use of both transactional and alternative data, removing the often opaque or patchy credit and financial histories of SMEs. In Europe these data-driven services are further supported by the Payment Services Directive 2 (Directive/EU/2015/2366), which allows non-bank providers to develop payment initiation and account information services through access to bank customers' account data. In a similar vein, the UK Open Banking project enables third party service providers to develop

[1] KPMG and University of Cambridge. (2016). *Global Insights from regional Alternative Finance studies*, October 2016, p. 3. Available at URL https://home.kpmg.com/content/dam/kpmg/uk/pdf/2016/10/global-alternative-finance-report-web.pdf

data and financial services based on consumer and SME account data, which should lead to both better choices for users and more competition in the market. Given that fintech start-ups are all leveraging cloud services, every time an SME makes use of fintech services across this space their digital data footprint is being captured. Through deeper data analytics, these firms can provide a more tailor-made financing service to SMEs, which particularly resonates with those SMEs that are becoming more tech-savvy. Innovations in this space spans across e-commerce, payments, microlending as well as new marketplace lenders. New forms of partnerships between fintech companies, banks and SMEs are also emerging, providing a broader set of tools to enable SME financing in more transparent and cost-effective ways. But, given the abundance of data collected and leveraged for the delivery of these new types of lending models, the importance of data privacy and compliance with enhanced European laws on data protection such as the General Data Protection Regulation (Regulation (EU) 2016/679) has to be kept in focus. This means that new types of complexities and risks associated with these alternative lending models will have to be recognised and properly managed.

A further noteworthy development is the technology innovation in the post-trade space where, for example, a consortium of financial institutions in Europe joined forces to create a joint venture that will deploy distributed ledger technology (DLT) in order to make post-trade processing for SME lending operations faster, cheaper and more efficient. The objective is to leverage this new technology in order to make access to capital markets by SMEs easier and less costly. In a similar vein, the recently announced initiative by Borsa Italiana and IBM circles around the same topic of leveraging blockchain technology for issuance of SME securities in Europe. The plan is to digitise securities certificate data in an effort to replace the traditional paper-based process and by virtue of the distributed ledger enable issuers, investors and regulators more transparent insights into the SMEs. The role of enhanced data is yet again a key driver in support of SMEs expanding their trading networks and enabling them to access more funding opportunities.

SME Financing Solutions That Can Help Today: Supply Chain Financing

After years of working capital deterioration, companies have realised that optimising working capital is crucial, and failure to manage it properly can have a serious impact on their ability to fund their day-to-day operations. All firms, regardless of the strength of their credit, ultimately prefer buying goods on credit terms as this provides them with an effective tool for generating working capital. Supply Chain Finance (SCF) in this regard is a well-established tool for providing financing and managing risk. Especially, after the global financial crisis, we witnessed a significant growth in the use of SCF. Some of the developed markets, like the UK for instance, operate on trade credit for 85 per cent of transactions.

Unfortunately, SME companies who tend to have greater needs of operating with efficient working capital often deploy expensive financing options, which in turn curtail their success and limit faster growth.

So, how does SCF work? The below infographic shows a step-by-step illustration of the SCF process.

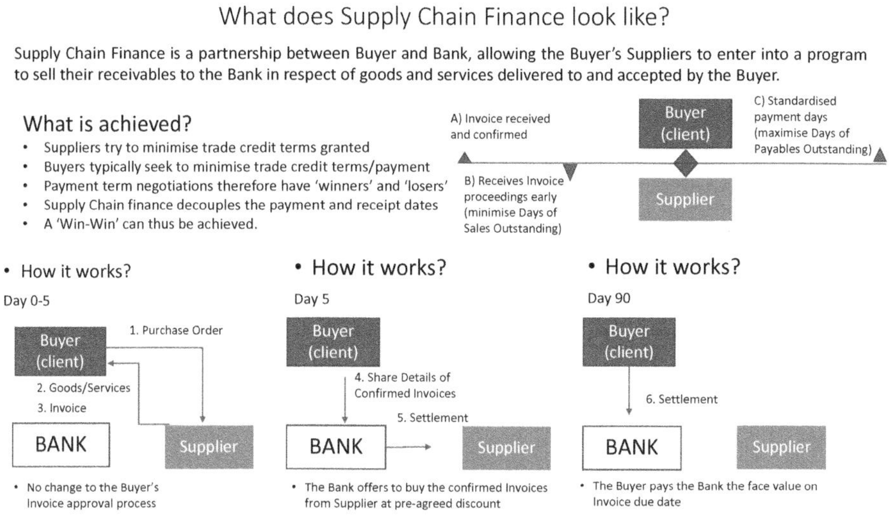

Source: Citi

When banks provide SCF they inject liquidity to the SME much earlier than the agreed payment terms of the buyer. This provides multiple benefits and most importantly ensures that SMEs have the liquidity they need to maintain and grow their business. The supplier universe therefore benefits directly as it can generate cash on acceptance and that at a much better rate than if they would have borrowed from their own sources. One of the main advantages of SCF programs is that they enable non-investment grade suppliers to benefit from investment-grade financing rates. At the same time SCF significantly increases the range of banks that would potentially provide financing to SMEs, that is, financing is provided to businesses not directly in the target market of many global banks (like Citi). In parallel new alternative investors are able to provide financing through syndicated financing structures, again a way to broaden the pool of potential providers of finance and hence increase the choice and availability for SMEs.

From an operational perspective, SCF financing is more easily scaled as the buyer will have to ensure legal agreements and due diligence, not the high volume of small suppliers. SCF also naturally matches timing of suppliers need for cash with financing. In a similar manner to an overdraft, the most popular source of SME finance, SCF financing is linked to the trade cycle.

Finance providers offer their services in the context of the financial requirements triggered by purchase orders, acceptance of invoices, receivables, and related pre- and post-shipment events along the supply chain. Consequently, SCF is largely 'event-driven'. The development of advanced technologies and procedures to track and control events in the physical supply chain creates opportunities to automate the initiation of SCF interventions.

Developed economies are early adopters of the SCF tool and have been able to achieve economies of scale with the end-to-end automation. They have also fine-tuned their operational processes over many years and adjusted their business model as needed. A number of economic, technological and regulatory forces have spurred its growth in the recent past. Working capital management becomes a top priority when there is a high paced growth coupled with a competitive environment.

Financial institutions continue to absorb regulatory changes with regard to capital requirements, which means that SCF has begun to be favoured over traditional trade loans since it takes out the performance risk of the suppliers. In addition, most financing remains within one year, which attracts much lower amounts of capital requirements compared to other forms of traditional lending.

Furthermore, the probability default factor for SCF is lower given the actual low default rates. Various independent reports confirm extremely low default rates given that financing is tied to a flow of goods and is generally done post-acceptance by buyers.

To make an SCF offering successful, apart from a large network and a strong balance sheet to support funding, it requires innovation, improved digital interfaces and tools connecting global counterparties on a single platform. Simplified implementation and on-boarding processes as well as adaptability to local needs in response to buyer and supplier feedback are vital ingredients to success.

Governments can play a key role in encouraging SCF propositions. An example of such a form of support would be the Betaalme.nu initiative in the Netherlands. Other countries actively supporting SCF for SMEs include, for example, Singapore, the USA and the UAE.

A Look Ahead: The EU Commission's Capital Market Union Project

In 2014, the European Commission adopted a milestone plan to create the European Capital Markets Union (CMU). The primary objective of this plan is to provide European businesses with a greater choice of lower cost funding and at the same time ensure that savers and investors have more opportunities through this initiative.

Overall, the expectation is that achieving CMU will contribute to the stability and resilience of the financial system in Europe. Arguably CMU also presents an opportunity for pursuing internationally coherent legislation, which should be a guiding principle for the Commission.

When we look specifically at the role of SME financing we find that the European Commission's key priority of enhancing Europe's equity markets, in particular for fast-growing medium-size enterprises, forms the bedrock of SME financing. In the future, public equity markets will be one of the key ingredients for a truly successful capital market. Declining trading volumes, in particular in non-equity securities, is a key issue for Europe. Vibrant secondary markets are essential to healthy primary markets, which can provide companies and countries with the financing they need.

A key element of supporting SME financing is to further facilitate SME listings on public markets. In that regard, the EU will examine different existing legislative measures with a view to proportionality in relation to SMEs.

The area of securitisation is another element of focus in the context of the CMU. This market remains moribund: with issuance in Europe as low as €237.6 billion in 2016, of which only €96.4 billion was placed with investors, according to Association for Financial Markets in Europe (AFME). This is largely because of the lack of a level playing field with similar fixed income products created by slightly challenging regulation, which does not recognise the strong performance of European securitisation through and since the financial crisis. It is therefore crucial to develop the European market to establish securitisation as a more efficient funding tool for SMEs as it frees up bank balance sheets. This goes hand-in-hand with improving relevant aspects of the prudential Basel III framework to ensure that appropriate relief for regulatory capital can be achieved through securitisation. Investments need to be economically viable and pricing needs to fairly compensate for taking credit and illiquidity risks.

Conclusion

SME financing in Europe is on the path of transformation. From traditional bank-led methods of financing, SMEs as well as start-ups are exposed to more choice of sources of funding across a broader array of providers. But we are far from a state of perfection. Access to financing still takes too long and few SMEs make use of the option to access national capital markets. What is more is the lack of a harmonised way of accessing the European Union's capital market, because this in itself does not yet exist. Obvious ways of alleviating financing challenges are offered by methods such as SCF, which would be able to unlock further financing flows, particularly if governments in Europe would also start to more actively support this method of financing. In the medium term, the revival of the securitisation market in Europe should be a priority to further support SME access to financing opportunities.

With technology innovation creating more opportunities for better and more granular data, and subject to appropriate data privacy and protection measures, SMEs are bound to benefit from better credit terms. Equally, the banking industry will be enabled to again play a more important role as dynamic credit scoring gives more clarity in terms of implications on risk-weighted assets on their balance sheets. The potential of DLT in providing more efficient and automated processes for the financial industry at large is an area that will unfold over the coming years. DLT could usher in a new era of financial services and potentially deliver significant improvements to the way SMEs can access financing in the future.

6

Funding Innovation in the Era of Weak Financial Intermediation: Crowdfunding and ICOs for SMEs in the Context of the Capital Markets Union

Dimitrios Psarrakis and Eva Kaili

In the fifth year of the European financial crisis, 2012, the World Bank published a book with a very interesting title: *Golden Growth: Restoring the Lustre of the European Economic Model.*[1] In this book, the authors I. S. Gill and M. Raiser identified the sources of economic growth of Europe, highlighted the reasons, both structural and cyclical, that led to poor economic performance and stagnation in terms of GDP, and suggested policies to revitalize the growth model of Europe. They focused on six economic parameters, namely trade, finance, enterprise, innovation, labor and government. The interconnection of these parameters in a coherent economic blend is what makes, according to them, the European growth model *unique*.

Economics is an endless optimization effort: a calculus exercise aiming to optimize both political and financial functions. This effort requires delicate political and economic skills in order to align issue-specific interests of a wide range of stakeholders. If this political economic exercise seems difficult at the national level, we can easily realize the complexity at a multinational level, like the European Union, where economic, financial and organizational arrangements evolved over time in completely different institutional

[1] Gill, I., and Raiser, M. (2012). *Golden Growth: Restoring the Lustre of the European Economic Model* (Washington, DC: World Bank Group Publications).

D. Psarrakis (✉) • E. Kaili
European Parliament, Brussels, Belgium
e-mail: dimitrios.psarrakis@ep.europa.eu; eva.kaili@ep.europa.eu

E. Kaili et al. (eds.), *New Models of Financing and Financial Reporting for European SMEs*,
https://doi.org/10.1007/978-3-030-02831-2_6

contexts, known as "variegated capitalisms".[2] Gill and Raiser view economic growth as an institutional arrangement. But is it all about institutions? The authors of this chapter have a slightly different view. In developed economies, like those of the EU, institutions play a significant role, but not as big as the institutional economists traditionally assume.[3] Similarly, we keep a distance from other explanations of growth, like the ones who emphasize the dimension of geography.[4]

In our view, the current economic environment of rapid technological change, accelerated by what many authors describe as "second machine age" or "fourth industrial revolution" resemble less the growth ideas of Adam Smith (the founder of the institutional tradition) and more the concepts articulated by Joseph Schumpeter.[5] We believe that we are in an era of transition from the Smithian to Schumpeterian growth.[6] This transition weakens traditional concepts of value chain, reassesses the worthiness of traditional business models and introduces new assumptions about the financial models that are necessary to be developed in order to finance this *new growth model.*

The Big Picture

What the *new growth model* is about? To be brief, it is the rearrangement of the aggregate production function (at the macroeconomic level), empowered by emerging digital technologies (such as AI, blockchain, IoT, etc.), in a way that the factor of capital becomes more and more important, whereas the factor of labor less and less significant. This rearrangement of the factors of production is of course originated to intra-firm value chain re-engineering and affects organizational relationships, business models, and capital structure preferences.

[2] There is a rich literature on this topic developed under the concepts of "varieties of capitalism" or "variegated neoliberalisms". Indicatively, look at: McCartney, H. (2015). *Variegated Neoliberalism: EU varieties of capitalism and International Political Economy* (New York: Routledge); Hall, P. (2001). *Varieties of Capitalism: Institutional Foundations of Comparative Advantage* (Oxford: Oxford University Press); Hanke, B. (2009). *Debating the Varieties of Capitalism* (Oxford: Oxford University Press).

[3] By institutional Economics tradition we mean the works originated from the ground-breaking approach of Douglass North. (1991). *Institutions, Institutional Change and Economic Performance* (Cambridge: Cambridge University Press).

[4] Jeffrey Sachs is the prominent scholar of the "geography" approach.

[5] Schumpeter, J. (1983). *Theory of Economic Development* (New York: Transaction Publishers).

[6] For an analytical account of this approach look at: Mokyr, J. (1990). *The Lever of Riches: Technological Creativity and Economic Progress* (Oxford: Oxford University Press); and Mokyr, J. (2017). *A Culture of Growth: The Origins of the Modern Economy* (New Jersey: Princeton University Press).

The discussion about the distribution between capital and labor, a fundamental subject in macroeconomics, directly links the new technological developments in the digital era with the subject of growth. This new era of digitization, which some authors describe as the Fourth Industrial Revolution[7] or the Second Machine Age[8] is characterized by the critical role played in the production process by the mobile internet, the smaller, more powerful and cheaper sensors, the artificial intelligence and machine learning.[9]

It is clear that the transformative power of digitization goes beyond the firm level. It redefines how we calculate the aggregate output, how we assess the aggregate consumer surplus, as well as how we define the aggregate supply in terms of labor and capital input.[10] Economics bibliography addresses this challenging topic under the headline of "the future of work" and how income inequality is affected by the race between education and technology.[11]

But from where does the *new growth* come if not from the labor? A very reasonable answer could be that it comes from the other factor of production, the capital, namely the infrastructure investments that firms have made to facilitate the production process. In the previous three industrial revolutions though (the period between the 1790s and the 2000s), the contribution of capital and labor in the aggregate output was fixed (see the famous Cobb-Douglas Theorem). Does the growth of the last one-and-a-half decades come from the digital infrastructures of the firms? If yes, then this would challenge Robert Solow (see the Solow Growth Model, named after him), who famously described the so-called *computer productivity paradox*, when he said, 20 years ago, that "*you can see the computer age everywhere but in the productivity statistics*".[12]

The answer comes from numerous empirical studies conducted in the last 15 years. The growth does not come monolithically from the contribution of labor or (digital) capital as the traditional growth models predicts, but from the intra- and inter-firm organizational rearrangements, enabled by investments in digital technologies, that firms designed and implemented. These rearrangements were changes that firms decided to make at some point after

---

[7] Schwab, K. (2016). *The Fourth Industrial Revolution* (New York: Crown Business).

[8] Brynjolfsson, E., and McAfee, A. (2016). *The Second Machine Age: Work, Progress, and Prosperity in a Time of Brilliant Technologies* (New York: Norton & Co).

[9] Schwab, K. (2016). ibid., p. 7.

[10] Brynjolfsson, E., and McAfee, A. (2016). ibid., pp. 97–146.

[11] Goldin, C., and Katz, L. F. (2008). *The Race Between Education and Technology* (Cambridge, MA: Harvard University Press).

[12] David, P. A. (1990). The Dynamo and the Computer: A Historical Perspective on the Modern Productivity Paradox. *American Economic Review. Papers and Proceedings*, 80 (2): 355–361.

the 2000s and started to deliver excess capital inflows and, consequently, increases in the aggregate output in five to seven years after their adoption.[13]

This is a critical observation because, suddenly, it is the well-designed organizational change of a firm that functionally incorporates the digital disruption has become the driving force for growth in the mature economies of the West. This has the following implications for Europe when we consider both its sources of growth in the long run and the sustainability of the competitive advantage of the European economy:

1. In the new growth model, SMEs stay in the core once again, but there is a qualitative shift: EU should not invest just in SMEs, but in SMEs that reflect the production characteristics of the Fourth Industrial Revolution.
2. The EU should make sure that financial markets can channel capital to start-ups and SMEs that research on the technologies of the Fourth Industrial Revolution, and find economically efficient ways that will accelerate technology transfer from the lab to the market.
3. The Capital Markets Union should not be *just* about the improvement of the allocation of capital to SMEs, but also about the allocation of capital to SMEs that develop certain technologies and improve their operational model.
4. The financial instruments used to serve the aforementioned purpose should take into account the riskiness of the projects (e.g. the uncertainty of the free cash flows in the short run and the difficulty in assessing the hurdle rate of the discount factor), and the fact that any improvement in the operations will be transformed into cash flows after five to seven years.
5. The European SMEs should realize the production characteristics of the new era, increase their demand for certain technological improvements, and gain access to finance that will make this improvements possible.

The five points we just stressed dictate that we should re-examine the adequacy of the current space of financial intermediation in Europe (the supply side of funds). Instinctively somebody could say that an improvement of the financial instruments and the channels of funding suffice to boost innovation in Europe, which means they translate the financing problem as a "supply side issue". In our view, this is not only a problem of supply side. It is also a "demand side" problem.

[13] Brynjolfsson, E., and Saunders, A. (2013). *Wired for Innovation: How Information Technology is Reshaping the Economy* (Cambridge, MA: MIT Press).

The (Weak) Demand Side of Funds for Innovation

This chapter focuses primarily on the supply side of the availability of funds for technological innovation. However, the demand side is also critical for the developed economies, especially in the case of Europe, and we need to briefly examine this dimension before proceeding further.

Various empirical studies have shown that the demand for funds for innovation requires, first and foremost, an intra-firm organizational decision to change its operations by adopting innovative technologies. It also requires the development of the firm's human capital.[14] A firm's demand to finance innovation derives from the demand for the innovation per se. Consequently, in an ecosystem that the demand for innovation is low, the overall supply of innovation is low.

A striking statistic of EUROSTAT reveals that from the overall funding directed to SMEs, only 6% goes to firms that create innovative digital products and services.[15] It is our view that if the EU aspires to be the global leader in the era of the Fourth Industrial Revolution, just like United States was the leader in the Third Industrial Revolution, it is of paramount importance not only to create a global regulatory competitive advantage, but also to make sure that financial markets will channel investments to Fourth Industrial Revolution technologies up to 12%, if not even higher.

We have significant statistics of the volume of money that goes to innovation (primarily funds for R&D) that are close to 3% of the EU's GDP. We also know that firms provide around 53% of this amount (the rest is funded by the government sector).[16] What is not clear is how these funds are distributed between incremental and disruptive innovations. This is a critical determinant of the demand for funds. As Clayton Christensen et al. underscore, firms indicate low preference in investing to disruptive innovation projects because of the biases inherent to the financial tools they use to measure their economic performance. In their seminal article *Innovation Killers: How financial tools destroy your capacity to do new things*, Christensen et al. indicate that (1) the discounted cash flow and net present value analysis, (2) the "unwise" use of sunk and fixed costs and (3) the "myopic" focus on earnings per share,

[14] Brynjolfsson, E., and Hitt, L. (2003). Computing Productivity: Firm-Level Evidence. *Review of Economics & Statistics*, 85 (4): 793–808; also Brynjolfsson, E., and Hitt, L. (2002). Digital Organization: The Seven Habits of Highly Competitive Companies. Working Paper, MIT and Bresnahan; Brynjolfsson, T. E., and Hitt, L. (2002). Information Technology, Workplace Organization and the Demand for skilled Labor: Firm-Level evidence. *Quarterly Journal of Economics*, 117 (1): 339–376.

[15] Source Eurostat: "Science, Technology and Innovation in Europe" (2013 Edition).

[16] Source Eurostat, ibid.

create a strong preference for certainty in the future cash flows and low risk appetite that result, altogether, to a business short-termism which aims to the maximization of the firm's current value, but inhibits its long-term prospects. In the aggregate, this low appetite for investments in disruptive innovation inhibits the long-term growth prospect of the economy as a whole.[17]

The (Even Weaker) Supply Side of Funds for Innovation

In the previous section we deliberately avoided making any reference to the supply and demand for loanable funds. The topic of the demand of loanable funds is a major subject in macroeconomics but it is not helpful to our discussion here. Obviously, the loans, and especially bank loans, have a minor impact in funding European innovation. Even if the availability of capital is abundant, investments in innovative start-ups and SMEs is considered as "un-bankable". The post-crisis regulatory framework of CRD III and CRD IV only widened the distance between bank-originated capital and innovation-oriented projects.

Even with the design of a strong SME Window in the framework of the European Fund for Strategic Investments (EFSI), it was still difficult to mobilize idle capital to SMEs, let alone to channel loanable funds to innovative SMEs, despite the fact that the SME Window was significantly more successful than the Infrastructure Window in absorbing the available capital.[18] The simple reason why EFSI was not successful in allocating capital to high risk SMEs is because the provision of guarantees of those loanable funds reflected the market interest rates and, thus, the interest rate of the instrument was prohibitive for investments in innovation.

Practically, as happens everywhere, the burden of risk-taking must fall on the shoulders of private equity schemes. However, the EU does not have a functionally developed venture capital industry, let alone a "Silicon-Valley-type" of risk mentality. With the inadequacy of loan instruments and the absence of venture capital funds the European innovative entrepreneurs have very few corridors to access deep pools of capital. Apparently, if a promising business idea or product is not sufficient condition to access capital, then it is not a mystery that only 6%

[17] Christensen, C., Kaufman, S. P., and Shih, W. (2008). Innovation Killers: How financial tools destroy your capacity to do new things. *Harvard Business Review*, 86 (1), 1–8.

[18] For updated statistics on the allocation of the EFSI, especially the SME Window, see the websites of the European Investment Bank (www.eib.org) and the European Investment Fund (www.eif.europa.eu).

of the funding of SMEs is directed to innovative projects. Also, if the old Keynesian dictum that "supply creates its own demand" is true, then the low supply of funds for innovation can only lead to lower demand for funds for innovation.

Financing Innovation with Innovative Financial Instruments: Crowdfunding and ICOs

It is not empirically (econometrically) proven that "supply creates its own demand". But Keynes would smile in the case of the Initial Coin Offerings (ICOs) that created a trend and hype in 2017 in Europe.

ICOs are crypto-assets (tokens) issued by a technology-oriented start-up to fund itself in the early (typically in the post-seed) stage. The start-ups publish a white paper in which they explain their product, in most of the cases a blockchain-based application, and they reach the crowds, usually technology enthusiasts, to sell their tokens (a promise of value) and raise the necessary capital for their firm. Using the traditional definitions, ICOs are (mainly) private placements. The token can be a "utility token", a "claim of ownership" or a "claim on the future cash flows" of the firm. Once the enthusiast has made the "investment", she keeps her tokens and expects that their value will go up. Practically, it is not a "valuation exercise", though. It is a "pricing exercise". The price of the token is determined in the open market with the forces of supply and demand. As more and more people review the white paper of the start-up, they assess to which extent the value proposition is reflected in the proposed code, they check if the code has glitches, they assess the originality of the project vis-à-vis other similar propositions, they estimate the size of the market and evaluate other related information that is publicly exchanged in online fora, blockchain events and private channels of communication.

The risk of ICOs as 'investment' is significantly high. First, the regulatory environment of the ICOs is not clear. There are different regulatory approaches in the EU. Some Member States have adopted a liberal approach towards ICOs whereas others are very conservative. This environment of legal uncertainty (1) intensifies the fluctuation of the crypto-assets, (2) intensifies the uncertainty regarding the best practices and the acceptable disclosure standards that should accompany the issuance of a token and a white paper, and (3) intensifies the uncertainty regarding the "nature of the claim" of the token-holder as well as the 'nature of the liability' of the token-issuer. In blear institutional environment, without regulation in place, and without regulatory authority responsible for the supervision of the token-market as well as the enforcement of law in case of fraud, many ICOs where proved to be just scams pursuing to exploit the hype, make some money and disappear. In a market of uncertain quality of information, where both the dynamics of adverse selection and moral hazard were apparent everywhere, many bad projects were capitalized and many good projects remain in obscurity and failed.

However, despite the regulatory and economic fog, suddenly, the European innovative start-ups found both a source of finance and hope. The very existence of the ICO as a funding instrument accelerated the willingness to initiate projects based on cutting-edge technologies that neither the banks nor the venture capitalists would ever finance.

The European Commission acknowledged the potential of ICOs as an instrument with strong potential to cover the financing gap for innovative start-ups and SMEs in the very ambitious FinTech Action Plan, published in March 2018 within the framework of the Capital Markets Union (CMU).[19] The communication of the Commission highlights that '*(a)n assessment of the suitability of the current EU regulatory framework with regard to Initial Coin Offerings and crypto-assets more generally is necessary. On the one hand, the aim should be to make sure, that EU firms, investors and consumers can take advantage of this technical innovation within a fair and transparent framework in order to make Europe a leading player in developing new ways to rapidly fund growing businesses. On the other hand, potential financial stability, market integrity, investor and consumer protection, personal data protection and money laundering and terrorist financing-related risks should be appropriately addressed*'.[20]

This was a very important development for the technological start-ups because it came in a period where other jurisdictions either adopted an approach that practically "was killing" the agility of the ICOs as an instrument (e.g. the case of the United States) or banned the ICOs altogether (e.g. South Korea and China). The idea of the European Commission, in contrary, was to start a consultation period with the regulatory authorities of the Member States, the European Central Bank (ECB), the European Supervisory Authorities (ESAs) and the European Security Markets Authority (ESMA) in particular, in order to explore best practices, optimal regulatory approaches, risks and standardization requirements in order to introduce a legislative proposal by 2019.

[19] European Commission, COM(2018)109: FinTech Action plan: For a more competitive and innovative European financial sector.

[20] European Commission, COM(2018)109, ibid., p. 6.

The European Parliament's view was even more supportive of ICOs. In the now famous Blockchain Resolution, adopted in May 2018, that the authors of this article were draftsperson and rapporteur respectively,[21] made a step forward. Article 60 of the Resolution describe ICOs *as an alternative investment instrument* and *distinct asset class* and calls on the Commission and *ESMA to provide guidelines, especially for the utility tokens*. Article 61 stresses the *importance of legal certainty, standardization and consumer/investor protection*. Article 62 identifies ICOs as *essential part of the Capital Markets Union and calls for a framework that will allow the blending of this instrument with other financial instruments in the funding of innovation projects*. Finally, Article 63 calls on the Commission *to establish an ICO and Crypto-assets Observatory*.[22]

It is interesting that both the Commission and the European Parliament did not delve into the details. They just remarked on the opportunities and the dangers and declared that, at least in principle, the ICOs comprise a welcome source of funding for innovation and they stressed their potential. However, they omitted to provide definitions. Are the ICOs securities or commodities? Different assumptions require different regulatory methods. Tokens that "look like" equities or bonds could be regulated as securities, but what about the "utility tokens" that are the majority of the crypto-assets issued in Europe? The United States identified ICOs as securities, increasing thus the disclosure requirements for the start-ups, and at the same time the legal and fixed costs of underwriting. Start-ups in the USA find their self in the predicament of spending their vital seed/angel capital to lawyers and accountants. Contrary to the USA, EU has not a mutually recognized definition of "security" among the Member States. Some Member States use a list of requirements in order to define if an asset qualifies as a security or, similarly to the USA, have developed a "test-methodology" to check if a "paper" is a security or not. Defining ICOs as "securities" would not be easy. On the other hand, defining them as "commodities" and putting them under the Consumer Protection Regulation would not be optimal either. Instead of waiting, the practical assumption of the EU Institutions (including ESMA) was the issuers of tokens, at list temporarily, to rely on the securities and consumer protection regulations already in place until we have dedicated legislative work on ICOs.

The FinTech Action Plan, along with the Communication of the Commission, includes also a list of legislative proposals and a regulatory road map. The first item on this list was the Crowdfunding Regulation. European

[21] European Parliament, EP(2017)2772(RSP): Motion for Resolution on Distributed Ledger Technologies and Blockchains: Building Trust with Disintermediation.

[22] European Parliament, EP(2017)2772(RSP): ibid., p. 10.

Commission recognized the potential of crowdfunding in closing the gap of financing for innovative start-ups and SMEs.[23] The legislative proposal of the Commission, though, was not about crowdfunding in general, but about the crowdfunding platforms.[24]

Crowdfunding is in the core of financial disintermediation and the greatest example of financial democratization that emerged from the difficulties of the financial crisis and the digitization of finance.[25] Michael Gierczak et al. define it "as an open call—mostly through the Internet—for the provision of financial resources by a group of individuals instead of professional parties either in form of donations, in exchange for a future product or in exchange for some form of reward".[26] The crowdfunding market becomes increasingly more and more robust with over 800 platforms globally and total volume of 5.1 billion dollars. In Europe, Germany and the Netherlands have the most developed crowdfunding markets.[27]

ICOs can be seen as a crowdfunding endeavor. The need for creating a legal framework around ICOs raised expectations that the Commission will include them into the Crowdfunding Regulation. However, DG FISMA, the Commission's Directorate General responsible for the Regulation, decided not to include ICOs into their first text. The reasoning was straightforward. First, the regulation was about the service providers (intermediaries) and not about (self-placement) instruments. Second, the legislative proposal suggested a limit of one million euros cap for every crowdfunding round per year whereas the average ICO in EU raises capital circa 12 million euros. Third, the priority of the Commission was to regulate lending activities, whereas ICOs are not primarily lending instruments. Finally, the idea of the regulation

[23] European Commission: FinTech Action Plan Fact Sheet. Look at: https://ec.europa.eu/info/sites/info/files/180308-action-plan-fintech-factsheet_en.pdf

[24] COM(2018)113, Proposal for a Regulation on European Crowdfunding Service Providers (ECSP) for Business.

[25] Despite the fact that crowdfunding is a comparatively new instrument of finance it has already attracted the interest of both the academia and practitioners. A significant source of theoretical and practical information can be found at: Bruntje, D., and Gajda, O. (2016). *Crowdfunding in Europe: State of the Art in Theory and Practice* (London: Springer); Freedman, D., and Nutting, M. (2015) *Equity Crowdfunding for Investors: A guide to risks, returns, funding portals, due diligence, and deal terms* (London: Wiley); or Bottiglia, R., and Pichler, F. (2016). *Crowdfunding for SMEs: A European Perspective* (London: Palgrave Macmillan).

[26] Gierczak, M. M., Bretschneider, U., Haas, P., Blohm, I., and Leimeister, J. M. (2016). Crowdfunding: Outlining the New Era of Fundraising, in Bruntje, D., and Gajda, O. (Eds.). *Crowdfunding in Europe: State of the Art in Theory and Practice* (London: Springer), p. 8.

[27] Gierczak, M. M., Bretschneider, U., Haas, P., Blohm, I., and Leimeister, J. M. (2016). ibid., p. 9.

was to harmonize the environment of crowdfunding in Europe so as to remove the barriers of the internal market fragmentation and allow to start-ups and SMEs coming from smaller Member States and "lacking the crowds", to raise capital in bigger Member States whereas ICOs are "borderless".

The Crowdfunding Platforms Regulation was voted by the Economic Committee of the European Parliament in November 2018. In general the regulation was welcome in the European Parliament and it was treated with enthusiasm. We expect the final draft of the Regulation to be agreed in the Trialogues (negotiations between the Commission, the Parliament and the Council) before the end of this Mandate by May of 2019. The modifications will be market-oriented and make sure that the legal framework will benefit the innovative start-ups and SMEs, no matter their size, origin and business model. Among the main market-related adjustments of the regulation will be the increase of the cap of crowdfunding rounds from 1 to 8 million euros per year (just under the threshold imposed by the Prospectus Directive). It is the intention of the European Parliament to introduce ICOs into this regulation.

European Union: The Leader of Financial Disintermediation?

In this chapter we focused on crowdfunding and ICOs, an absolutely interesting and challenging topic of the Capital Markets Union that aims not only to improve the allocation of finance and the distribution of risk using the pioneering tools of fintech, but also to inspire a new wave of innovative tools of funding. In our view both crowdfunding and ICOs are only the first phase of a period of transition that will shape the global financial markets in such a way that the funding of innovation will gradually include not merely the traditional intermediation models we already know, but also the "wisdom of crowds". This transition requires a fresh look on the main characteristics of financial regulation. ICOs are a clear example of this new reality. From the USA to China traditional regulators try to fit this brand of new instrument to old definitions and old regulatory boxes.

The European Union, it seems, will not follow that example. Every technological innovation challenges old concepts of value proposition and business models. It is clear that technologies like blockchain and artificial intelligence challenge incumbents and their business models. It is the responsibility of the regulator to be *technology neutral* (to regulate not the technology per se but its uses) and *business model neutral* (let the market—not the regulator or the government—to decide which business model will survive). With these two principles, technology neutrality and business model neutrality, EU will build its global regulatory competitive advantage not only to accelerate the channeling of good quality of capital to the innovative European SMEs and start-ups, but also to inspire the regulatory initiatives of other jurisdictions around the world.

Part II

Financial Reporting

7

Towards Business Model Reporting for SMEs

Colin Haslam

Introduction

In Europe small and medium-sized enterprises (SMEs) represent 99 per cent of all businesses in the EU and roughly 58 per cent gross value added (GDP) and two-thirds of total employment. The definition of an SME is important for access to finance and EU support programmes targeted specifically at these enterprises.

Within Europe the application of International Financial Reporting Standards (IFRS) for SMEs, whilst supported by a number of member countries, has also been resisted by others. Objections include the complexity of IFRS reporting, its cost of implementation for SMEs, and its relevance, given that IFRS tends to be more appropriate for large corporations that operate in a global market.

Financialising SME Financial Reporting

The objective of adopting International Financial Reporting Standards (IFRS-5) issued by the International Accounting Standards Board (IASB) for use in the EU was to improve the efficient functioning of the EU capital markets and the internal market.

C. Haslam (✉)
Queen Mary University of London, London, UK
e-mail: c.haslam@qmul.ac.uk

E. Kaili et al. (eds.), *New Models of Financing and Financial Reporting for European SMEs*,
https://doi.org/10.1007/978-3-030-02831-2_7

> The objective of the International Accounting Standards (IAS) Regulation was to harmonise the financial reporting of listed companies by ensuring a high degree of transparency and comparability of their financial statements in order to enhance the efficient functioning of EU capital markets and of the internal market. The Regulation attached importance to IFRS becoming globally accepted so that EU companies would be able to compete on an equal footing for financial resources in the world capital markets.[1]

At the time of its adoption the implementation of International Accounting Standards (IAS) was seen as being more applicable to EU listed companies. But the idea of expanding IFRS into SMEs has found traction and justified on the grounds that this will enhance information transparency for investors and providers of capital.

> The concepts and principles of IFRS for SMEs are based on the Framework for the Preparation and Presentation of Financial Statements (the Framework) and therefore are very similar to full IFRS. Likewise, the statements needed to comprise a complete set of financial statements under IFRS for SMEs are also very similar to that required by IFRS.[2]

It is somewhat taken for granted that the application of IFRS will contribute to improving capital market efficiency; that is, reducing the cost of capital to potential or existing investors. The evidence itself is mixed as to whether or not adopting IFRS impacts on the costs of capital when other factors such as financial market conditions are also influential. Overall, it is argued that the adoption of IFRS is sensible because the benefits of adoption and implementation outweigh the costs of adoption—although this might not be the case for SMEs.

The IASB's financial reporting project is primarily focused on improving the efficiency of capital markets and has been less concerned with the impact of accounting standards applied within the context of financialised firms. The

---

[1] European Commission to the European Parliament and Council. (2015). *Evaluation of Regulation EC No 1606/2002 on application of international accounting standards.* 18 June 2015. Available at https://eur-lex.europa.eu/legal-content/EN/ALL/?uri=CELEX:32002R1606

[2] EY, IFRS for Small and Medium-Sized Entities. Available at http://www.ey.com/Publication/vwLUAssets/IFRS_for_SMEs_Comparison/$FILE/IFRS_for_SMEs_Comparison.pdf

Maystadt report[3] highlights the possibility that financial reporting practices played a role in exacerbating financial market instability in the last financial crisis. Former research[4] suggests that the IFRS standards that adjust historic costs of assets to their fair value (FV) increase the potential for financial instability in reporting entities because in financialised organisations dividends and share buy-backs are hollowing out reserves relative to the inflated value of their assets.

The IASB's project contributes to the financialisation of financial reporting because its primary focus is with capital market efficiency and recalibrating reporting entity accounts to their market value, such that the reporting entity looks increasingly like a tradable financial instrument.

Towards SME Business Model Reporting

The object of this section is to present an alternative framework within which SMEs might report their financial and non-financial results. This is grounded in a business models approach to reporting entities disclosures. The value proposition of an SME business model is about how relations with key material stakeholders are helping to secure value creation and value capture for their reporting entity. Fundamentally this is about managing stakeholder relations instrumentally to generate a financial return of capital invested and normatively about sustaining trust relationships. A business model approach to financial reporting for SMEs would capture how stakeholder relations have an ongoing impact on financial viability both instrumentally and normatively.

[3] European Commission, *Maystadt report* (2013). Available at http://ec.europa.eu/internal_market/accounting/docs/governance/reform/131112_report_en.pdf

[4] Haslam, C., et al. (2017). *The Routledge Companion to Critical Accounting, Stress testing the adoption of Fair Value Accounting (FVA): Fragility and instability in financialized firms*, Routledge Companions in Business, Management and Accounting, London: Routledge.

The SME world. Source: Author

With business model financial reporting the object is to capture information about how material stakeholder relations are impacting on financial viability. This would contribute to securing:

- SME accounting disclosures for business intelligence gathering
- Informing investors about viability
- Informing policymakers about how material stakeholder relations underwrite growth and financial viability in SME business models.

Our proposal for SME financial disclosures is organised around the idea of an *integrated financial viability statement* (IFVS) that is informed by the SME business model (stakeholder relations and market conditions).

This would take the form of a simplified but integrated financial statement with accompanying information about material stakeholder and market relations that contribute to or put at risk the viability of the SME's value proposition. With the rollout of digital XBRL reporting this information would be collected more rapidly and processed into useful risk-evaluation toolkits for policy informing intelligence reports in addition to investment risk evaluation.

XBRL involves the application of computer-readable tags that connect to data disclosed by business. This 'tagging' of disclosed data enables it to be processed automatically by software tools in an efficient way, thereby facilitating high-quality analysis of business information.

Our suggestion is for SMEs to disclose financial information using the nature of expenses format (rather than function of expenses) which allows discrimination between internal value retained and external costs. International Accounting Standard 1 (IAS1) outlines the disclosure of financial statements by the function of expenses and in the notes suggests that these disclosures might also be by their nature.

> An entity shall present an analysis of expenses recognised in profit or loss using a classification based on either their nature or their function within the entity, whichever provides information that is reliable and more relevant.[5]

Why Move Towards Business Model Financial Reporting for SMEs?

- The object is to get us to start thinking about SME accounting disclosures within a relatively simple but integrated viability statement.
- It can provide a useful intelligence gathering toolkit informing us about material stakeholder relations that underwrite SME financial viability.
- It reveals how market conditions impact upon the financial performance and sustainability of SMEs.
- It generates innovative policy interventions and financing strategies for SME viability.

		Integrated financial viability statements stakeholder driven SME statement		
		Financials	Stakeholders	Market risk drivers
http://rvaconsulting.se/		CU	Descriptions	Descriptions
	Sales	X	Customer demand	Product market (price, volume)
Minus	External costs	X	Suppliers	Procurement market (price, volume)
Equals	Value retained	X	Value captured	*Position in the economy*

(continued)

[5] European Commission, *International Accounting Standard 1*. Available at http://ec.europa.eu/internal_market/accounting/docs/consolidated/ias1_en.pdf

(continued)

		Integrated financial viability statements stakeholder driven SME statement		
		Financials	Stakeholders	Market risk drivers
http://rvaconsulting.se/		CU	Descriptions	Descriptions
Minus	Employment expenses	X	Employees	Labour market (no of employees, salary)
Equals	Cash from primary activity	X	Primary EBITDA	*Gross profit position in the economy*
Plus/ minus	Realised holding gains/losses	X	Other firms	Secondary product markets
Minus/ plus	Pensions and other cash adj.	X	Employees	Demographics, asset and liabilities
Equals	Cash from secondary activity	X	Secondary EBITDA	
Equals	Cash from operations	X	EBITDA	
Minus	Cash taxes	X	Government regulation	Tax rate, fiscal policy
Minus/ plus	Change in working capital	X	Customers, suppliers, employees	Product, procurement & labour market
Minus	CAPEX, sale of assets	X	Suppliers	Product market (price, volume)
	Cash flow to investors	X	Investors	
Minus/ plus	Net interest, amortisation	X	Credit institutions	Capital market (interest rate, risk appetite)
Minus/ plus	Dividends, share buy-backs	X	Shareholders/ owners	Capital market (cost of capital/risk appetite)
	Retained cash	X	*Management*	

Source: Author

The income statement is simple and reveals how total income is distributed to cover external costs and then reveal value captured. This is distributed to cover employee costs and then reveals cash from operations. This cash then distributed to cover other claims. These line items correspond also to key stakeholders: suppliers, employees, government, and investors. Commentary about these relations reveals how these stakeholder relations are changing and impacting on financial viability.

		Financials	Stakeholders	Market risk drivers
Statement of financial position		CU	Descriptions	Descriptions
Tangible assets				
	Property	X	Consolidating entity	Property market valuations
	Plant	X	Consolidating entity	Cost and supplier dependency
	Equipment	X	Consolidating entity	Cost and supplier dependency
Financial				
	Leases	X	Consolidating entity	Lessor risks
	Marketable securities	X	Consolidating entity	Asset market risks
	Investments	X	Consolidating entity	Subsidiary company risks
	Pension funds	X	Employees	Bonds and equities markets (Actuarial risk)
Intangible	Goodwill	X	Consolidating entity	Business unit cash earnings or market valuation risk
	Brands patents licenses	X	Consolidating entity	Future earnings capacity risks
Current	Stock	X	Consolidating entity	Suppliers and product market
	Debtors	X	Consolidating entity	Debtor credit rating and repayment risk
	Cash	X	Consolidating entity	Investment performance
Total assets		X		
Liabilities ST				
	Borrowings	X	Consolidating entity	Remortgaging, etc.
	Loans	X	Consolidating entity	Banks, etc.
	Creditors	X	Consolidating entity	Credit ratings
	Family loans	X	Consolidating entity	Details
	Credit cards	X	Consolidating entity	Details
Liabilities LT				
	Loans	X	Consolidating entity	Credit ratings and credit markets

(*continued*)

(continued)

Statement of financial position		Financials CU	Stakeholders Descriptions	Market risk drivers Descriptions
	Provisions	X	Consolidating entity	Risks attached to asset and product markets
Reserves	Paid in funds	X	Consolidating entity	Access to refinancing
	Accumulated earnings	X	Consolidating entity	Equity market conditions at IPO
	Minus treasury stock	X	Consolidating entity	Equity market conditions
	Holding gains/ losses	X	Consolidating entity	Capital and asset market conditions
	Fair value adjustment	X	Consolidating entity	Capital and asset market conditions
Total reserves		X	Risk to value in excess of paid in capital	Risk to value in excess of paid in capital

Source: Author

Information about the line items in the statement of financial position would help inform users about how relations with stakeholders are impacting upon both assets and liabilities.

Specifically the statement of financial position would provide additional insight into the key material stakeholders underwriting assets and liabilities in SMEs.

The European Financial Reporting Advisory Group's (EFRAG) position is that a business model framework would contribute towards 'cohesiveness'.

> The need to understand an entity's business model is further increased by development of integrated reporting, which suggests that investors need to rely on a cohesive set of information, encompassing more than only financial statements. (EFRAG[6])

The International Integrated Reporting Council report *Integrated Reporting* also defines an organisations business model as a 'system of transforming inputs, through its business activities, into outputs and outcomes that aims to

[6] EFRAG, The role of the business model in financial statements. Available at https://www.efrag.org/Assets/Download?assetUrl=%2Fsites%2Fwebpublishing%2FSiteAssets%2FBusiness%2520Model%2520Research%2520Paper.pdf

fulfil the organization's strategic purposes and create value over the short, medium and long term'.[7]

Central to understanding the viability of SMEs is the need for information about stakeholder interactions and how these are contributing to value creation and value capture for cash earnings. In this respect there is a significant role for the accounting profession and its professional bodies because a business model disclosure project would enhance our understanding of SME financial viability.

There is a need for a closer alignment between the financial statements and stakeholders to make visible how stakeholder relations contribute to SMEs financial viability. Most reporting entities do not disclose the nature of expenses in their income statements but prefer to disclose expenses by their function. This may be the result of the IAS1 suggesting that a functional approach to disclosure provides superior information of relevance to investors and demands of capital markets. Our argument is that reporting the nature of expenses is an equally valuable disclosure method because it increases the visibility of stakeholders. In addition we are able to construct a financial boundary that discriminates what is inside and outside the SME reporting entity. This provides intelligence about changes in the balance of value capture between the SME and its other stakeholders in the business model network of financial relations.

The objective of SME financial reporting would become that of revealing information about stakeholder relations and how these are contributing to (or frustrating) an SME business model value proposition; that is, its financial viability. This is a different project to that being pursued by the IASB, which is about information for capital market efficiency and the financialisation of accounting.

[7] Integrated Reporting, *Business Model*. Available at http://integratedreporting.org/wp-content/uploads/2013/03/Business_Model.pdf

8

New Relevance of Accounting and Reporting: SMEs, Ethics and Sustainability

Olivier Boutellis-Taft

Introduction

SMEs have recently taken the centre stage in many political debates. It was due time as they form the core of the EU economy and are the real engine of job creation, wealth generation and innovation. Although discussions in policy circles on how to steer the EU economy and its regulatory framework towards more sustainable directions are growing, many policymakers and regulators remain largely focused on big business and there is still some way to go to make the motto "think small first" an operational principle of day-to-day policymaking.

SMEs encompass a large and heterogeneous group, which, according to some, accounts for 99 per cent of enterprises. This makes it uneasy to *pinpoint precisely a typical SME, especially in today's changing world (1)*. What remains certain is that *financial (and non-financial) information are essential to business, including for SMEs (2)*. It is important that corporate reporting evolves with changed circumstances, needs and technologies—this is why Accountancy Europe is engaged in a project on the *future of corporate reporting (3)*; this project already helped identify some key *recommendations for policymakers (4)*. Change is a collective responsibility and we also see necessary *evolutions in the accountancy profession (5)*.

O. Boutellis-Taft (✉)
Accountancy Europe, Brussels, Belgium
e-mail: olivier@accountancyeurope.eu

E. Kaili et al. (eds.), *New Models of Financing and Financial Reporting for European SMEs*,
https://doi.org/10.1007/978-3-030-02831-2_8

What Is an SME in Today's World?

From the shop around the corner to the high-tech start-up, SMEs are an extraordinarily diverse crowd. While everybody talks about SMEs, it is not always clear whether we all mean the same thing. Therefore, first and foremost it is important to reflect how an SME should be defined today in our globalising and changing economies where technology and its transformation of conventional business models further complicates the matter. However, concerns around financing seem to be a key element of commonality.

Most of the attention tends to be absorbed by the high-growth potential innovative start-ups. They are a fascinating group but still only account for a small minority of SMEs. Even in this elite group, situations and needs differ widely, for example between the IT start-up set up by three friends in a garage to look for the "killer app", the high-tech pharma company with large human and financial capital in search of a new miraculous cancer drug or the sophisticated fintech active on global financial markets.

Next to these outliers in the spotlight, the search for the typical SME is equally in vain. There is little in common between my baker making these delicious croissants with the help of just one apprentice and his wife at the cashier, a professional services firm with 3 partners and 10 employees providing services all around the country, a broker trading oil tankers globally over the phone and a German Mittelstand with 200 staff outsourcing part of its production in neighbouring EU member states and exporting to China.

All these businesses may be below the quantitative threshold by which regulators define SMEs; but their business model, their target markets, their ownership and corporate governance structure, their strategy, risk level and growth potential, the complexity of their transactions and their social and environmental impact differ widely. Nonetheless, most regulatory approaches continue to focus only on size to define SMEs. I personally, however, doubt that such an approach is still fully relevant.

Furthermore, purely numerical criteria may not match the complexity of a business model. Consider, for example, the 10-staff threshold established by the Accounting Directive (2013/34/EU): In today's economy, there are companies with less than 10 staff operating on a global scale with complex structure and business models. On the other side of the spectrum, there are companies employing more than the 500-staff threshold that are fairly simple and straightforward, with few external stakeholders and low risk.

Thresholds give little indication, if any, of the future growth potential and aspirations these businesses may have. In the examples above, the fintech or the German Mittelstand will probably seek to further grow and expand internationally. By contrast, the likes of my baker have—in most instances—no appetite to grow and have different needs. They, however, play a fundamental role in our economies (not only because they provide me with excellent croissants, but they are the fabric of our local economies and social lives). Their stakeholders are also different. This diversity beside size does not justify that their lives be complicated with all sorts of excessive legal and administrative requirements shaped for large companies.

The above-mentioned Accounting Directive nonetheless classifies these companies in accordance with the same method of size thresholds. Once it has put them in a box, it treats them in more or less the same manner. However, today there may be much more relevant criteria than size, including, for example:

- Business model, types of activity and complexity of transactions, risk profile
- Sectors and markets (local, EU Single Market, global markets)
- Impact and stakeholders (investors and other providers of finance, employees, business partners, communities, resources, biodiversity, etc.)
- Sources and nature of funding (public or private, etc.).

The latter makes a key difference. The existence of external investors and the status of limited liability company bring the public interest into the equation with particular prominence. In fact, external investors deserve protection whatever the size of the company.

Our economies have evolved steadily and the pace of change has accelerated in recent years not the least because of technology, therefore SMEs are not (always) what they used to be. The drivers of value creation have also evolved. In many sectors, intangibles (e.g. R&D, knowledge, leadership, sustainability, employee commitment, brand, goodwill) are often considered to be getting more important than property, plant and equipment. However, these factors are more complex to address than mere size, which lawmakers, perhaps understandably, continue to hold on to, although it is becoming less relevant.

This evolution also creates specific challenges when it comes to measuring and reporting how a company creates value.

The European Parliament is right in promoting this debate. It is the right time to have this discussion: with technology changing business model and financing logic (and in fact, changing just about everything we do including gradually the way we think without us really noticing), it is also important we embrace a future that is coming sooner than ever before.

The Importance of Financial (and Non-financial) Information

Information is key for (proper) decision-making and successful management of businesses. It should be noted this is true for financial but also increasingly for non-financial information. A small business owner, managing his own finance, needs information. A banker, lending to a craftsman, a professional, a merchant or a small industry requires information. A venture capitalist, investing in a start-up, requires information. A citizen, putting money in local development via a crowdfunding platform, requires information.

There is no commerce and social life without proper information and trust—and information and trust are also the lifeblood of our sophisticated and changing economies. There is no sustainable business and long-term investment without financial—and growingly non-financial—information. Corporate reporting is therefore essential to the development of our economies and in particular to what constitutes the largest part of European enterprises: SMEs.

The first thing to bear in mind is that corporate reporting is a means to an end—not an end in itself. Financial information is first and foremost a critical management tool. Indeed, the lack of good quality financial information is behind many business failures. Therefore, while reducing reporting requirements may initially sound like a good idea to reduce red tape, it may indeed prove fatal in the long run. Quality of regulation matters a lot more than quantity, but designing better regulation is a lot more difficult and carries less communicative value than just striking the delete button.

Furthermore, transparency is essential to external stakeholders who, for various reasons, want to understand how a business is managed, what impacts it has and how it performs. Such information is particularly important when considering providing financing to a company, but also when signing an employment contract or a supplier agreement.

Although today's discussions around company reporting focus mainly on listed SMEs, I would like to outline that reporting remains relevant to all SMEs—including the smaller local ones. Reporting should not be seen merely as a formal compliance exercise detached from these SMEs' needs. It is the needs of SMEs and their various stakeholders (including policymakers) and the value of the information for decision-making that should drive proportionate reporting. For instance, non-financial information is increasingly used, even when it is not required by existing regulations.

Compliance-driven reporting, based on purely administrative requirements disconnected from evolving market needs, collected redundantly via outdated means and with no other reason than habits, is doomed to lose its relevance, and risks becoming a mere administrative burden bringing little value, if any, to the business and to society.

It is important to ensure that reporting is relevant and comparable while avoiding an information overload and mitigating costs (administrative and other). It is a difficult balance to strike and this is why users and stakeholders must drive this debate.

To contribute to these objectives, Accountancy Europe produced a paper *Disclose what truly matters—Model disclosures under the non-financial and diversity information directive* in November 2016. Our intention was to provide ideas and examples of best practices to companies that will have to comply for the first time with the EU Directive on the disclosure of non-financial and diversity information by certain large undertakings and groups. In line with our belief that public policy and regulation should be pragmatic and rooted in market realities, instead of writing long explanations, we produced a short "mock-up" management report of a fictional company in the food industry to reflect how the Directive's requirements would effectively operate in practice.

The Directive 2014/95/EU on non-financial and diversity information disclosures is the most significant legislative initiative to promote consistent reporting of environmental, social, and governance (ESG) issues across Europe.

The European Commission estimated that the Directive would directly impact around 6, 000 of the largest public interest entities (PIEs) across Europe. However, as Member States have the flexibility to reduce the threshold criteria, the final number of PIEs affected could be considerably higher. Of these companies, many will already have gone down the route of disclosing ESG information, either in response to national requirements or voluntarily—"voluntarily" includes responding to market pressure, whether it results from stakeholders' demands or competitive pressure. There will be many other companies, however, that have little or no prior experience in this field of reporting and may be wondering how they will be able to meet the requirements that entered into force on 1 January 2017.

This demonstrates that reporting needs to evolve to respond to markets needs and that such evolution can only happen if there is space for experimentation and flexibility.

The Future of Corporate Reporting

In times of rapid changes, we need to look ahead. Accountancy Europe has therefore undertaken a project to explore the future of corporate reporting and is also working on a series of follow-up papers.[1]

In the project, we outline that we see the array of stakeholders of corporate reporting is increasing. Many stakeholders are taking a keen and legitimate interest in reporting: first and foremost, providers of finance, but also for example, consumers, local communities, and various interest groups, such as environmental non-governmental organisations.

In parallel, technology is radically changing the ways in which we access, obtain, process, compare and analyse information. Its potential is unfortunately insufficiently leveraged as legislation was written with a very different world in mind.

Today's reporting is too much centred around only shareholders and compliance. However, the needs of different providers of finance (ranging from loans to crowdfunding), employees, business partners and civil society appear as growingly important and must be taken into account.

Unfortunately, many users also find reporting too complex and too voluminous; some would argue that reporting brings too little, too late, while others worry that it is incomplete and drives short-termism. Given such diverging views on the matter, the impossibility of pleasing everyone must be accepted from the outset. Compromises have to be made.

However this is also where technology can help. Rather than thinking in linear terms of information requirements to be presented in the form of a sequence of pages which come in increasing number, IT would enable more flexible solutions. However, IT cannot serve the never-ending appetite for always more and more diverse information in financial reporting, but also non-financial information (NFI) and Country by Country Reporting (CBCR). There is a need for clearly hierarchising information needs.

Technology is a very promising enabler but we shouldn't fool ourselves: it will never compensate for poor law-making and inconsistencies across EU Member States.

The Future of Corporate Reporting discussion paper suggests developing what we called a "core and more" approach, whereby a concise summary report is provided whilst technology will enable interested users to drill down into the details. In this respect, we see great potential in integrated reporting.

---

[1] Accountancy Europe. Available at www.accountancyeurope.eu

An "integrated report" (<IR>) properly prepared as proposed by the IIRC[2] would be an excellent example of a core report.

The strategic report required by the new Companies Act (2013) in the UK is also a most interesting and welcomed development. Along a similar line as <IR>, strategic report provides a holistic and meaningful picture of a company's business model, strategy, development, performance, position and future prospects.

Recommendations for Policymakers

Our discussion paper on the Future of Corporate Reporting project also puts forward a set of recommendations for policymakers.

First, the Hippocratic principle, 'first do no harm', deserves due consideration in the world of corporate reporting too. This means that regulation and standards should avoid inhibiting innovation. Obstacles to change should be addressed. Reporting should be free to evolve with stakeholders' needs and developments in new technology: if cast in stone, it risks becoming irrelevant and obsolete.

Second, policymakers should adopt a more principles-based approach to corporate reporting. We believe that focusing on principles and outcomes is more effective than detailed prescriptions that foster a tick-the-box mindset. A proportional application of standards should be encouraged by all involved, including regulators, companies, auditors and enforcers.

We believe that the International Financial Reporting Standards (IFRS) adequately respond to this objective and are scalable—but only insofar as enforcers allow an application based on relevance and proportionality (and not mechanical formalism).

With markets steadily globalising (in spite of a few political hiccups) and with the view of furthering the Single Market, greater consistency in company reporting remains highly valuable and instrumental to fostering investment.

Finally, we need to allow experimentation. There is no innovation without experimentation and risk-taking. Innovation is not something you govern by decree. History shows that it is rarely a top-down standardised process. This is not something everybody is comfortable with outside of science and business but it is the price to pay for evolution, relevance and progress. Regulators should not stifle change but encourage—or at least make possible—experimentation so that better solutions can be found.

---

[2] International Integrated Reporting Council. Available at http://integratedreporting.org

At this very moment, such innovation is unfolding in the world of corporate reporting: integrated reporting (<IR>). <IR> is the best concrete example of innovation in motion in the world of reporting. It is an attempt to bring together financial and non-financial information and report in an integrated manner on a company's capacity to create value in the short- and long-term. Although <IR> is still work in progress, we have identified it in our project on the future of corporate reporting as the most promising way forward.

Evolutions in the Profession

Technology is radically transforming our social and professional lives. This of course equally applies to the accountancy profession. In the debate on SMEs, it is too often forgotten that most accountants are SMEs themselves. They know SMEs from their day-to-day work being the prime advisor of millions of SMEs, but they also learn from their direct experience as SMEs themselves.

Technology is opening up new opportunities, especially for small accountancy firms that depend less on size and location to create value.

The profession is also leveraging technology to better help clients. For instance, more accountancy firms are experimenting and using cloud technology. As a result, both the accountant and her clients are able to access financial information in real time to provide an instant picture of how the business is performing. This can be used to help clients adjust their strategy and improve their future profitability. Improved insight also allows for better advice to SME clients. This marks a key evolution from serving clients to collaborating with them.

Increasingly, basic accountancy and compliance work is automated. To remain relevant, accountants are moving away from being inputters and processors of financial information to providing the bridge between the information and clients' business needs. The profession is ideally placed not only to interpret the (big) information available to clients but also to help design those analytics (such as Key Performance Indicators (KPIs) and client specific dashboards) most relevant to them.

Although cloud technology has the potential for simplifying accounting for clients, it is apparent that many clients remain unwilling or unable to keep their own accounting records and will still seek the services of an accountant.

The accountancy world is moving towards "zero entry"—where customers and vendors enter information directly. With access to online services (providing e.g. ERP, CRM, accounting or tax software), clients can amend personal information, input data directly (perhaps using apps), and download documents and reports from the system themselves. Consequently, the profession will spend less time dealing with client administration and data entry, and can concentrate on providing value-added services, such as providing strategic advice and improving SMEs' access to finance.

The cloud offers smaller businesses access to services and tools previously available only to large organisations, such as Big Data analytics. These services are often offered on demand, using a pay-as-you-go approach, which allows for experimentation and adaptation as required.

In these times of disruptive innovation, the profession is, like other sectors, reflecting on what the future holds. Since the clay tokens of around 7000 BC, the accountancy profession has a good track record of adapting to technological innovation. As with all waves of change, many say this time it is different; it may, however, be true in that for the first time, the human brain—the main asset of professionals—is losing some of its monopolies.

Developments in artificial intelligence and machine learning, data analytics and natural language interaction bring new prospects … for robots. These innovations do more than automating processes and replacing clerical staff: they open up new ways of doing things and create new things to do. While digitalisation represents a massive change, it is only one of the mega-trends currently reshaping the world. To make sense of what is happening, we must consider it in the light of other transformations taking place:

- Environmental destruction is directly impacting us through resource scarcity, the rising death toll due to pollution, and new risks related to rising climate change.
- Security threats make fighting against terrorism financing, money laundering, and other financial crimes a collective imperative.
- Income inequalities, the malfunctioning of tax systems and corruption are having a negative impact on society and the economy through sluggish demand, exclusion, and costly social unrest.
- Corporate or governmental information can be analysed—or leaked—more easily than ever, and are expected to be available and widely shared. With unprecedented scrutiny, public opinion increases political pressure.

What we see today is a growing demand from society for trust, ethical behaviour, and social and environmental responsibility. The hard truth is that any professional activity, including accounting, only exists if it creates value and responds to the needs of society. In such a changing environment, professionals and professions need to reinvent themselves. Five directions appear to be worth exploring further.

Differentiating Between Means and Ends

Machines can replace most of the tasks that professional accountants currently do, except deciding what these tasks are. Computers and robots can do many things except inventing their own purpose. Humans get to define what we want computers to do. However, once the task is defined and standardised, the need for human beings to perform it diminishes or even disappears, except where adaptability and flexibility are required (e.g. to change plans or stop a process), at which point the need for human judgement and emotional intelligence returns.

Defining and Discovering the (Real) Problem

The most intelligent person or machine cannot solve an unidentified problem. Troubleshooting systems and self-help tools can do wonders, except when the user leads those systems to answer the wrong question. All professionals dealing with clients know that the true problem is not always what the customer thinks it is. Accountants still need professional judgement and emotional intelligence to understand and decipher the issue they are asked to solve. Over the past few decades, the profession has mostly focused on technical expertise—precisely the bit that is easiest to replace by robots. Soft skills and emotional intelligence matter a lot more today.

Providing Ethical Judgement

Machines have no notion of right and wrong; they cannot (yet) respond to society's demand for more ethics and moral values. At least when they attempt to do so it is on the basis of what we humans defined. This leaves an opportunity for accountants whose professional values are more important than ever. At the end of the day, the profession's purpose is to provide transparency, integrity, and trust—more than technical expertise, which is simply one of the means to that end.

Promoting Responsible Business

At a time when business is expected to and must become socially and environmentally responsible, rigorous measurement and reporting become even more instrumental, including on matters such as the United Nations Sustainable Development Goals (SDGs). Independent assurance, a core area of expertise of professional accountants, is also a critical tool to provide trust and prevent much detrimental greenwashing. We need technology to help us bring some clarity to the impact of business on the SDGs, but algorithms on their own will not provide the answers we are looking for. And they will not provide any answer other than what we ask them for. Trained professionals who can assess the impact of business decisions on other parties and stakeholders, on the public interest, and on future generations remain indispensable.

Over the last 40 years, the evidence is that accounting and financial information only is not enough to explain how companies create value. The International Integrated Reporting Council (IIRC) outlines the role other capitals (natural, human, manufactured, social and relationship, and intellectual capitals) play alongside financial capital in value creation. Modern technologies, such as cloud, mobile, and big data analytics, are rapidly multiplying the information that is being picked up across all the capitals. But someone needs to make sense of these capitals, making sure that business is assimilating the growing volumes of data and making good decisions in the short, medium, and long term. Clearly, the accountancy profession is in an excellent place to be the conduit and arbiter between multi-capital data and sustainable value creation. This will require the profession to move beyond finance as its primary focus.

Building on the profession's long-time commitment to the public interest, there is a unique occasion to refocus on what matters most by responding to an acute demand of society and become more relevant than ever. However, to be able to seize the opportunities, it is critical that regulation doesn't impede innovation and change. With its daily involvement with SMEs, the accountancy profession is uniquely placed to understand the needs and challenges SMEs face in today's environment and is committed to playing an important role to help modernise regulation. However, the profession can only play its full role if it not only embraces change, but also reinvents its ways of thinking and acting—like all other players.

9

Financial Reporting for Small Listed Companies

Darrel Scott

Introduction

The IFRS Foundation is a not-for-profit, public interest organisation. The primary objective of the Foundation, as set out in its *Constitution*, is 'to develop, in the public interest, a single set of high quality, understandable, enforceable and globally accepted financial reporting standards based upon clearly articulated principles'. The *Constitution* also specifies another objective of the organisation as being 'to take account of, as appropriate, the needs of a range of sizes and types of entities in diverse economic settings'.

Accounting standards are a set of principles companies follow when they prepare and publish their financial statements, providing a standardised way of describing a company's financial performance. Publicly accountable companies (those listed on public stock exchanges) and financial institutions are typically required to publish their financial reports in accordance with agreed accounting standards. The Board, which is the independent standard-setting body of the Foundation, has developed IFRS Standards for such companies.

The views expressed in this chapter are those of the author, and do not necessarily reflect the views of the International Accounting Standards Board (Board) or the IFRS Foundation (Foundation). This chapter reflects in large part the submission made by the Foundation in response to the Green Paper, Building a Capital Markets Union, issued in February 2015 by the European Commission (Commission).

D. Scott (✉)
IASB, London, UK
e-mail: dscott@ifrs.org

E. Kaili et al. (eds.), *New Models of Financing and Financial Reporting for European SMEs*,
https://doi.org/10.1007/978-3-030-02831-2_9

Totalling around 250 printed pages, the length of the *IFRS for SMEs®* Standard is much shorter than the full IFRS Standards. The SMEs Standard is tailored for companies that are not publicly accountable. It focuses on the information needs of lenders, creditors and other users of SME financial statements who are interested primarily in information about cash flows, liquidity and solvency. It also takes into account the capabilities of SMEs to prepare financial information.

Setting the Global Context: The Importance of International Comparability

In its October 2014 response to the Commission's consultation on the effects of using IFRS Standards in the EU, the Foundation commented that the use of a single set of financial reporting requirements is essential to the successful achievement of a Capital Markets Union (CMU). The Foundation has previously noted its belief that, in order to facilitate global investment, a financial reporting regime must provide for transparent and reliable financial information that is internationally comparable.

The importance of that international comparability continues to be stressed. For example, the Maystadt Report in 2013 observed a 'wide consensus among stakeholders on the commitment to global quality accounting standards', with the global character of IFRS Standards being the most significant factor.[1] A review of the responses to the Commission's public consultation in 2014 on the effects of using IFRS Standards in the EU also reveals the importance that stakeholders attach to the establishment of a single set of globally accepted, high-quality financial reporting standards. IFRS Standards have the twin advantage of being the single financial reporting language both for the EU and for much of the world at large.

IFRS Standards are applied across the world. The Foundation has been developing profiles on the use of IFRS Standards. Of 150 jurisdictions profiled to date, 126 mandate the use of the Standards for all or most public companies and 12 more permit their use.[2] In other words, market participants around the world are familiar with, and use, IFRS Standards. The use of the

[1] Maystadt, P. (October 2013) *Should IFRS Standards be More 'European'? Mission to Reinforce the EU's Contribution to the Development of International Accounting Standards*. Available at URL http://ec.europa.eu/finance/accounting/docs/governance/reform/131112_report_en.pdf

[2] IFRS, *Who uses IFRS standards*. Available at URL www.ifrs.org/use-around-the-world/use-of-ifrs-standards-by-jurisdiction/

Standards in the EU already contributes to the promotion of Europe as an internationally competitive and attractive place to invest, as does its use in other jurisdictions. The global reach of IFRS Standards and the positive effects that they have brought in terms of the quality, transparency and comparability of financial reporting is core to this promotion. The use of the Standards in the EU also helps EU companies in search of capital and investment from elsewhere. In addition, the use of IFRS Standards globally by EU companies, without the need for reconciliations, is generally considered to have benefited those companies with improved group reporting and administrative savings through having to report only under one accounting framework.

Public Accountability and Meeting the Needs of Investors

Experience around the world shows that a key factor to the success of capital markets is the level of trust placed in them by investors.

However, in relation to smaller companies wanting access to dedicated trading venues such as Multilateral Trading Facilities (MTFs), some commentators have raised concerns about the perceived additional costs of applying full IFRS Standards.

While the application of IFRS Standards does require a company to incur the costs of preparing financial statements, the Foundation has previously expressed the view that this is a necessary investment if a company decides to enter a public capital market. Such markets, whether regulated or MTFs, bring together companies that seek capital and investors who are not involved in managing the company and who are considering whether to provide capital, and at what price. Those investors do not have the power to demand the financial information they might find useful for investment decision-making and so must rely on the company's general purpose financial statements.

A company's decision to enter a public capital market makes it publicly accountable, regardless of size. In this circumstance, the company must provide the outside debtors and equity investors with a broader range of financial information than may be needed by users of financial statements of companies that obtain capital only from private sources.

The Commission's report in 2008 on the operation of the IAS Regulation[3] noted, on the evidence of a 2007 study by the Institute of Chartered

[3] European Commission. (2008). *Report on the Operation of Regulation 1606/2002 on the Application of International Accounting Standards*. http://ec.europa.eu/finance/accounting/docs/ias/com-2008-0215_en.pdf

Accountants in England and Wales (ICAEW),[4] that smaller quoted companies faced more difficulties than do larger enterprises in applying IFRS Standards because of limited resources and a lack of prior experience. Nevertheless, the level of implementation and recurrent application costs 'remains at an acceptable level'. Elsewhere, evidence of the Canadian transition to IFRS Standards reveals that costs were 'significant, but manageable' and that, for smaller listed companies, the transition to IFRS Standards was 'generally straightforward'.[5] The application of IFRS Standards is straightforward when a company's business model is simple. Unsurprisingly, the costs of application are greater where a company's business model is complex, but those costs are arguably necessary in order for such a company to provide investors with a faithful representation of that complexity.

Other jurisdictions with major capital markets deem all listed companies, regardless of size, as being publicly accountable and so require them to apply the full suite of applicable financial reporting standards. This is the case, for example, in Australia, Canada, Hong Kong and Korea, where full IFRS Standards[6] are required to be applied by all listed companies. It is also the case in the US, where all domestic companies whose debt or equity securities are traded in a public market are required to follow US Generally Accepted Accounting Principles (US GAAP), regardless of their size.

In the US, smaller listed companies are provided with relief from regulatory requirements other than the financial reporting standards to be applied. For example, in September 2010, the US Securities and Exchange Commission removed the requirement for 'non-accelerated filers' (smaller issuers)[7] to obtain an independent auditor's report on the effectiveness of their internal control over financial reporting under Section 404(b) of the Sarbanes-Oxley Act 2002. As another example, the US Jumpstart Our Business Startups Act 2012 created a new category of issuer, called an emerging growth company (EGC), and provides regulatory relief to EGCs to encourage initial public offerings (IPOs).

---

[4] ICAEW. (2007). *EU Implementation of IFRS and the Fair Value Directive.* http://ec.europa.eu/internal_market/accounting/docs/studies/2007-eu_implementation_of_ifrs.pdf

[5] FEI. (2013). *The Cost of IFRS Transition in Canada.* https://portal.feicanada.org/enews/file/CFERF%20studies/2012-2013/The%20cost%20of%20IFRS%20transition%20in%20Canada%20-%20July%204,%202013%20-%20final.pdf

[6] HKFRS in Hong Kong are identical to IFRS Standards.

[7] SEC Final Rule Release No. 33-9142, *Internal Control Over Financial Reporting in Exchange Act Periodic Reports of Non-Accelerated Filers.* While 'non-accelerated filers' is not defined in Commission rules, it refers to issuers that have aggregate worldwide market values of voting and non-voting equity of less than US$75 million, as of the last business day of the issuer's most recently completed second fiscal quarter. https://www.sec.gov/rules/final/2010/33-9142.pdf

One of the reliefs available to EGCs allows for an extended phase-in for the application of new or revised accounting standards. However, an EY report in 2014[8] reveals that less than 20% of EGCs have elected to retain the ability to delay the effective date of new or revised accounting standards. The report notes that many EGCs seem to want to ensure investors that their financial statements will remain comparable with those of other public companies.

The application of US GAAP by such companies does not, therefore, appear to have been a barrier to growth in the US markets.

Any proposal to develop a common accounting standard for SMEs listed on MTFs will, therefore, need careful consideration, given that such companies are publicly accountable. The definition of an SME, as set out in the Markets in Financial Instruments Directive (Directive 2014/65/EU) (also known as 'MiFID II') encompasses some sizeable companies. For the purposes of the Directive, an SME is a company with an average market capitalisation over a three-year period of up to €200 million.

Public accountability requires such companies to prepare and publish financial information compiled in accordance with financial reporting standards that are viewed by market participants as being credible, authoritative, comparable and familiar to investors. (This requirement is particularly important where companies are seeking to raise funds outside their home jurisdiction.) A key principle of any reporting framework for publicly accountable companies should be to ensure an effective level of investor confidence and protection, including through the financial reporting standards to be applied. IFRS Standards meet all these requirements. Any alternative financial reporting regime would also need to meet these requirements.

A Single Set of Financial Reporting Standards for All Listed Companies

A number of companies which seek to have their securities listed on non-regulated markets do so in the expectation that they may eventually seek a listing on a regulated market. This is particularly the case where the purpose, and consequently limitation, of the non-regulated market is premised on the size of the company, rather than the nature or type of its business activity.

---

[8] EY. (August 2014). *The JOBS Act: 2014 Mid-year Update—An Overview of Implementation and an Analysis of Emerging Growth Company Trends*, p. 13. http://www.ey.com/Publication/vwLUAssets/EY-the-JOBS-Act-2014/$FILE/EY-the-JOBS-Act-2014.pdf

This implied mobility suggests that these companies would benefit from the application of the same or a similar financial accounting framework on both regulated and unregulated markets. The same, or a similar, financial reporting framework would allow companies to move between markets with limited or no changes to their systems, would facilitate any prelisting information requirements, and would allow those companies to maintain and present a historical set of meaningful, verified comparative reports.

Companies listed on non-regulated exchanges often compete for investment funds with companies that are listed on regulated markets. Investors frequently invest in both regulated and unregulated markets, and make their investment decisions based on comparisons of investment performance across both platforms. Since many companies listed on non-regulated exchanges differ from competitors listed on regulated markets only in terms of size, and not in terms of either nature or type of business activity, such comparisons are valid and would benefit from the application of a single or a similar accounting framework.

Consequently, it would seem that there is benefit to be sought in applying the same, or similar, financial accounting framework to companies on both regulated and unregulated markets. Such cross-market application facilitates both comparability and mobility.

The Foundation Has Acknowledged the Principle of Differential Reporting

Differential reporting for various categories of companies is not a new idea. Indeed, the Board has established its own differentiation with the issue in 2009 of the SMEs Standard. The publication of the *IFRS for SMEs* Standard represented the culmination of a project begun by the Board shortly after its inception in 2001, which included two major rounds of consultation, together with further outreach activities and field tests.

As mentioned previously, the primary objective of the Foundation is 'to develop, in the public interest, a single set of high quality, understandable, enforceable and globally accepted financial reporting standards based upon clearly articulated principles', but also 'to take account of, as appropriate, the needs of a range of sizes and types of entities in diverse economic settings'. Considering these two objectives together, the Board has stated that 'single set' means that all companies in similar circumstances globally should follow the same standards. However, the Board has noted that the circumstances of

SMEs can be different from those of larger, publicly accountable companies.[9] An acknowledgement of such differences was part of the Board's rationale for its development of a separate reporting framework for SMEs.

When it developed the SMEs Standard, the Board concluded that 'public accountability' (or a lack thereof) was the principle for identifying the companies for which the Standard is intended. A company has public accountability if its debt or equity instruments are traded in a public market, or if it is in the process of issuing such instruments for trading in a public market, or if it holds assets in a fiduciary capacity for a broad group of outsiders as one of its primary businesses. The Board decided that it would not be appropriate to define an SME by reference to quantified size criteria; in relation to accounting requirements, the Board noted, the needs of the users of financial statements are more important than is the size of a company. The Board also concluded that it was not feasible to develop quantified size tests that would be applicable across numerous countries.

As part of its recent review of the SMEs Standard, the Board considered whether some or all publicly accountable companies should be permitted to apply it. The Board observed that the SMEs Standard was specifically designed for SMEs and users of SME financial statements. In contrast to non-publicly accountable companies, public investors and stakeholders generally are not involved in managing the business and do not have the power to demand information that they might find useful for investment decision-making. They must rely on general purpose financial statements. Many of the simplifications, expedients and reduced disclosure requirements in the SMEs Standard are due to users' different needs.

As a consequence, the Board noted two interrelated reasons for not allowing publicly accountable companies to use the SMEs Standard:

- If the scope was widened to include some or all publicly accountable companies, this might lead to pressure to make changes to the SMEs Standard to accommodate the needs of the users of financials statements of the companies in that wider group, which would increase the complexity of the Standard. Even excluding concerns that may be raised from other interested parties, the Board noted that in its own deliberations it would be difficult, if not impossible, to ignore the existence of public users of a subset of financial statements prepared under the SMEs Standard; and

[9] *IFRS for SMEs* Basis for Conclusions, paragraph BC42.

- There are specific risks associated with the inappropriate use of the SMEs Standard. The Board noted that if publicly accountable companies were allowed to use the SMEs Standard, and, as a consequence of not being the intended user group, were producing financial statements of insufficient quality or usefulness, this would have the effect that a subgroup of financial statements, prepared under the IFRS brand, would essentially not be fit for purpose. This would have the further consequence that some financial statements produced applying the requirements of an IFRS Standard would not meet the objectives of the Foundation.

As part of the review of the SMEs Standard, the Board consulted the IFRS Advisory Council and its specialist SME Implementation Group (SMEIG). The majority of members of both groups shared the Board's concerns and recommended keeping the requirement in the SMEs Standard that prevents publicly accountable companies from stating compliance with the Standard.

The Board concluded that the present position should be maintained and that the scope of the SMEs Standard should remain restricted to non-publicly accountable companies. A company with public accountability should use full IFRS Standards.

Approaches

In seeking to consider separately the needs of smaller, but nonetheless publicly accountable companies, a jurisdiction has several options.

Jurisdictions can incorporate the SMEs Standard into their local GAAP to allow certain publicly accountable companies to use it. However, those companies would be required to state compliance with local GAAP, not with the SMEs Standard. A jurisdiction may also consider adopting an entirely new framework for such companies, or it could elect to use an existing framework already available within the jurisdiction.

However, in either case, alternative accounting frameworks such as these would potentially fail to achieve the objective of attracting capital if they did not garner a similar level of international understanding and acceptance to that enjoyed by full IFRS Standards. So, if contemplating an alternative accounting framework, a jurisdiction would almost certainly need to consider whether, and to what extent, investors drawn to the market are likely to be non-domestic. Another alternative approach may be to permit companies the choice between a local GAAP and full IFRS Standards, and thereby permit those companies to evaluate for themselves the investor market they are targeting.

Allowing the use of IFRS Standards for companies listed on MTFs ensures that the benefits of using IFRS Standards that I have outlined above are extended to this important group of companies.

Conclusion

The Foundation and the Board have followed with interest the Commission's publications and discussions to date on this topic. We remain very interested in this topic and continue to be willing to engage with the Commission as it develops its views in this area.

10

Financial Reporting by Quoted SMEs

Andrew Watchman

Introduction

Since 2005 the EU's 'IAS Regulation' has required companies quoted on an EU regulated market to prepare their consolidated financial statements in accordance with International Financial Reporting Standards (IFRS) as endorsed in the European Union. The IFRS has harmonised financial reporting in these markets and the European Commission's 2015 review of the IAS Regulation concluded that IFRS has brought overall net benefits.[1]

The IAS Regulation applies to equally to all companies quoted on a regulated market regardless of their size. However, the situation is different for the (mostly smaller) companies quoted on one of the EU's so-called multilateral trading facilities (MTFs). These companies are not subject to the IAS Regulation (although the Regulation includes various member state options to extend the use of IFRS) and therefore prepare financial statements under

Andrew Watchman is Chairman of the Technical Expert Group of the European Financial Reporting Advisory Group (EFRAG) and EFRAG CEO. The views expressed are entirely his own.

[1] The European Commission issued on 18 June 2015 its report on the evaluation of Regulation (EC) No. 1606/2002 (the 'IAS Regulation' or Regulation on the application of International Financial Reporting Standards). The report can be found at: http://eur-lex.europa.eu/legal-content/EN/TXT/?uri=COM:2015:301:FIN

A. Watchman (✉)
EFRAG, Brussels, Belgium
e-mail: andrew.watchman@efrag.org

E. Kaili et al. (eds.), *New Models of Financing and Financial Reporting for European SMEs*,
https://doi.org/10.1007/978-3-030-02831-2_10

various different frameworks. The applicable framework is determined by the member state laws and regulations (including the effect of the member state's use of options in the IAS Regulation), in conjunction with the MTF's own rules if applicable. At least one MTF, the UK's Alternative Investment Market (AIM) currently requires the use of IFRS. Some other MTFs permit companies a choice between IFRS and the applicable national accounting standards, examples being the Entry Market and Alternext. National accounting standards in the EU are harmonised only to the extent of the Accounting Directive.

In view of the importance of smaller companies to the EU economy, the European Commission's 2015 Green Paper 'Building a Capital Markets Union' (the 2015 Green Paper) asked whether there is value in developing a common EU-level accounting standard for small and medium-sized companies (SMEs) listed on MTFs and whether such a standard should become a feature of 'SME Growth Markets' (see below).

This chapter considers whether a new accounting solution is needed to help achieve the CMU's ambitions for the successful development of the quoted SME sector.[2] I offer my analysis of where we are today on this question, and of some of the various options for moving forward.

Quoted SME Accounting: A Big Issue?

It is well-documented that, in relative terms, very few European SMEs have listed on a stock market to date. It is estimated around 3000 of Europe's 20 million or so SMEs are currently listed, i.e. around 0.015%.

Based on 2014 data reported by the World Federation of Exchanges,[3] Europe's 10 largest 'SME markets' by total market capitalisation shown in the table.

[2] In this chapter I use the term 'quoted SMEs' in a broad sense to refer to smaller companies listed on any public market. This term is not intended to necessarily correspond to a particular legal definition of 'SME' or category of stock market.

[3] See World Federation of Exchanges, https://www.world-exchanges.org/home/index.php/research/wfe-research

World Federation of Exchanges, Europe's 10 largest 'SME markets' by total market capitalisation

Exchange name	Name of SME market	Number of companies	Total market cap (USD million)
London SE group	*AIM*	1104	111,406
Irish stock exchange	*Enterprise securities market*	26	56,732
Deutsche Börse	*Entry standard*	168	18,752
Euronext	*Alternext*	191	10,293
NASDAQ OMX Nordic exchange	*First north*	174	6078
Warsaw stock exchange	*New connect*	431	2572
Wiener Börse	*Second regulated market and third market (MTF)*	30	2512
BME Spanish exchanges	*MAB expansion*	26	2178
Oslo Børs	*Oslo Axess*	35	1646
Cyprus stock exchange	*Emerging companies market*	20	807

These numbers suggest that Europe's SME markets have not yet been hugely successful. Moreover the UK's AIM is by far the largest, so the post-Brexit numbers for the EU/EEA will be significantly lower still. On this basis it is debatable whether the quoted SME sector is of a sufficient scale to justify development of a new, EU-wide accounting solution or other major change to the status quo.

However, these data reflect the past and current state of the quoted SME sector in Europe. The CMU Action Plan, among its various goals, seeks to make it easier for SMEs to list their shares on public markets. Linked to this, a new category of MTF—the SME Growth Market—is being created under MiFID II and will apply from 2018.[4] The key point is therefore whether a new accounting solution—potentially bringing with it a more harmonised system—could play a role in creating the conditions for future growth.

The success of the SME Growth Markets will depend, among other factors, on the proportionality of the applicable listing requirements—including the applicable financial reporting rules. A proportionate approach requires striking a balance between consumer protection, including ensuring that investors

[4] SME Growth Markets are expected to comprise a sub-category of multilateral trading facilities that meet specified criteria, in particular that at least 50% of the issuers whose financial instruments are traded are SMEs as defined.

are provided with the information they need to make decisions, and a regulatory regime that not unduly burdensome on the SMEs. Financial reporting requirements are highly relevant in this context.

There is at least one positive to be drawn from the variety of accounting frameworks in use in the quoted SME sector today: this variety could provide a valuable resource to help research the advantages and disadvantages of alternative models and the case for far-reaching change. In particular, where quoted SMEs are offered a choice between IFRS and national accounting standards, research into the choices made, their impact on the entities concerned and on the investors in those entities, could be very instructive.

I suggest that finding the right way forward depends on the answers to the following questions:

- How important is financial reporting to investors in quoted SMEs?
- Is a change to the status quo needed for quoted SMEs?
- If so, is 'full' IFRS suitable for quoted SMEs?
- Or is a customised approach needed for quoted SMEs?

Importance of Financial Reporting to Investors in Quoted SMEs

There is a common perception that investors in SMEs pay little attention to financial statements. However, a recent exercise by the UK's Financial Reporting Council (FRC) on financial reporting by smaller quoted companies[5] in fact indicates the opposite. The lack of readily-available alternative sources of information about quoted SMEs in fact places increased emphasis on the annual report as investors' main source of knowledge and they rely on it when making decisions. For example, in its response to the FRC's Discussion Paper an organisation representing the asset management sector explained that:

> The annual report is a vital tool in demonstrating management's accountability. Management is entrusted with shareholders' funds and the Annual Report shows how effectively it put those funds to use and the performance derived from those funds. An investor is more likely to provide capital if the Annual Report clearly conveys a company's business model and financial position, and

[5] FRC. (2015). Consultation: Improving the Quality of Reporting by Smaller Listed and AIM Quoted Companies. Available at https://www.frc.org.uk/Our-Work/Publications/FRC-Board/Consultation-Improving-the-Quality-of-Reporting-b-File.pdf

> has clear accounting policies that provide insight into management's judgements. Investors can better understand the quality of management from seeing how directors have exercised their professional judgement in determining what is important and how it should be reported.
>
> [...] It is precisely because there is often little, if any, coverage by analysts and an absence of other publicly available information that the annual reports of smaller quoted companies are particularly important to investors.[6]

High quality financial reporting therefore matters to investors in quoted SMEs. A perception—whether or not justified—that financial reporting is of lower quality in this sector compared to larger quoted companies would surely act as a deterrent to investors and thus inhibit growth in the quoted SME sector.

Is a Change to the Status Quo Needed for Quoted SMEs?

Although investors in quoted SMEs need high quality financial reporting, it does not automatically follow that the applicable requirements need to be harmonised across borders (either at a European or at a wider international level). The EU Accounting Directive already establishes a minimum level of financial information that must be provided under national accounting standards and ensures a certain degree of harmonisation.

In a number of ways the case for further harmonisation of financial reporting requirements among quoted SMEs seems less compelling than for the larger quoted companies that are the mainstay of Europe's regulated markets—at least as of today. Harmonisation provides a common language for communicating an entity's financial position and performance. The benefits of such a common language seem self-evident when the companies operate, or seek investment, internationally. The case for a common language diminishes if the companies in question have a predominantly domestic focus.

Quoted SMEs typically have fewer operations and activities outside their country of domicile, and fewer cross-border investors in comparison to larger quoted companies (although this may vary among member states). A European Commission staff working document accompanying the CMU mid-term review[7] explains:

[6] From the response of the Investment Association to the FRC's 2015 Discussion Paper 'Improving the Quality of Reporting by Smaller Listed and AIM Quoted Companies'.

[7] European Commission. (2017). On the Mid-Term Review of the Capital Markets Union Action Plan. Available at URL https://ec.europa.eu/info/sites/info/files/staff-working-document-cmu-mid-term-review-june2017_en.pdf

> Investments in equity markets are also subject to home bias, i.e. the tendency to overweight domestic stocks. Although this is a common feature of equity investments, the lack of cross-border investments may be more pronounced for SME IPO markets. Empirical research shows that foreign investors prefer large stocks. Hence, market fragmentation further curtails SMEs access to equity markets.

That said, there are indications that smaller companies are increasingly seeking investment from outside their country of domicile, suggesting that the case for harmonisation might become stronger over time. In addition, it is hoped the CMU initiative and the creation of the SME Growth Market concept will provide further impetus towards cross-border investment in SMEs and alleviate the market fragmentation referred to above. All else being equal, a common accounting language can reasonably be expected to stimulate these developments—but only if implemented in a way that avoids excessive burdens on the SMEs.

Suitability of 'Full' IFRS for Quoted SMEs

There are various arguments for requiring all quoted companies, including quoted SMEs, to use 'full' IFRS:

- Investors in quoted companies, including investors in quoted SMEs, need high quality financial statements and, despite various controversies, most commentators agree that IFRS is a high quality system.
- IFRS is a proven system—well-established and widely understood and accepted in the EU and beyond.
- Some commentators argue that any company that chooses to offer its shares or debt on public markets should accept the same high standards of transparency.
- An entity's size is not always a good indicator of the complexity of its business model or transactions. SMEs sometimes enter into complex transactions such as derivatives, share-based payments, complex financing instruments, business combinations and sophisticated customer contracts. IFRS is designed to cope with these and many other types of complex transactions as well as more routine ones.

Although these arguments seem sound, I remain unconvinced that full IFRS is the right answer for all quoted SMEs—at least for the time being. My doubts relate to whether IFRS is sufficiently scalable, and whether the core information objective on which IFRS is founded is optimised for quoted SMEs.

The question of scalability relates to complexity—both of the standards themselves and their application. The type of skills and level of resources necessary to apply a set of accounting standards is not just a function of the standards themselves: the most important determinant of accounting complexity is the scale and complexity of the business. It follows that IFRS is scalable to a substantial degree. This observation is supported by a simple comparison of the typical length of a set of IFRS financial statements for smaller and larger companies. IFRS financial statements prepared by companies listed on the UK's AIM (an MTF that has required the use of IFRS since 2007) are typically 20 to 40 pages long—far shorter than financial statements of most large listed companies.

Despite this, the question remains as to whether the cost-benefit trade-off—evaluated as favourable in the European Commission's 2015 review in the context of the EU's regulated markets—would also be favourable for the quoted SME sector taken as a whole. There is a fixed or minimum level of cost that any company applying IFRS must incur in order to develop and maintain a sufficient knowledge of these comprehensive and frequently changing standards. Inevitably this base cost is proportionately higher for smaller entities. The FRC 2015 Discussion Paper referred to above noted that:

> Generally, the cost of being listed or admitted to AIM (in particular in relation to preparation of IFRS financial statements) is proportionately greater for smaller companies than for their larger counterparts. The size and expertise in the finance function does not necessarily increase post listing or admission to offset the increased requirements.

The issue of information objective is more subtle. Today, the primary objective of the IFRS is to provide information that is useful in estimating future cash flows (a valuation objective). The question is whether this objective is fully consistent with the information needs of investors in quoted SMEs. Many quoted SMEs are start-ups that seek to commercialise a particular idea or new business model. Investors are backing the idea and the management team behind it. The most relevant information to help investors in assessing the future cash flow prospects of a quoted SME is likely to be found elsewhere in the annual report—such as information on strategy, business model, risks and various intangible resources (many of which are not recognised in the financial statements today).

These arguments may seem to contradict my earlier assertion that financial statements are very important to investors in quoted SMEs. I maintain this view but contend that the primary role of the financial statements of quoted SMEs should be to provide confirmatory value and enable shareholders to hold management to account (i.e. a stewardship objective). I should not overemphasise this: information deemed useful for assessing cash flow prospects, for confirmatory purposes and for stewardship is often the same. Nonetheless, a recent study jointly sponsored by EFRAG and the Institute of Chartered Accountants of Scotland (ICAS) does indicate that the information objective matters.[8]

It is also encouraging that work underway by the International Accounting Standards Board (IASB) holds out promise to alleviate some of the concerns about scalability and complexity. In particular, the IASB's 'Disclosure Initiative' (despite its rather slow progress—see below) has potential to enhance the scalability of IFRS by introducing a more flexible and principle-based approach to disclosures. Meaningful progress in this direction would certainly strengthen the case for wider use of IFRS among quoted SMEs.

The IASB's Disclosure Initiative: A Solution?

The IASB's 'disclosure initiative' is an umbrella title for a portfolio of IASB projects aimed at improving the effectiveness of the disclosures in IFRS financial statements.[9] The disclosure initiative was started in 2013, following an increasing level of concern among stakeholders that the disclosures in IFRS financial statements had become excessive and ineffective. Several organisations (including EFRAG—see below) have contributed reports, studies and position papers drawing attention to the issues, assessing the underlying root causes and recommending ways forward.

Although the IASB has made important progress since 2013, including completing two minor amendments to existing standards, the disclosure initiative still has a long way to run in overall terms. A milestone was reached in March 2017 with the publication of an IASB Discussion Paper 'Principles of Disclosure' (the IASB Discussion Paper). The IASB Discussion Paper (DP) explores a number of issues linked to the disclosure debate and seeks input to inform a more comprehensive review of the IFRS disclosure requirements.

The IASB's discussion paper is a consultation document, open for comment until early October 2017, and EFRAG will respond from a European

[8] EFRAG. (2016). *Professional investors and the decision usefulness of financial reporting*. Available at http://www.efrag.org/Assets/Download?assetUrl=%2Fsites%2Fwebpublishing%2FSiteAssets%2FProfessional%2520investors%2520and%2520the%2520decision%2520usefulness%2520of%2520financial%2520reporting.pdf

[9] The ongoing projects have recently been reclassified under the heading of the IASB's even broader "Better Communication in Financial Reporting" initiative.

perspective. At the time of writing EFRAG has published a draft comment letter which sets out tentative views. This is itself a consultation document on which stakeholders are invited to provide feedback. In its tentative views EFRAG expresses some disappointment with (what we consider to be) the limited progress made to date, and comments that:

> EFRAG considers that the remaining aspect of the disclosure problem as of today is mainly one of overload. It is therefore concerning that the IASB DP makes no mention of the extent to which the proposals in the IASB DP might address concerns about disclosure overload. EFRAG considers the IASB's primary focus for the next phases of this project should be to tackle disclosure overload through a comprehensive review of standards-level requirements. The objective of this review should be to develop a clear, effective, coherent and comprehensive but concise package of disclosure requirements. This review should, in particular, aim to identify and remove any disclosure requirements that are disproportionate or redundant. EFRAG considers that the standards-level review is the most critical remaining element of the Disclosure Initiative.

It therefore remains to be seen whether the IASB's disclosure initiative will make much of a difference to the question of proportionality of full IFRS for quoted SMEs. That said, one idea in the IASB Discussion Paper that is of interest is a 'two-tiered' approach to disclosure requirements. The main features of this approach, which was developed by the staff of New Zealand Accounting Standards Board and is directionally consistent with one of the approaches suggested by EFRAG and its partners in a 2012 joint discussion paper (see below), are:

- The inclusion of disclosure objectives, comprising an overall disclosure objective for each standard and more specific ones for each type of information required to meet that overall disclosure objective;
- The division of disclosure requirements into two tiers:
  - a level of summary information, that all entities would be required to provide subject only to materiality, to give an overall picture; and
  - a level of additional information, which an entity would consider disclosing if that information is necessary to meet the overall disclosure objective in the standard.

In its draft comment letter EFRAG calls on the IASB to develop this approach further.

A Customised Approach for Quoted SMEs

If the balance of cost and benefits arising from mandating full IFRS for quoted SMEs is assessed as unfavourable, could a differential (simplified) regime achieve a favourable trade-off?

A differential regime could, of course, take any number of forms but, for the purpose of this discussion, I will consider three broad approaches, each of which is in some sense 'IFRS-based':

- Approach 1—IFRS with reduced disclosures
- Approach 2—IFRS with broader simplifications
- Approach 3—IFRS for SMEs

Approach 1: IFRS with Reduced Disclosures

There are various precedents for developing customised versions of IFRS that simplify the disclosure requirements while retaining the recognition and measurement principles in full IFRS (a reduced disclosure regime). The broad rationale for this partial simplification is to retain the perceived advantages of a single set of accounting principles (including comparability, transparency and relevance), while reducing disclosure burdens and costs. In the context of quoted SMEs, an IFRS-based approach of this type could reduce frictions for entities that might 'graduate' from an MTF to a regulated market and for investors making investment choices from both categories of market.

The FRC has introduced a reduced disclosure regime that is available, as a matter of choice, to eligible subsidiaries and parent entities in their individual financial statements. This enables groups that use IFRS for their consolidated financial statements to streamline to use the same recognition and measurement principles for the individual financial statements of the UK group entities, but with fewer disclosures. The use of the same recognition and measurement principles at the consolidated and individual level helps to streamline the overall financial reporting process. Although the UK's reduced disclosure regime cannot be used in consolidated financial statements, it is available to quoted companies that have no subsidiaries (and hence do not prepare any consolidated financial statements). As such, the UK has determined that a reduced disclosure regime can be compatible with public accountability.

Australia and New Zealand have also implemented reduced disclosure regimes. However, in contrast to the UK, these regimes are limited to entities that do not have public accountability (accordingly, they cannot be used by entities whose shares or debt securities traded on any public market).

Some commentators argue that a reduced disclosure regime should be developed for smaller listed companies. In 2011, the French national standard setter *Autorité des Normes Comptables* (ANC) published a proposal for the simplification of the IFRS accounting requirements for small listed companies.[10] The ANC proposed a reduced disclosure regime for 'small listed companies', arguing that the application of IFRS requirements is often burdensome for these entities. The ANC paper did not distinguish between small listed companies quoted on regulated markets and those quoted on MTFs for this purpose. The ANC proposal was to eliminate a series of disclosure requirements considered superfluous for small listed companies and develop simplified notes to the financial statements, designed to provide the minimum expected information. The benefit of this proposal, in the ANC's view, was to alleviate current disclosure requirements assessed as having been developed principally with large listed companies in mind.

Specifically, the ANC's 2011 paper recommended two developments:

- Reduce the volume of the notes in nine specified areas compared to the current disclosure requirements under IFRS.
- Facilitate the preparation, and improve the readability and relevance of the notes to the financial statements by proposing in particular an illustrative set of simplified financial statements.

The differential disclosure question was also raised in the 2012 EFRAG/ANC/FRC joint discussion paper 'Towards a Disclosure Framework for the Notes' (the 2012 EFRAG/ANC/FRC Paper). In this Paper, various bases of differentiation were referred to—including individual versus consolidated financial statements, interim and year-end financial statements, the size of the reporting entity, the industry of the entity and public accountability. The 2012 EFRAG/ANC/FRC Paper also noted the some of the challenges of differential disclosure regimes. In particular, if such regimes were to be generally applied it would be challenging to identify suitable differentiating criteria and to fulfil users' needs in different circumstances. The Paper noted that some believe such an approach could only lead to arbitrariness and a lack of proper

[10] ANC. (2010). *Consultation sur la norme internationale d'information financière pour les petites et moyennes entreprises*. Available at http://www.anc.gouv.fr/files/live/sites/anc/files/contributed/ANC/1.%20Normes%20fran%C3%A7aises/Travaux%20autres/CE_12mars2010_Lettre_Consultation_sur_la_norme_IFRS_pour_les_PME.pdf

fulfilment of users' needs. Feedback received on the 2012 EFRAG/ANC/FRC Paper also indicated rather limited support for this approach.

The 2012 EFRAG/ANC/FRC Paper also discussed a 'tiered' approach that sets different levels of requirements for each IFRS standard. Under this approach there would be a minimum set of requirements (assuming the item was material to the entity) and each entity would add more layers of information based on the relative importance of the item in the context of its own financial statements. Again, the 2012 Paper noted some challenges in particular around the different materiality judgements required to put such an approach into practice. It is nonetheless encouraging that the IASB's 2012 Discussion Paper further develops and seeks feedback on a tiered approach.

Approach 2: IFRS with Broader Simplifications

The 2015 Green Paper noted that:

> International Financial Reporting Standards (IFRS) have played a key role for promoting a single accounting language in the EU, making it easier for large listed EU companies to have access to global capital markets. Imposing full IFRS on smaller companies, in particular those wanting to access dedicated trading venues, would, however, be a source of additional cost. The development of a simplified, common, and high quality accounting standard tailored to the companies listed on certain trading venues could be a step forward in terms of transparency and comparability, and if applied proportionally, could help those companies seeking cross-border investors to be more attractive to them. The standard could become a feature of SME Growth Markets, and be available for wider use.

The 2015 Green Paper also included a question on whether there is value in developing a common EU level accounting standard for small and medium-sized companies listed on MTFs, whether such a standard should become a feature of SME Growth Markets and, if so, under which conditions.

The European Commission's Feedback Statement,[11] which provides a summary of responses, reported that:

[11] European Commission. (2015). *Feedback Statement on the Green Paper "Building a Capital Markets Union"*. Available at http://ec.europa.eu/finance/consultations/2015/capital-markets-union/docs/summary-of-responses_en.pdf

> Some respondents considered that the current situation is appropriate and should not be changed. Currently, SMEs listed on most MTFs prepare their financial reports according to national accounting standards, although there are already MTFs that require SMEs to apply the International Financial Reporting Standards (IFRS). Most respondents considered, however, that some kind of initiative or incentive, legislative or other, is needed to render EU SMEs listed on MTFs more attractive to European and international investors through enhanced transparency and comparability of relevant financial information. Rather than a full application of the IFRS or use of the IFRS for SMEs, many respondents suggested that a pragmatic IFRS-based solution be found in order to deliver for SMEs listed on MTFs the advantages of a high-quality, comparable, international set of accounting rules, whilst avoiding excessive administrative burden and costs, particularly in relation to disclosure.

In summary, responses to the 2015 Green Paper revealed no strong consensus for any particular course of action in the financial reporting area. Many of the respondents advocating some form of new accounting solution stressed the need for it to be founded on full IFRS. Interestingly, the European Commission's June 2017 communication on the Mid-Term Review of the CMU Action Plan[12] includes as an ongoing action 'Monitor progress on IASB commitment to improve disclosure, usability and accessibility of IFRS'. The June 2017 communication makes no reference to developing a customised accounting standard for MTFs.

Approach 3: IFRS for SMEs

In the debate generated by the 2015 Green Paper so far, it seems that little attention has been paid to the IFRS for SMEs. The IFRS for SMEs is a self-contained standard of less than 250 pages, designed by the IASB to meet the needs and capabilities of SMEs around the world. Simplifications in the IFRS for SMEs, compared to full IFRS, are in the following broad areas:

- Topics considered not relevant for SMEs are omitted, for example, earnings per share, interim financial reporting and segment reporting.
- Various recognition and measurement principles have been simplified, for example, goodwill is amortised systematically rather than subject to the 'impairment-only' approach in full IFRS.

[12] European Commission. (2017). *On the Mid-Term Review of the Capital Markets Union Action Plan.* Available at https://ec.europa.eu/info/sites/info/files/communication-cmu-mid-term-review-june2017_en.pdf

- Disclosures are reduced by around 90 per cent.
- Efforts have been made to use clearer language.
- The IASB has stated its intention to revise the IFRS for SMEs only every three years (in fact the original version was published in 2009 and the first revision appeared in 2015).

Given that a simplified, international standard is available today, why has the IFRS for SMEs not gained more traction as a possible solution for quoted SMEs? One explanation is that, despite the name, the IASB designed this standard for non-publicly accountable entities (which includes unquoted entities) rather than for entities below a certain size. The IASB has indeed stated that publicly accountable entities are not permitted to claim that they are in conformity with the IFRS for SMEs.

Looking at the substance of the differences between the IFRS for SMEs and full IFRS, some of the topics omitted, such as earnings per share and segment reporting, are generally considered to be relevant for all quoted companies. Those topics could, of course, be reinstated in a version targeted at quoted SMEs. In many of the other areas of simplification, it is debatable whether the resulting outcome is conceptually or practically unsuitable for quoted SMEs.

The main objection to the IFRS for SMEs is perhaps simply that it deviates too far from full IFRS. This gap might reduce or widen in future depending on whether, in future reviews, the IASB decides to bring the IFRS for SMEs into line with full IFRS in areas where full IFRS has been overhauled in recent years (for example, revenue recognition and lease accounting).

Conclusion

To summarise and conclude, my main observations are that:

- Despite the limited harmonisation of financial reporting requirements for Europe's quoted SME sector, the case for far-reaching change to the status quo is not clear-cut;
- The variety of accounting frameworks used in the quoted SME sector today can provide a valuable research resource to help assess the advantages and disadvantages of alternative models and the need for further harmonisation;
- To the extent that evidence calls for a more harmonised financial reporting regime for quoted SMEs, full IFRS seems viable only with further progress

to address concerns around proportionality. The IASB's agenda, in particular the IASB's disclosure initiative, holds out promise to deliver this but the outcome remains to be seen; and

- If more harmonised financial reporting regime is needed but concerns around proportionality are not addressed satisfactorily, further consideration should be given to developing a customised solution for quoted SMEs. If this course of action is pursued, the balance of argument seems to favour an IFRS-based model with reduced disclosures.

11

The IFRS for Small and Medium-Sized Entities

Veronica Poole, Laurence Rivat, and Jens Berger

Introduction

Overview of the IFRS for SMEs

The *International Financial Reporting Standard for Small and Medium-sized Entities* (IFRS for SMEs) is a self-contained Standard, incorporating accounting principles that are based on full IFRSs but that have been simplified to suit the entities within its scope. The IFRS for SMEs provides an alternative framework that can be applied by eligible entities in place of full IFRSs. The IFRS for SMEs is separate from full IFRSs and is, therefore, available for any jurisdiction to adopt, whether or not it has adopted full IFRSs.

V. Poole (✉)
Deloitte, London, UK
e-mail: vepoole@deloitte.co.uk

L. Rivat
Deloitte, Paris, France
e-mail: lrivat@deloitte.fr

J. Berger
Deloitte, Frankfurt, Germany

E. Kaili et al. (eds.), *New Models of Financing and Financial Reporting for European SMEs*,
https://doi.org/10.1007/978-3-030-02831-2_11

The 2015 Amendments to the IFRS for SMEs

The IFRS for SMEs was most recently amended in May 2015 by the *2015 Amendments to the International Financial Reporting Standard for Small and Medium-sized Entities*. The amendments resulted from a comprehensive review of the IFRS for SMEs, which specifically considered (1) implementation issues identified in the application of the Standard since it was issued in 2009, and (2) other new and amended IFRSs issued in the intervening period. In addition, Q&As issued by the SME Implementation Group (SMEIG—see section "Maintenance of the IFRS for SMEs") have been incorporated into the body of the Standard and/or the IFRS Foundation's educational material [see IFRS for SMEs: BC227].

Meaning of the Term "Small and Medium-Sized Entities"

The title of the IFRS for SMEs may appear to suggest that the Standard applies only to small and medium-sized entities; however, this is not the case. The scope of the Standard is much broader and is not determined by reference to the size of the reporting entity but rather by reference to the extent to which the reporting entity has public accountability. The IFRS for SMEs is intended for use by any entity, even a very large corporation, provided that (1) the entity does not have public accountability, and (2) it is required, or chooses, to publish general purpose financial statements for external users. Essentially, an entity is considered to have public accountability if its debt or equity instruments are publicly traded, or if it holds and manages financial resources entrusted to it by a number of clients as one of its primary businesses (see section "Scope" in this chapter for further discussion).

Therefore, throughout this chapter, the term "SME" refers to an entity within the scope of the Standard, rather than describing the size of the entity under consideration.

Which Entities Should Apply the IFRS for SMEs?

Ultimately, the decisions regarding which entities should use the IFRS for SMEs in a specific jurisdiction and the timing for adoption rest with national regulatory authorities and standard-setters, and those bodies may specify more detailed eligibility criteria, including quantified criteria based on revenue and assets. However, the International Accounting Standards Board (IASB) intends that the application of the IFRS for SMEs should be limited to entities with no public accountability. Consequently, the Standard states that, even if law or regulation in a jurisdiction permits or requires the IFRS for SMEs to be used by a publicly accountable entity, that entity's financial statements should not be described as conforming to the IFRS for SMEs (see section "IFRS for SMEs Not Appropriate for Entities with Public Accountability").

Entities eligible to adopt the IFRS for SMEs and that are considering such adoption should first of all consider whether the IFRS for SMEs is suitable for their circumstances. Among other issues, an entity should consider:

- whether adopting the IFRS for SMEs will result in financial statements that are appropriate for the needs of its users;
- whether adopting the IFRS for SMEs will result in financial statements that are more or less comparable with those of its competitors;
- the cost and other effects on its business of adopting the IFRS for SMEs (including the effect on key performance indicators, banking covenants, staff bonus arrangements, tax payable, etc.); and
- for entities that are part of a group, any group reporting requirements.

Focus of This Chapter

A full discussion of all aspects of the IFRS for SMEs is beyond the scope of this chapter. The purpose of this chapter is to provide an overview of the IFRS for SMEs to enable users that have already adopted (or are familiar with) IFRSs to understand the key differences between the IFRS for SMEs and full IFRSs. This may be of assistance when:

- considering the implications of adopting the IFRS for SMEs, when permitted; and
- considering what adjustments are required to the financial statements of a subsidiary prepared in accordance with the IFRS for SMEs for the purposes of preparing consolidated financial statements in accordance with full IFRSs.

[The complete IFRS for SMEs (together with the Basis for Conclusions, Illustrative Financial Statements, and a Presentation and Disclosure Checklist) can be downloaded free of charge at the following address: http://www.ifrs.org/IFRS-for-SMEs/Pages/IFRS-for-SMEs-and-related-material.aspx. It is available in English and several other languages].

Scope

Scope: General Requirements

Entities Targeted by the IFRS for SMEs

The IFRS for SMEs is intended for use by entities that [IFRS SMEs: 1.1 & 1.2]:

- do not have public accountability; and
- publish general purpose financial statements for external users. Examples of external users include owners who are not involved in managing the business, existing and potential creditors, and credit rating agencies.

Entities that Have Public Accountability

IFRS for SMEs Not Appropriate for Entities with Public Accountability

If a publicly accountable entity uses the IFRS for SMEs, its financial statements should not be described as conforming to the IFRS for SMEs—even if law or regulation in its jurisdiction permits or requires the IFRS for SMEs to be used by publicly accountable entities [IFRS for SMEs: 1.5].

The IASB believes that the IFRS for SMEs is only appropriate for an entity that does not have public accountability. A jurisdiction that wishes to allow publicly traded entities or some entities that hold assets in a fiduciary capacity for a broad range of outsiders (e.g. small entities) to use the IFRS for SMEs could incorporate the requirements of the IFRS for SMEs into its local generally accepted accounting principles (GAAP) for those entities. However, if this is done, the financial statements should be described as conforming to local GAAP. The IFRS for SMEs prohibits the financial statements of a publicly traded entity or an entity that holds assets in a fiduciary capacity for a broad range of outsiders as one of its primary businesses, however small, from being described as being prepared in accordance with the IFRS for SMEs.

Public Accountability: Definition

An entity has public accountability if [IFRS for SMEs: 1.3]:

(a) its debt or equity instruments are traded in a public market or it is in the process of issuing such instruments for trading in a public market (a domestic or foreign stock exchange or an over-the-counter market, including local and regional markets—see section "Interpretation of 'Traded in a Public Market'"); or

(b) it holds assets in a fiduciary capacity for a broad group of outsiders as one of its primary businesses. Most banks, credit unions, insurance companies, securities brokers/dealers, mutual funds and investment banks would meet this second criterion.

> The wording of [IFRS for SMEs: 1.3(b)] was amended as part of the 2015 Amendments to clarify that the types of entities listed are not automatically considered to meet this criterion—there may be some circumstances in which an entity of one of the types listed does not have public accountability. The SME Implementation Group (SMEIG) (see section "Maintenance of the IFRS for SMEs"), which previously considered this question, suggested that this might be the case, for example, for some captive insurance companies and investment funds with only a few participants.

If an entity holds assets in a fiduciary capacity for a broad group of outsiders for reasons incidental to a primary business (as may be the case, for example, for travel or real estate agents, schools, charitable organisations, co-operative enterprises requiring a nominal membership deposit, and sellers that receive payment in advance of delivery of the goods or services such as utility companies), that does not make them publicly accountable [IFRS SMEs: 1.4].

Interpretation of "Traded in a Public Market"

> The SMEIG (see section "Maintenance of the IFRS for SMEs") has considered how broadly the term 'traded in a public market' should be interpreted in the context of [IFRS SMEs: 1.3(b)] (see section "Public Accountability: Definition"). The conclusion of the SMEIG, set out below, was not incorporated into the IFRS for SMEs as part of the 2015 Amendments but has been added to the IFRS Foundation's educational material (see section "IFRS Foundation Training Material") as non-mandatory guidance.
>
> > 'Public market' is defined in paragraph 1.3 as 'a domestic or foreign stock exchange or an over-the-counter market, including local and regional markets'. A 'public market' is not restricted to recognised and/or regulated stock exchanges. It includes all markets that bring together entities that seek

(*continued*)

(continued)

capital and investors who are not involved in managing the entity. For a market to be public it must be accessible by a broad group of outsiders. If the instruments can only be exchanged between parties involved in the management of the entity, such as key management personnel or shareholders, the instruments are not traded in a public market. In some jurisdictions, a shareholder of a small or medium-sized entity is permitted by law to publicly advertise those shares for sale, for example, on a website or in a newspaper, without any active involvement (or sometimes without even the knowledge) of the entity issuing those shares. Because the entity did not take an affirmative step to permit public trading of shares (such as, but not limited to, share registration), such advertising by a shareholder does not, by itself, create an over-the-counter public market and would not prevent an entity that otherwise meets the criteria in Section 1 from using the *IFRS for SMEs*. Furthermore, the availability of a published price does not necessarily mean that an entity's debt or equity instruments are traded in a public market. For example, in some countries over-the-counter shares have a quoted price, but the market has no facility for trading and so buyers and sellers deal with each other directly. This would not constitute trading in a public market. However, if trading occurs only occasionally in a public market, even only a few times a year, this would constitute trading. The assessment of whether an entity's debt or equity instruments are traded in a public market, or are in the process of being issued for trading in a public market, should be an ongoing one.

Are Subsidiaries in Groups Using Full IFRSs Within the Scope of the IFRS for SMEs?

A subsidiary whose parent uses full IFRSs, or that is part of a consolidated group that uses full IFRSs, is not prohibited from using the IFRS for SMEs in its own financial statements if it does not have public accountability [IFRS SMEs: 1.6].

The fact that the ordinary shares of an entity's parent are listed on a stock exchange does not, by itself, make that subsidiary publicly accountable. Entities assess their eligibility to use the IFRS for SMEs on the basis of their own circumstances, even if they also submit financial information in accordance with full IFRSs to a parent for consolidation purposes. The same is true for associates and joint ventures, which may need to submit financial information in accordance with full IFRSs to an investor.

A subsidiary may wish to apply the IFRS for SMEs in its own financial statements, if prepared, to benefit from reduced disclosures and because full IFRS information is only prepared at a higher materiality threshold (see section "Potential Benefits of the IFRS for SMEs for Subsidiaries" for further detail). A subsidiary will usually find that the circumstances in which the IFRS for SMEs mandates a recognition or measurement principle that is different from recognition or measurement under full IFRSs are limited (see section "Mandatory Differences Between Full IFRSs and the IFRS for SMEs").

Are Non-Publicly Accountable Parents of Groups Using Full IFRSs Within the Scope of the IFRS for SMEs?

A parent entity (including the ultimate parent or any intermediate parent) that is required to present consolidated financial statements in accordance with full IFRSs (or another set of generally accepted accounting principles) is not prohibited from using the IFRS for SMEs in its own separate financial statements if the parent entity itself does not have public accountability. The parent entity assesses whether it is eligible to use the IFRS for SMEs on the basis of its own status, without considering whether other group entities have, or the group as a whole has, public accountability [IFRS for SMEs: 1.7].

Any financial statements prepared in accordance with the IFRS for SMEs should be clearly distinguished from financial statements prepared in accordance with full IFRSs or other requirements [IFRS for SMEs: 1.7].

Content

The IFRS for SMEs is organised by topic, with each topic presented in a separate section, to make it more like a reference manual—intended by the IASB to be more user-friendly for SME preparers and users of SME financial statements.

The Standard contains the following sections.

Preface

(a) Small and Medium-sized Entities (comprises the scope)
(b) Concepts and Pervasive Principles (similar to the IASB's Conceptual Framework)
(c) Financial Statement Presentation
(d) Statement of Financial Position
(e) Statement of Comprehensive Income and Income Statement
(f) Statement of Changes in Equity and Statement of Income and Retained Earnings
(g) Statement of Cash Flows
(h) Notes to the Financial Statements
(i) Consolidated and Separate Financial Statements
(j) Accounting Policies, Estimates and Errors
(k) Basic Financial Instruments
(l) Other Financial Instruments Issues
(m) Inventories
(n) Investments in Associates
(o) Investments in Joint Ventures

(p) Investment Property
(q) Property, Plant and Equipment
(r) Intangible Assets other than Goodwill
(s) Business Combinations and Goodwill
(t) Leases
(u) Provisions and Contingencies
Appendix—Guidance on recognising and measuring provisions
(v) Liabilities and Equity
Appendix—Example of the issuer's accounting for convertible debt
(w) Revenue
Appendix—Examples of revenue recognition under the principles in Section 23
(x) Government Grants
(y) Borrowing Costs
(z) Share-based Payment
(aa) Impairment of Assets
(bb) Employee Benefits
(cc) Income Tax
(dd) Foreign Currency Translation
(ee) Hyperinflation
(ff) Events after the End of the Reporting Period
(gg) Related Party Disclosures
(hh) Specialised Activities (comprised of agriculture, exploration for and evaluation of mineral resources, and service concession arrangements)
(ii) Transition to the IFRS for SMEs
Glossary of terms

Comparison with Full IFRSs

IFRS for SMEs: A Separate and Distinct Framework

The IFRS for SMEs is a self-contained set of accounting principles, based on full IFRSs but simplified to reflect the needs of users of the financial statements of SMEs, and also limitations in both the technical and financial capabilities available to SMEs. The IFRS for SMEs and full IFRSs are separate and distinct frameworks.

No General "Fallback" to Full IFRSs

Entities that are eligible to apply the IFRS for SMEs, and that choose to do so, must, with one exception, apply that framework in full (i.e. they are not permitted to "mix and match" the requirements of the IFRS for SMEs and full IFRSs). The only exception is that the IFRS for SMEs includes an option to apply the requirements of IAS 39—*Financial Instruments: Recognition and Measurement* in respect of the recognition and measurement of financial instruments (see section "Option to Apply Full IFRSs for Recognition and Measurement of Financial Instruments").[1]

The IFRS for SMEs includes requirements for the development and application of accounting policies in the absence of specific guidance on a particular subject. An entity may, but is not required to, consider the requirements and guidance in full IFRSs on similar and related issues.

The SMEIG (see section "Maintenance of the IFRS for SMEs") has considered the scenario in which a jurisdiction permits all entities meeting the definition of an SME to follow the IFRS for SMEs; however, the jurisdiction adds a requirement that, when the recognition and measurement requirements for a particular transaction, other event or condition are not specifically covered by the IFRS for SMEs, but are covered in full IFRSs, an SME must follow the recognition and measurement requirements in full IFRSs for that transaction, event or condition. The question addressed was whether SMEs in that jurisdiction may state compliance with the IFRS for SMEs.

The conclusion of the SMEIG, set out below, is included in the IFRS Foundation's educational material (see section "IFRS Foundation Training Material") as non-mandatory guidance.

"Whether an SME can assert compliance with the *IFRS for SMEs* in such a case will depend on management's assessment of relevance and reliability as required by paragraph 10.4 of Section 10 *Accounting Policies, Estimates and Errors*. In the absence of specific requirements in the *IFRS for SMEs*, paragraph 10.4 requires management to use its judgement in developing an accounting policy that is reliable and results in information that is relevant to the economic decision-making needs of users. Paragraph 10.5 establishes the following hierarchy for an entity to follow in deciding on the appropriate accounting policy:

(a) the requirements and guidance in the *IFRS for SMEs* dealing with similar and related issues; and
(b) the definitions, recognition criteria and measurement concepts for assets, liabilities, income and expenses and the pervasive principles in Section 2 *Concepts and Pervasive Principles*

Paragraph 10.6 notes that, in making the judgment described in paragraph 10.4, management may also consider the requirements and guidance in full IFRSs that deal with similar and related issues. Taken together, paragraphs 10.4 to 10.6 allow the full IFRS principles to be used in the absence of specific guidance in the *IFRS for SMEs*, provided that they do not conflict with requirements in the hierarchy in paragraph 10.5. This scenario is different from allowing a free choice to follow full IFRS requirements when specific requirements exist in the *IFRS for SMEs* for a transaction, other event or condition. Where there are such specific requirements in the *IFRS for SMEs,* they must be applied even if they differ from full IFRSs. If the entity follows a requirement in full IFRSs for that transaction, other event or condition for which the *IFRS for SMEs* contains different guidance, it will not be able to state compliance with the *IFRS for SMEs* unless the effect is not material."

[1] IAS 39 remains the "fallback" for SMEs, pending the next comprehensive review of the IFRS for SMEs.

Key Types of Simplifications to Full IFRSs

In developing the IFRS for SMEs, the key types of simplifications made to full IFRSs are as follows:

- some topics in IFRSs are omitted because they are not relevant to typical SMEs (see section "Omitted Topics");
- some accounting policy treatments in full IFRSs are not allowed because a simplified method is available to SMEs (see section "Accounting Policies Not Permitted");
- simplification of many of the recognition and measurement principles that are in full IFRSs (see section "Simplification of Recognition and Measurement Principles");
- substantially fewer disclosures (see section "Substantially Fewer Disclosures"); and
- simplified language and explanations throughout.

Sections "Omitted Topics", "Accounting Policies Not Permitted", "Simplification of Recognition and Measurement Principles", "Substantially Fewer Disclosures", and "Additional Issues Addressed in the IFRS for SMEs" summarise the key differences between the IFRS for SMEs and full IFRSs resulting from the simplifications described above.

Omitted Topics

The IFRS for SMEs does not address the following topics that are dealt with in full IFRSs, because these topics are not generally relevant to SMEs:

- earnings per share;
- interim financial reporting;
- segment reporting; and
- insurance (because entities that sell insurance contracts to the public will generally be classed as publicly accountable).

Accounting Policies Not Permitted

The IFRS for SMEs does not allow the following accounting treatments that are available under full IFRSs (generally because a simplified method is available to SMEs):

- the revaluation model for intangible assets;
- for investment property, measurement is driven by circumstances rather than allowing an accounting policy choice between the cost and fair value models. Under the IFRS for SMEs, if an entity can measure the fair value of an item of investment property reliably without undue cost or effort, it must use fair value. Otherwise cost is applied;
- various options for government grants permitted by full IFRSs;
- measurement of non-controlling interests (NCI) in consolidated financial statements at fair value;
- the fair value option for financial instruments; and
- certain hedging strategies (e.g. option-based hedging strategies, hedge accounting for portfolios and hedge accounting using debt instruments).
- However, entities can choose to apply the recognition and measurement provisions of IAS 39 in their entirety, which would enable the accounting policies in the last two bullet points in this list to be adopted (see section "Additional Issues Addressed in the IFRS for SMEs").

Simplification of Recognition and Measurement Principles

Simplification of Recognition and Measurement Principles: General

The main simplifications to the recognition and measurement principles in full IFRSs are as set out in the following table.

Topic	Simplification of recognition and measurement principles when compared to full IFRSs
Financial instruments (if an entity chooses the option to apply IAS 39's recognition and measurement requirements, these simplifications do not apply)	• Most 'basic' financial instruments (i.e. those that meet specified criteria) are measured at cost or amortised cost. All other financial instruments are measured at fair value through profit or loss. The available-for-sale and held-to-maturity classifications in IAS 39 are not available. • A simple principle is established for derecognition; the "pass-through" and "continuing involvement" tests in full IFRSs are dropped. • Hedge accounting requirements, including the detailed calculations, are simplified and tailored for SMEs. Periodic recognition and measurement of hedge ineffectiveness is required, but under conditions less strict than those in full IFRSs. • The IFRS for SMEs does not require separate accounting for embedded derivatives. However, non-financial contracts that include an embedded derivative with economic characteristics not closely related to the host contract are required to be accounted for in their entirety at fair value.

(continued)

(continued)

Topic	Simplification of recognition and measurement principles when compared to full IFRSs
Investments in associates and jointly controlled entities	An accounting policy to measure such investments at cost can be applied for all investments without published price quotations (if published price quotations exist, fair value must be used).
Property, plant and equipment and intangible assets	Residual value, useful life and depreciation/amortisation method for items of property, plant and equipment and intangible assets only need to be reviewed if there is an indication they may have changed since the most recent annual reporting date (full IFRSs require an annual review).
Research and development costs	All costs are expensed.
Goodwill and other intangible assets	• Such assets are always considered to have finite useful lives; consequently, they are amortised over their estimated useful lives. If the useful life of an asset cannot be established reliably, the asset should be amortised over its useful life determined based on management's best estimate; in any case, the useful life is not permitted to exceed 10 years. For entities that have not adopted the 2015 Amendments (see section "The 2015 Amendments to the IFRS for SMEs"), if the useful life cannot be estimated reliably, goodwill and intangible assets are amortised over 10 years. • An impairment test is performed only if there is an indication of impairment (full IFRSs would require the test at least annually). • If goodwill cannot be allocated to individual cash-generating units (or groups of cash-generating units) on a non-arbitrary basis, it is tested for impairment by determining the recoverable amount of either: – the acquired entity, if the goodwill relates to an acquired entity that has not been integrated; or – the entire group of entities excluding any entities that have not been integrated, if the goodwill relates to an entity that has been integrated. In this context, "integrated" means that the acquired business has been restructured or dissolved into the reporting entity or other subsidiaries.
Leases	A lessee is not required to recognise lease payments under operating leases on a straight-line basis if the payments to the lessor are structured to increase in line with expected general inflation to compensate for the lessor's expected inflationary cost increases.
Borrowing costs	All costs are expensed.

(continued)

(continued)

Topic	Simplification of recognition and measurement principles when compared to full IFRSs
Share-based payments	• The directors use their judgement to apply the most appropriate valuation method to determine the fair value of an equity-settled share-based payment if observable market prices are not available. • Arrangements in which the counterparty has a choice of settlement in cash or equity are treated in the same way as arrangements in which the entity has the choice of settlement (i.e. they are classified as cash-settled unless the option lacks economic substance or the entity has a past history of settling in equity); full IFRSs require such arrangements to be accounted for as compound financial instruments. • Group entities are permitted to measure the share-based payment expense arising from awards granted to their employees by another group entity on the basis of a reasonable allocation of the expense for the group, provided that the group presents consolidated financial statements using either the IFRS for SMEs or full IFRSs.
Defined benefit plans	• Subsidiaries are permitted to recognise a reasonable allocation of the expense recognised for the group for benefits provided by a parent that presents consolidated financial statements under the IFRS for SMEs or full IFRSs. • The projected unit credit method is only required to be used to measure the defined benefit obligation and the related expense if it is possible to do so without undue cost or effort. Otherwise the entity is permitted to make the following simplifications in measuring the defined benefit obligation with respect to current employees: – ignore estimated future salary increases; – ignore future service of current employees (i.e. assume closure of the plan for existing as well as any new employees); and – ignore possible in-service mortality of current employees between the reporting date and the date employees are expected to begin receiving post-employment benefits (i.e. assume all current employees will receive the post-employment benefits). Mortality after service (i.e. life expectancy) must still be considered. Entities following the simplifications above are still required to include both vested and unvested benefits in measuring the defined benefit obligation. Entities that have used any of the simplifications described above are required to disclose that fact and the reasons why using the projected unit credit method to measure their obligations and cost under defined benefit plans would involve undue cost or effort.
Income tax	Requirements for income tax are drafted in simple language with less application guidance than full IFRSs and with simplified disclosures.

(*continued*)

(continued)

Topic	Simplification of recognition and measurement principles when compared to full IFRSs
Exchange differences relating to a foreign operation	Exchange differences recognised in other comprehensive income on a monetary item that forms part of a reporting entity's net investment in a foreign operation or on translating the financial statements of a foreign operation into the group presentation currency are not reclassified to profit or loss on disposal of the related investment. This eliminates the need for tracking to which foreign operation such exchange gains or losses relate after initial recognition.
Biological assets	The fair value through profit or loss model is required for biological assets only when fair value is readily determinable without undue cost or effort. Otherwise, the cost-depreciation-impairment model is used.
Non-current assets held for sale	There is no separate held for sale classification and, therefore, there are no special measurement requirements. Instead, holding an asset (or a group of assets) for sale is an impairment indicator.
First-time adoption	There is an "impracticability" exemption with respect to the adjustments required at the date of transition to the IFRS for SMEs.

Meaning of "Undue Cost or Effort"

The IFRS for SMEs contains an "undue cost or effort" exemption that an entity may apply to certain requirements in the Standard. There is guidance on applying this exemption in practice, as follows [IFRS SMEs: 2.14A–2.14C]:

- The undue cost or effort exemption is not a general principle/exemption that can be applied throughout the IFRS for SMEs. The exemption can only be applied to specified requirements, and is not to be used for any other requirements in the Standard.
- The determination as to whether the exemption can be applied will depend on the specific facts and circumstances of the entity and management's judgement in assessing the costs and benefits of obtaining the information necessary to comply with the requirement. Management's assessment should include a consideration of how the economic decisions of the users of the financial statements could be affected by not having the information. Applying a requirement would result in undue cost or effort if the incremental cost (e.g. valuers' fees) or additional effort (e.g. endeavours by employees) substantially exceed the benefits that the users of the entity's financial statements would receive from having the information.

- An assessment of undue cost or effort by an SME in accordance with the IFRS for SMEs would usually constitute a lower hurdle than an assessment of undue cost or effort by a publicly accountable entity because SMEs are not accountable to public stakeholders.
- An assessment as to whether a requirement would involve undue cost or effort on initial recognition in the financial statements should be based on information about the costs and benefits of the requirement at the time of initial recognition. If the undue cost or effort exemption also applies subsequent to initial recognition (e.g. to a subsequent measurement of an item), a new assessment of undue cost or effort is required at that subsequent date, based on information available at the date of the subsequent measurement.

The IASB added the clarifying guidance to the IFRS for SMEs to emphasise that the undue cost or effort exemption is not intended to be a low hurdle. This is because an entity is required to carefully weigh the expected effects of applying the exemption on the users of the financial statements against the cost or effort of complying with the related requirement. In particular, the IASB observed that it would expect that if an entity already had, or could easily and inexpensively acquire, the information necessary to comply with a requirement, any related undue cost or effort exemption would not be applicable. This is because, in that case, the benefits to the users of the financial statements of having the information would be expected to exceed any further cost or effort by the entity [IFRS SMEs: BC232].

The 2015 Amendments also introduced a requirement that whenever an entity uses an undue cost or effort exemption, that fact should be disclosed, together with the reasons why applying the requirement would involve undue cost or effort [IFRS SMEs: 2.14D].

Substantially Fewer Disclosures

The disclosure requirements in the IFRS for SMEs are substantially reduced when compared with those in full IFRSs. Disclosures required by full IFRSs have been omitted from the IFRS for SMEs for two principal reasons, namely, either

- they relate to topics or accounting policy options in full IFRSs that are omitted from the IFRS for SMEs, or they relate to recognition and measurement principles in full IFRSs that have been replaced by simplifications in the IFRS for SMEs; or

- they are not considered appropriate based on users' needs and/or cost-benefit considerations. For example, some disclosures in full IFRSs are more relevant to investment decisions in public capital markets than to the transactions and other events and conditions encountered by typical SMEs.

Additional Issues Addressed in the IFRS for SMEs

The IFRS for SMEs covers several issues that, in the IASB's judgement, are relevant to SMEs but are not addressed in full IFRSs. These are

- combined financial statements (which are a single set of financial statements of two or more entities under common control);
- original issue of shares or other equity instruments;
- sale of options, rights and warrants; and
- capitalisation or bonus issues of shares and share splits.

Option to Apply Full IFRSs for Recognition and Measurement of Financial Instruments

The IFRS for SMEs only allows an entity to apply the requirements of full IFRSs, instead of those in the IFRS for SMEs, in one area—the recognition and measurement of financial instruments. An entity must choose to apply either [IFRS SMEs: 11.2]

(a) the relevant requirements of the IFRS for SMEs (both Section 11 *Basic Financial Instruments* and Section 12 *Other Financial Instruments Issues*) in full; or
(b) the requirements for recognition and measurement of IAS 39 and the disclosure requirements of Sections 11 and 12 of the IFRS for SMEs, to account for all of its financial instruments.

An entity's choice between (a) and (b) under IFRS SMEs: 11.2 of the IFRS for SMEs is an accounting policy choice, not a mandatory fallback to full IFRSs. Therefore, it does not detract from the stand-alone status of the IFRS for SMEs.

In either case, the disclosure requirements in the IFRS for SMEs must be followed, not those in IFRS 7—*Financial Instruments: Disclosures*. The IASB decided not to require IFRS 7 disclosures, even for those SMEs applying IAS 39's recognition and measurement requirements, because many of the IFRS 7 disclosures are designed for entities that hold assets in a fiduciary capacity for a broad range of

(*continued*)

(continued)

members of the public, such as banks, or for entities whose securities are traded in public capital markets. Neither of these types of entities is eligible to use the IFRS for SMEs (see section "Scope").

The IASB's reasons for allowing SMEs the option to apply the recognition and measurement requirements of IAS 39 are as follows [IFRS SMEs:BC106]:

- Some of the simplifications in Sections 11 and 12 of the IFRS for SMEs involve eliminating options that are available to entities with public accountability under IAS 39 (e.g. the fair value option, held-to-maturity classification, certain hedging strategies). The IASB is currently reconsidering IAS 39 in its entirety and concluded that SMEs should be permitted to have the same accounting policy options as in IAS 39 pending completion of the comprehensive IAS 39 project.
- Because the default category for financial instruments in the scope of Section 12 of the IFRS for SMEs is fair value through profit or loss, and cost or amortised cost is permitted only when specified conditions are met, some items measured at cost or amortised cost under IAS 39 would be measured at fair value through profit or loss under the IFRS for SMEs. Some SMEs might find this added fair valuation burdensome.
- Sometimes, an entity makes what it views as a "strategic investment" in equity instruments, with the intention of establishing or maintaining a long-term operating relationship with the entity in which the investment is made. Those entities generally believe that the available-for-sale classification of IAS 39 is appropriate to account for strategic investments. Under the IFRS for SMEs requirements, however, these strategic investments would be accounted for either at fair value through profit or loss or at amortised cost.
- The derecognition provisions of the IFRS for SMEs would not result in derecognition for many securitisations and factoring transactions that SMEs may enter into, whereas IAS 39 would result in derecognition.

It is expected that most stand-alone SMEs will choose to apply the provisions of Sections 11 and 12 of the IFRS for SMEs in full so as to avoid the greater complexity in IAS 39. However, the ability to combine IAS 39's recognition and measurement requirements with the Section 11 and 12 disclosures is likely to be attractive to many subsidiaries who wish to apply the IFRS for SMEs in their own financial statements, but are required to submit financial information for consolidation purposes in accordance with full IFRSs (such entities are considered in more detail in section "Use of the IFRS for SMEs by Subsidiaries in Groups Using Full IFRSs"). This is because such subsidiaries will be able to align their accounting policies for financial instruments with those used in the consolidated financial statements, yet still benefit from the reduced disclosure requirements in the IFRS for SMEs in their own financial statements. This will be particularly beneficial for entities with numerous and more complex financial instrument transactions (e.g. treasury entities within a group).

The IFRS for SMEs (2015) clarifies that entities that opt to apply option (b) under paragraph 11 of the IFRS for SMEs, should apply the following:

- until IAS 39 is superseded by IFRS 9—*Financial Instruments*, the version of IAS 39 that is in effect at the entity's reporting date[2]; and
- when IAS 39 is superseded by IFRS 9, entities should apply the version of IAS 39 that applied immediately prior to IFRS 9 superseding IAS 39.

Income Tax

The IFRS for SMEs requires a temporary difference approach, similar to IAS 12—*Income Taxes*.

The main differences between IAS 12 and Section 29—*Income Tax* of the IFRS for SMEs are as follows:

- Section 29 is drafted in more simple language, and has simplified presentation and disclosure requirements; and
- Section 29 contains additional clarification that "substantively enacted" means that the remaining steps in the enactment process historically have not affected the outcome and are unlikely to do so.

There is an undue cost or effort exemption (see section "Meaning of 'Undue Cost or Effort'") whereby entities are not required to offset income tax assets and liabilities if significant, detailed scheduling would be required.

Use of the IFRS for SMEs by Subsidiaries in Groups Using Full IFRSs

Potential Benefits of the IFRS for SMEs for Subsidiaries

Provided that a jurisdiction does not otherwise prohibit it, a subsidiary whose parent uses full IFRSs, or that is part of a consolidated group that uses full IFRSs, will be entitled to apply the IFRS for SMEs in its own financial state-

[2] As of 1 August 2018, IAS 39 remains the "fallback" financial instruments standard in the context of the IFRS for SMEs.

ments if that subsidiary does not itself have public accountability. If the subsidiary opts to use the IFRS for SMEs then, apart from the exception relating to IAS 39—*Financial Instruments: Recognition and Measurement* (see section "Option to Apply Full IFRSs for Recognition and Measurement of Financial Instruments"), it will be required to follow the Standard in its entirety, that is, the subsidiary cannot pick and choose between the requirements of the IFRS for SMEs and those of full IFRSs in order to minimise differences between its accounting policies and those in the group's consolidated financial statements. For example, a subsidiary would not be permitted to apply the recognition and measurement requirements of full IFRSs and the disclosure requirements of the IFRS for SMEs.

In many countries, subsidiaries, even those that are wholly owned, are subject to the same general requirements concerning the preparation and audit of annual financial statements as other entities. In general, subsidiaries are required to apply all of the detailed disclosure requirements in full IFRSs. This means that their own financial statements are lengthy documents, with pages of detailed note disclosures, most of which will rarely be looked at. Most interested parties only look at the consolidated financial statements of the group, particularly when there are no minority shareholders or significant creditors in the subsidiary.

If a subsidiary chooses to apply the IFRS for SMEs in its individual financial statements, the group would be required to restate the subsidiary's financial information under full IFRSs for consolidation purposes. However, this does not automatically mean that it is more efficient in terms of time and costs from the group's perspective for the subsidiary to prepare its own financial statements under full IFRSs. The following are some of the reasons why the group may still benefit from a subsidiary using the IFRS for SMEs.

- The financial information produced for consolidation purposes under full IFRSs has a different materiality threshold from that necessary for the subsidiary's own financial statements. Therefore, particularly when the subsidiary is small in relation to the group of entities, some amounts may not need to be determined, or may be approximated, for consolidation purposes (e.g. if they are immaterial to the consolidated financial statements). However, those amounts may be material at the subsidiary level and so they would need to be determined accurately for the subsidiary's own financial statements under the subsidiary's accounting framework. Applying the IFRS for SMEs would allow the subsidiary to make use of the more simplified requirements when determining measurement for its own financial statements.
- Presenting full IFRS note disclosures in the subsidiary's own financial statements is very time consuming, notwithstanding that many of the required amounts will need to be determined for consolidation purposes. Applying the IFRS for SMEs would allow subsidiaries to benefit from significantly less note disclosures in comparison to full IFRSs.

(continued)

(continued)

- The IFRS for SMEs allows accounting policy choices for some recognition and measurement principles, so that differences from full IFRSs can be minimised by aligning the accounting policies used in the group's consolidated financial statements and the accounting policies in the subsidiary's own financial statements where possible (section "Mandatory Differences Between Full IFRSs and the IFRS for SMEs" lists the areas for which alignment is not possible). By aligning policies where possible, an entity may find only a few adjustments are required to the financial information maintained under the IFRS for SMEs in order to provide information suitable for consolidation purposes under full IFRSs.

Mandatory Differences Between Full IFRSs and the IFRS for SMEs

Although the IFRS for SMEs contains many simplifications from full IFRSs, the circumstances in which the IFRS for SMEs would mandate a recognition or measurement principle that is different from full IFRSs are limited. In many cases accounting policies may be chosen that are appropriate under both the IFRS for SMEs and full IFRSs. The Basis for Conclusions on the IFRS for SMEs identifies the principal circumstances when there would necessarily be a difference between the two accounting frameworks—the table below highlights those major circumstances. As a result, in these circumstances, consolidation adjustments will always be required (subject to materiality considerations) if a subsidiary of a full IFRS group chooses to apply the IFRS for SMEs in its own financial statements.

The third column in the table below explains the impact for the preparer of the full IFRS consolidated financial statements if a subsidiary of the group chooses to apply the IFRS for SMEs in its own financial statements.

The items listed in the table will only result in consolidation adjustments when the subsidiary actually has the transactions/balances under consideration, and the related amounts in the subsidiary's financial statements are material to the consolidated financial statements either in the current year or any prior years presented.

Differences between full IFRS and the IFRS for SMEs || Impact for the preparer of full IFRS consolidated financial instruments

Topic	Difference between full IFRSs and the IFRS for SMEs	Impact for the preparer of full IFRS consolidated financial instruments
Non-current assets (or groups of assets and liabilities) held for sale	• IFRS for SMEs: Holding assets for sale triggers an assessment for impairment, but otherwise there is no held for sale classification and there are no special accounting requirements. • IFRS 5—*Non-current Assets Held for Sale and Discontinued Operations*: Measured at the lower of carrying amount and fair value less costs to sell. Depreciation stops when assets are classified as held for sale.	Under the IFRS for SMEs, non-current assets (or groups of assets and liabilities) held for sale are treated in the same way as if they were not held for sale, except that an expected sale triggers an impairment assessment. Therefore, on consolidation, any non-current assets (or groups of assets and liabilities) of the subsidiary that meet the held for sale classification requirements under IFRS 5, either in the current or prior periods, must be identified, remeasured under IFRS 5 and presented separately in the consolidated financial statements.
Borrowing costs	• IFRS for SMEs: Must be recognised as an expense immediately. • IAS 23 [IAS 35] *Borrowing Costs*: Costs directly attributable to the acquisition, construction or production of a qualifying asset must be capitalised.	Although the IFRS for SMEs requires all borrowing costs to be expensed when incurred, when a subsidiary has any qualifying assets the group will need to keep a record of the borrowing costs eligible for capitalisation on those assets under IAS 23 for consolidation purposes. Such borrowing costs will need to be tracked during the period they qualify for capitalisation under IAS 23 and also while the asset is held by the group. Such borrowing costs will affect the carrying amount of the asset as well as any depreciation and potential impairment loss recognised in the consolidated financial statements. Any interest incurred on intragroup borrowings would not need to be tracked because it would not qualify for capitalisation in the consolidated financial statements.

(*continued*)

(continued)

Topic	Difference between full IFRSs and the IFRS for SMEs	Impact for the preparer of full IFRS consolidated financial instruments
Development costs	• IFRS for SMEs: Must be recognised as an expense immediately. • IAS 38—*Intangible Assets*: Requires capitalisation of development costs meeting specified criteria.	Although the IFRS for SMEs requires all development costs to be expensed, if a subsidiary incurs development costs and these meet the criteria for capitalisation under IAS 38, the group will need to keep a record of these development costs for consolidation purposes. Therefore, an assessment as to whether the development project is commercially viable would be required for the consolidated financial statements. Such development costs would need to be tracked during the period they qualify for capitalisation under IAS 38 and while the intangible asset is held by the group. An intangible asset will be recognised in the consolidated financial statements and amortisation/impairment losses will need to be recognised.
Investment property	• IFRS for SMEs: Must be measured at fair value through profit or loss if fair value can be measured reliably without undue cost or effort; otherwise the cost model is applied. • IAS 40—*Investment Property: Accounting* policy choice of fair value through profit or loss or cost model. If the fair value model is used and an investment property is acquired whose fair value is not reliably determinable on a continuing basis (meaning comparable market transactions are infrequent and alternative reliable estimates of fair value are not available), the cost model is used for that property—this will only occur in exceptional circumstances. If the cost model is used, the entity must disclose the fair value of investment property in the notes to the financial statements.	Under the IFRS for SMEs, the accounting treatment for investment property is determined by an entity's ability to determine the fair value of its properties. It is up to the preparer of the subsidiary's financial statements to determine what is 'undue cost or effort' (see section "Meaning of 'Undue Cost or Effort'"). Different entities will have differing interpretations. Unless investment properties are immaterial from a group perspective, a subsidiary will in any case need to provide fair value information for its properties to its parent to meet the disclosure requirement in IAS 40. In such circumstances, the subsidiary is less likely to conclude that measuring properties at fair value in its own financial statements would involve "undue cost or effort". If cost measurement is appropriate for an investment property in the consolidated financial statements, due to its fair value not being reliably measurable under IAS 40 (when the group uses the fair value model to measure investment property), then the cost model would also be applied to that property in the subsidiary's own financial statements under the IFRS for SMEs.

Biological assets	• IFRS for SMEs: Measure at fair value through profit or loss only if fair value is readily determinable without undue cost or effort; otherwise the cost model is applied. • IAS 41—*Agriculture*: Presumption that fair value can be reliably measured. Can be rebutted only on initial recognition if market-determined prices or values are not available and alternative estimates of fair value are clearly unreliable (in which case the cost model is used).	Similar considerations as for investment property apply to biological assets. When a subsidiary is required to disclose fair value information for biological assets to its parent, it is less likely to conclude that measuring biological assets at fair value in its own financial statements would involve "undue cost or effort". If cost measurement is appropriate for a biological asset in the consolidated financial statements due to its fair value not being reliably measurable under IAS 41, then cost measurement would also be appropriate for that asset in the subsidiary's own financial statements under the IFRS for SMEs.
Share-based payments with cash alternatives in which the terms of the arrangement provide the counterparty with a choice of settlement	• IFRS for SMEs: Account for the transaction as a cash-settled share-based payment unless either the entity has a past practice of settling by issuing equity instruments or the option to settle in cash has no commercial substance. • IFRS 2—*Share-based Payment*: Accounting similar to a compound instrument.	This point only refers to share-based payment awards granted by the subsidiary. If a share-based payment award is granted by an entity to the employees of one or more group entities, and the group presents consolidated financial statements using either the IFRS for SMEs or full IFRSs, the group entities are permitted to measure the share-based payment expense in their own financial statements on the basis of a reasonable allocation of the expense for the group. If share-based payment awards with cash alternatives are granted by the subsidiary where the counterparty (e.g. the subsidiary's employees or a supplier of the subsidiary) has choice of settlement, separate records will need to be kept for preparation of the consolidated financial statements.
Goodwill and other indefinite-lived intangible assets	• IFRS for SMEs: All intangible assets, including goodwill, are considered to have a finite useful life. If the useful life cannot be estimated reliably, it is determined based on management's best estimate, but the period shall not exceed 10 years. • IAS 38—*Intangible Assets*: Intangible assets with an indefinite useful life are not amortised but must be tested annually for impairment. IFRS 3—*Business Combinations* requires that goodwill is not amortised but is tested annually for impairment.	For consolidation purposes, any amortisation charged on the intangible assets in the subsidiary's own financial statements will need to be added back and an impairment test performed at the reporting date (or other designated date during the year). Care would be needed to ensure that goodwill or intangible assets that had been fully written off through amortisation are reinstated if necessary for consolidation purposes.

(*continued*)

(continued)

Topic	Difference between full IFRSs and the IFRS for SMEs	Impact for the preparer of full IFRS consolidated financial instruments
Timing of recognition of government grants	• IFRS for SMEs: A government grant is not recognised until the conditions attached to the grant are actually satisfied. The grant may not be matched with the expenses for which it is intended to compensate or the cost of the asset that it is used to finance. • IAS 20—*Accounting for Government Grants and Disclosure of Government Assistance*: A government grant is not recognised until there is reasonable assurance that the entity will comply with the conditions attached to it and the grant will be received. A grant is recognised as income over the periods necessary to match it with the related costs for which it is intended to compensate, on a systematic basis.	The different recognition criteria may result in a grant being recognised earlier or later under full IFRSs in comparison to the IFRS for SMEs. If this is the case, and recognition of part or all of the grant falls into different accounting periods under full IFRSs, then adjustments will be required on consolidation. IAS 20 permits additional options for measuring and presenting certain grants, but if accounting policies are aligned with the IFRS for SMEs where possible, the difference can be reduced to the timing of recognition of the grant.
Exchange differences on a monetary item that forms part of the net investment in a foreign operation	This difference refers only to the financial statements that include the foreign operation and the reporting entity (e.g. consolidated financial statements when the foreign operation is a subsidiary). • IFRS for SMEs: Recognise in other comprehensive income and do not reclassify to profit or loss on disposal of the investment. • IAS 21—*The Effects of Changes in Foreign Exchange Rates*: Reclassify to profit or loss on disposal of the investment.	Exchange differences on a monetary item that forms part of a subsidiary's net investment in a foreign operation do not need to be tracked by the subsidiary for its own financial statements because the differences are not reclassified under the IFRS for SMEs on disposal. When the foreign operation is still a foreign operation in the consolidated financial statements under full IFRSs (i.e. the functional currency of the foreign operation differs from the group's presentation currency), the exchange differences will need to be tracked because reclassification is required under full IFRSs. If the group applies the direct method of including the foreign operation in the consolidated financial statements, this will be more straightforward. If the step-by-step method is used, the group must ensure that the exchange differences are tracked so that when the subsidiary disposes of the foreign operation, a consolidation adjustment can be made to the subsidiary's financial information. The above difference is more likely to arise if the foreign operation is a foreign associate or foreign joint venture of the subsidiary applying the IFRS for SMEs. If the foreign operation is a subsidiary of the subsidiary applying the IFRS for SMEs, the latter may follow the exemption in Section 9.2 of the IFRS for SMEs not to prepare consolidated financial statements.

The differences between the IFRS for SMEs and full IFRSs listed in the table above are those that are unavoidable, that is, they cannot be eliminated by judicious selection of accounting policies. However, often small subsidiaries will not be involved in transactions or arrangements of the types discussed. For example, defined benefit plans and share-based payment arrangements are often set up at a group rather than a subsidiary level, and biological assets, government grants and investment property are only usually encountered by certain types of entity.

Other differences may arise between the group's accounting policies and the subsidiary's accounting policies because it will not always be practical, or desirable, for the group to choose accounting policies that are in compliance with the IFRS for SMEs. For example, the group may wish to revalue intangible assets traded in an active market to be comparable to competitors in the same industry. Revaluation of such intangible assets is not permitted under the IFRS for SMEs. The need for the group to make accounting policy choices which diverge from the IFRS for SMEs should also be considered when deciding whether to adopt the IFRS for SMEs.

Transition to the IFRS for SMEs

The IFRS for SMEs includes a separate section dealing with first-time adoption. Section 35—*Transition to the IFRS for SMEs* applies to a first-time adopter of the IFRS for SMEs, regardless of whether its previous accounting framework was full IFRSs, or another set of generally accepted accounting principles (e.g. the entity's national accounting standards), or another framework (e.g. a local income tax basis) [IFRS SMEs: 35.1].

A first-time adopter of the IFRS for SMEs applies Section 35 in the first annual financial statements in which that entity makes an explicit and unreserved statement of compliance with the IFRS for SMEs. If an entity using the IFRS for SMEs stops using it for one or more reporting periods, but is required or chooses to adopt it again for a later reporting period, the entity can either apply Section 35 in that later accounting period, or apply the IFRS for SMEs retrospectively in accordance with Section 10—*Accounting Policies, Estimates and Errors* as if the entity had never stopped applying the IFRS for SMEs [IFRS SMEs: 35.2–4].

Apart from when certain exemptions are provided, Section 35 requires an entity, in its opening statement of financial position as of its date of transition to the IFRS for SMEs (i.e. the beginning of the earliest period presented) [IFRS SMEs: 35.7]:

- to recognise all assets and liabilities whose recognition is required by the IFRS for SMEs;
- not to recognise items as assets or liabilities if the IFRS for SMEs does not permit such recognition;
- to reclassify items that it recognised under its previous financial reporting framework as one type of asset, liability or component of equity, but which are a different type of asset, liability or component of equity under the IFRS for SMEs; and
- to apply the IFRS for SMEs in measuring all recognised assets and liabilities.

The approach in Section 35 is similar to that under IFRS 1—*First-time Adoption of International Financial Reporting Standards*. Section 35 also contains most of IFRS 1's optional exemptions from, and mandatory exceptions to, the full retrospective application that would otherwise be required. Section 35 also has an additional optional exemption with respect to deferred income tax, allowing first-time adopters to apply Section 29—*Income Tax* prospectively from the date of transition to the IFRS for SMEs.

Section 35 provides additional relief regarding comparative information by including an "impracticability" exemption (which is not in IFRS 1). Section 35 states that if it is impracticable for an entity to make one or more of the adjustments required by the bullet points above at the date of transition, the entity should apply the adjustments in the earliest period for which it is practicable to do so [IFRS SMEs: 35.11].

Maintenance of the IFRS for SMEs

The initial implementation review of the IFRS for SMEs has been completed and resulted in the IASB issuing the 2015 Amendments (see section "The 2015 Amendments to the IFRS for SMEs").

In future, the revision of the IFRS for SMEs will be limited to once in approximately three years; these periodic reviews will consider new and amended IFRSs that have been developed in the previous three years, as well as specific issues that have been identified as possible improvements. On occasion, the IASB may identify a matter for which amendment of the IFRS for SMEs needs to be considered outside the periodic review process. Until the IFRS for SMEs is amended, any changes made or proposed with respect to full IFRSs do not apply to entities applying the IFRS for SMEs.

The SME Implementation Group (SMEIG) was established in 2010 to support the international adoption of the IFRS for SMEs and monitor its implementation, develop non-mandatory implementation guidance in the form of Q&As, and make recommendations to the IASB on the need to amend the IFRS for SMEs. As of 1 August 2018, there are no current Q&As; however, prior to the 2015 Amendments (see section "The 2015 Amendments to the IFRS for SMEs"), the SMEIG had issued seven Q&As, which have either been incorporated into the IFRS for SMEs (and made mandatory) or the IFRS Foundation's educational material (and remain non-mandatory guidance).

In June 2017, the SMEIG issued draft guidance (the first to be published since the 2015 Amendments—see section "The 2015 Amendments to the IFRS for SMEs") addressing the accounting treatment for a financial guarantee issued by a parent in that parent's separate financial statements.

IFRS Foundation Training Material

To support the implementation of the IFRS for SMEs, the IFRS Foundation has developed comprehensive training material, which can be downloaded free of charge from the following address: https://www.ifrs.org/supporting-implementation/supporting-materials-for-the-ifrs-for-smes/modules/sme-modules-english/

12

Conclusion: Closing the Circle of Financing and Financial Reporting for SMEs. Our Formula

Raz van Hoinaru

The book presented and united financing with financial reporting, a merger which looked obvious to us; however, it is not common among other publications. Our research discovered that there is a 'myopic' thinking in terms of net present value and (future) cash flows, generating short-termism and low risk appetite for business. This is not an accounting issue, but rather a preference toward certain financial tools. A segment of SMEs, the ones that seek the high end of funding possibilities, as well as modern technologies (MTFs listing, blockchain, ICOs, etc.) do require, even without knowing, IFRS for SMEs. Of course one can argue that there is a self-fulfilling prophecy, an old Keynesian saying that 'supply creates its own demand'. Yet, by this standard the IASB created a high quality set of financial reporting standards, meant to improve business networks and transparency. Professor Haslam, in his chapter, argues that IFRS connects with market efficiency and generate policies and business strategies for SMEs.

Therefore, a straightforward answer to a great question launched as part of Accountancy Talks by ICAEW 'Is IFRS for SMEs good for SMEs?' is yes, however, for the top SMEs only. This happens in spite of some shortages of harmonisation and other known critics, some of them unsubstantiated. Generally,

R. van Hoinaru (✉)
European Parliament, Brussels, Belgium

Queen Mary University of London, London, UK
e-mail: razvan.hoinaru@europarl.europa.eu

E. Kaili et al. (eds.), *New Models of Financing and Financial Reporting for European SMEs*,
https://doi.org/10.1007/978-3-030-02831-2_12

IFRS for SMEs contributes to the internationally competitive image Europe has. A global set of standards brings positive effects, among the most common being transparency, promotion and investment. The business environment impacts on the SMEs' activities and the SMEs answers back to these conditions. There are 23 million SMEs in the European Union, making 99% of the total registered companies. Most of them are traditional in the way they do business, economic growth being connected with institutional arrangements and general economic trends. This top-down approach perspective is not shared by the editors of this book, who recognise the value of traditional business models and of EU funding; they do, however, understand the transition period that we now traverse. We are now facing a *new growth model. It has been important to grasp practitioners' views on the subject, and our aim has been to develop a comprehensive theory.*

The contributors of the first part of this volume present their views about the financing environment for the SMEs in the post-financial-crisis period and in the light of the developments introduced by the Capital Markets Union and the digitisation of the financial markets. The title speaks about *new models.* The chapters give a clear sense of the notion of new models of financing for SMEs. The old models are well known. The SMEs, especially in Continental Europe, were highly dependent on the system of universal banks. The banks provided funds for investments in Property, Plant, and Equipment (PP&E) and more. The banks provided also the necessary financial facilities for the SMEs operations.

The traditional model was very well adapted to the habits of the SMEs. A significant part of the capital investments was based on their retained earnings but the banks contributed a significant part when necessary. The bank was (and still is), however, an essential partner of the SMEs in the everyday life of the firm, especially in the "smoothing" of the liquidity needs with products like invoice prepayment accounts, business credit cards, credit lines extensions and so on. The bank was like a 'supermarket' of financial products and its marketing was simple and straightforward: maximise the revenue as much as possible per SME. This system works perfectly when the business cycle is booming and when the recession is not dramatic. But when the recession is sharp and ends up becoming a long depression, the SME's exposure to the bank becomes a trap and the outcome can be dramatic. The systemic consequences of this situation are everywhere in the popular media and they are epitomised by notions like "debt overhang" and the huge stocks of non-performing loans (NPLs). The banks and the SMEs of Italy and Greece are vivid examples of this turmoil.

When the banks were unable to perform their traditional role, due to their incapacity to function in the interbanking space during the crisis, or because of the regulatory constraints imposed on them after the crisis, they gradually lost markets and new entrants, the fintechs, harnessed the digital technology and started selling products, like payment services, to the SMEs. This is the *first type of 'new model' of financing*: the replacement of the bank as the sole provider of traditional financial services for SMEs.

However, the banks did not stay idle. They attempted to renovate their products and also capitalise on the new opportunities that digitisation creates. Many banks automated their procedures and digitised the relationship between the bank and the SME. They also tried to be creative and bypass the regulatory constraints imposed by the regulator by creating new instruments like those of the supply chain finance (SCF) and sponsoring the 'minibonds'. This is a *second type of 'new model' of financing* of SMEs. Both the first and the second type of those 'new models' became a source of significant regulatory work for the EU institutions and led to very significant improvements for many important fields like the Payment Services Directive (PSD) or the Anti-Money Laundering Directive (AMLD).

The major impact of the financial crisis though, was that it incentivised SMEs not only to try to find new providers for the old products; SMEs, as well as policymakers or associations working with SMEs, started to explore alternative sources of finance beyond the banks and the 'plain vanilla' banking services. The Capital Markets Union attempted (intentionally or unintentionally) to cover the inefficiencies created in the financial space by the fact that the EU does not have a genuine and functional banking union. The European firms, no matter what their size, location and business model, had to be able to reach vital capital for their survival and growth. This was even more important for SMEs and start-ups, especially in the cases where we had the development of significant innovation ecosystems but weak supply of funds (e.g. in Estonia, Malta or Cyprus). The result has been that, since 2012, everybody in the EU speaks about the need to develop, ab initio when necessary, robust private and public equity markets. This was a common point of agreement among all the contributors of this volume. The emergence of equity as the necessary alternative to banking was *the third, and possibly major, type of 'new model' for financing of SMEs*.

The post-financial-crisis era in Europe opened the discussion on financial disintermediation. From all the types of 'new models' we have described so far, only *the fourth type is truly innovative, and possibly the only new model of financing for SMEs deserving to be written without quotation marks*. Sources of finance based on crowdfunding and ICOs are indicators that, sooner or later, one part of the financing needs for SMEs, and especially the ones that are dedicated to the quest of disruptive innovation, will be carried on the shoulders, not of the financial specialists, but of the enthusiastic crowds. The promise that these innovative financial instruments bring is great. It is paramount though, to educate both regulators and investors about these new types of investment and understand the sources or risk, the systematic dangers, and the new investor protection requirements. The European Union seems to be in the forefront of this effort and everybody, from the European Commission and the Parliament to the European Supervisory Authorities and the European Central Bank, work closely and hard to keep all the options open and make the EU a global leader and source of inspiration for the financial jurisdictions around the world.

The second part of the book showed that financialised financial reporting is an imperative to the way modern business is conducted at a certain level. Nowadays, opportunities are in high growth international markets, and financing, being it investment or sales, must benefit from proper recognition. It is also useful to consider the implications for a self-contained standard like IFRS for SMEs, both in comparison with full IFRS and also with local GAAPs. Even though IFRS for SMEs is a lighter version of full IFRS, and the inner technical complexities are simplified, Deloitte representatives mentioned in their contribution that 'the IASB added the clarifying guidance to the IFRS for SMEs to emphasise that the undue cost or effort exemption is not intended to be a low hurdle'. A common standard for SMEs, listed on MTFs, have some specific risks attached to it. Accordingly to the MiFID II Directive, SMEs are ample companies, and therefore capable of creating some societal dangers. There are also risks related to unsuitable use and actual misuse of this set of standards, especially among the group and subsidiary accounting approaches and interplays and the presence of the so-called public users of certain subsets of accounts. There may be a slight difference of views between the issuer, preparers and users. However, any change in the standard is delicate, neither the oversimplification of the standard, nor increasing its complexity being desired solutions, while the purpose is still SMEs and the intended users are the investors.

Nowadays, there is a trend where stakeholders and stakeholder relations are taken into consideration. This higher visibility of stakeholders make companies better consider both inside and outside values in their business models and commercial activities. Some authors called for a balance between investors' needs and decision usefulness, consumer protection and, moreover, environmental care. To what extent this is within the scope of the IASB and the IFRS Foundation is arguable. Principle-based accounting involves expertise, of course, but also business intuition and emotional intelligence for a responsible business. Accounting has departed from the traditional way of being purely technical. Financial reporting has been developed for the public good, helping not only companies, but also regulators and governability, and maybe even society at large. In this way, SMEs and SMEs accounting can contribute to regulatory changes, accounting having its own business logic and point of view.

Lastly, chartered accountants must not be forgotten. The question that the profession faces today is that of remaining relevant.[1] There is a difference between the means and the ends in accounting and ethical considerations are still very important, especially when judging non-financial reporting. This extension and qualitative version of accounting offers information that can be used in financial ways by investors, but also contributes to value creation and stakeholder (relationship) disclosure. Whether professionally trained accountants have the right sets of skills to prepare non-financial reports is another great question. Considering reinvention of the profession by innovation, fostering knowledge and advancement in the guild trade look like prospects to consider, arbitrating between new types of data and business sustainability. For now, certain gaps have to be bridged, harmonisations taken care of and disclosures prepared, in a world where SMEs are key changing factors.

At the end, the reader has to keep in mind 10 concluding points:

On SMEs

1. SME is not a one-size-fits-all concept. It encompasses small and medium-size companies, with micro companies being mentioned aside. It is therefore hard to address SMEs both business-wise and regulatory-wise due to its artificial construction, defined in legal and business standards.
2. In the European Union, SMEs are rather 'little big business' with revenues that can reach up to 200 million euros in capitalisation over a 3-year period, 50 million euros in revenue per year, and they can have 250 employees. Some old fashioned perception that SMEs are small businesses generally persists as the vast majority of them still are;

[1] Nixon, R. (2015). *Remaining Relevant - The future of the accounting profession*, Vivid Publishing.

On Financing

3. In the European Union, which is a rich and highly competitive environment, regulation, business, innovation and funding go hand in hand.
4. Banks are still the traditional source for SMEs to obtain finance. However, due to certain new banking requirements SMEs are put at a disadvantage compared to larger firms.
5. Europe needs to adapt to new approaches such as fintech and blockchain, to ensure future competitiveness, sustainable societies and maintain a global leadership role. In addition, new regulatory boxes are required.

On IFRS for SMEs

6. IFRS for SMEs is not aimed at small companies, but at the very high end of the SMEs, where size matters, but also business models and management style;
7. IFRS for SMEs is largely considered a set of standards that are of high quality, with the acknowledgement of the deficiencies and questions that appear when they are gamed into and used for certain business activities;
8. IFRS has a market efficiency component, reducing costs and generally aiming at investment and growth.
9. Non-financial reporting is important as well and it can be used by investors in the most financial way possible.
10. Digitalisation and Big data created challenges to professional accountants, but the remaining relevant argument for now is obsolete due to ethnic, soft skills set needed and judgement required in financial reporting and business in general.

Bibliography

Abdulsaleh, A. M., & Worthington, A. C. (2013). Small and Medium-Sized Enterprises Financing: A Review of Literature. *International Journal of Business and Management, 8*, 36–54. Retrieved from https://www.researchgate.net/publication/227462778_SMES'_SECTOR_ACCESS_TO_FINANCE_AN_OVERVIEW

Accountancy Europe. Retrieved from www.accountancyeurope.eu

African SME Organisation. *About African SME*. Retrieved from https://africansme.org/index.php/about/about-african-sme

Alvarez, F., & Fridson, M. (2011). *Financial Statement Analysis: A Practitioner's Guide* (p. 378). New Jersey: John Wiley & Sons.

ANC. (2007). *ED IFRS for SMEs*. Retrieved from http://www.anc.gouv.fr/files/live/sites/anc/files/contributed/ANC/2.%20Normes%20internationales/NI%202007/IASB_2007ED_ifrs_sme.pdf

ANC. (2010). *Consultation sur la norme internationale d'information financière pour les petites et moyennes entreprises*. Retrieved from http://www.anc.gouv.fr/files/live/sites/anc/files/contributed/ANC/1.%20Normes%20fran%C3%A7aises/Travaux%20autres/CE_12mars2010_Lettre_Consultation_sur_la_norme_IFRS_pour_les_PME.pdf

Andersson, T., Haslam, C., Tsitsianis, N., Katechos, G., & Hoinaru, R. (2016). Stress Testing International Financial Reporting Standards (IFRSs): Accounting for Stability and the Public Good in a Financialized World. *Accounting, Economics and Law – A Convivium, 6*(2), 93–118.

Atkinson, R., & Ezell, S. (2012). *Innovation Economics: The Race for Global Advantage* (p. 31). New Haven and London: Yale University Press.

Baldarelli, M. (2012). Accounting Harmonization for SMEs in Europe: Some Remarks on IFRS for SMEs and Empirical Evidences. *Economic Research – Ekonomska Istrazivanja, 25*(1), 1–26.

E. Kaili et al. (eds.), *New Models of Financing and Financial Reporting for European SMEs*,
https://doi.org/10.1007/978-3-030-02831-2

Bauwhede, H., & van Cauwenberge, P. (2015). Financial Reporting Quality and the Cost of Debt of SMEs. *Small Business Economics, 45*(1), 149–164.

BDO. (2015). *IFRS for SMEs at a Glance at 1 July 2015*. Retrieved from https://www.bdo.global/getmedia/8760a193-5417-4497-84c7-a77d412d1006/IFRS-for-SMEs-at-a-Glance_July2015.pdf.aspx

Bluhn, K., & Smith, R. (2008). *Change in SMEs: Towards European Capitalism*. Retrieved from https://www.palgrave.com/us/book/9780230515895

Bogner, E. (2011). Machiavelli: 16 Lessons from the Master Manipulator. *Business Insider*, June 20. Retrieved from https://www.businessinsider.com/machiavelli-the-prince-2011-5

Boreiko, D. *Alternative Finance: ICOs as New Financing Mechanism*. Retrieved from https://www.researchgate.net/project/Alternative-Finance-ICOs-as-new-financing-mechanism

Bottiglia, R., & Pichler, F. (Eds.). (2016). *Crowdfunding for SMEs: A European Perspective*. Palgrave Macmillan. Retrieved from https://www.palgrave.com/de/book/9781137560209; https://www.palgrave.com/gp/book/9781137331199

Bouvier, S. (2018). *Accounting Roundup: IFRS Questions EU Plans to Modify Rules*. Retrieved from https://www.ipe.com/pensions/pensions/pensions-accounting/accounting-roundup-ifrs-questions-eu-plans-to-modify-rules/10023979.article

Brem, A., Kreusel, N., & Neusseu, C. (2008). Performance Measurement in SMEs: Literature Review and Results from a German Case Study. *International Journal of Globalisation and Small Business, 2*(4), 411–427.

Bresnahan, T., Brynjolfsson, E., & Hitt, L. (2002). Information Technology, Workplace Organization and the Demand for Skilled Labor: Firm-Level Evidence. *Quarterly Journal of Economics, 117*(1), 339–376.

Bruntje, D., & Gajda, O. (2016). *Crowdfunding in Europe: State of the Art in Theory and Practice*. London: Springer.

Brynjolfsson, E., & Hitt, L. (2002). *Digital Organization: The Seven Habits of Highly Competitive Companies*. Working Paper, MIT.

Brynjolfsson, E., & Hitt, L. (2003). Computing Productivity: Firm-Level Evidence. *Review of Economics & Statistics, 85*(4), 793–808.

Brynjolfsson, E., & McAfee, A. (2016). *The Second Machine Age: Work, Progress, and Prosperity in a Time of Brilliant Technologies*. New York: Norton & Co.

Brynjolfsson, E., & Saunders, A. (2013). *Wired for Innovation: How Information Technology Is Reshaping the Economy*. Cambridge, MA: MIT Press.

Buda, D. (2016). *Raport de Activitate si Ghid de Finanțare UE* [Romanian Language]. Retrieved from http://www.danielbuda.ro/ro/raport-de-activitate-2014-2016/

Bușoi, C., & Țurcanu, M. (2016). *Ghid pentru accesarea fondurilor europene* [Romanian Language]. Retrieved from http://www.cristianbusoi.eu/publicatii/

Carraher, S., & van Auken, H. (2013). *The Use of Financial Statements for Decision Making by Small Firms*. Retrieved from https://www.researchgate.net/publication/272532573_The_use_of_financial_statements_for_decision_making_by_small_firms

Chishti, S., & Barberis, J. (2016). *The FinTech Book*. Chichester, UK: John Wiley & Sons.

Christensen, C., Kaufman, S. P., & Shih, W. (2008). Innovation Killers: How Financial Tools Destroy Your Capacity to Do New Things. *Harvard Business Review* 86(1), 1–8.

David, P. A. (1990). The Dynamo and the Computer: A Historical Perspective on the Modern Productivity Paradox. *American Economic Review. Papers and Proceedings, 80*(2), 355–361.

Deloitte. (2007). *ACCA Detailed Summary of Proposed IFRS for SMEs*. Retrieved from https://www.iasplus.com/en/news/2007/August/news3157

Devrimi, K., & Koch, M. (2015). Countries' Adoption of the International Financial Reporting Standard for Small and Medium-Sized Entities (IFRS for SMEs) – Early Empirical Evidence. *Accounting and Business Research, 45*(1), 93–120.

Di Bitetto, M., Gilardoni, G., & D'Anselmi, P. (Eds.). (2013). *SMEs as the Unknown Stakeholder*. London: Palgrave Macmillan.

Di Pietra, R., McLeay, S., & Ronen, J. (Eds.). (2014). *Accounting and Regulation. New Insights on Governance, Markets and Institutions* (p. 412). New York and London: Springer.

Dugan, R., & Gabriel, K. (2013). Special Forces Innovation: How DARPA Attacks Problems. *Harvard Business Review, 91*(October), 74–76.

EFRAG. (2016). *Professional Investors and the Decision Usefulness of Financial Reporting*. Retrieved from http://www.efrag.org/Assets/Download?assetUrl=%2Fsites%2Fwebpublishing%2FSiteAssets%2FProfessional%2520investors%2520and%2520the%2520decision%2520usefulness%2520of%2520financial%2520reporting.pdf

EFRAG. *The Role of the Business Model in Financial Statements*. Retrieved from https://www.efrag.org/Assets/Download?assetUrl=%2Fsites%2Fwebpublishing%2FSiteAssets%2FBusiness%2520Model%2520Research%2520Paper.pdf

Eshima, Y. (2003). Impact of Public Policy on Innovative SMEs in Japan. *Journal of Small Business Management, 41*(1), 85–93.

Europe Commission. *Horizon 2020*. Retrieved December 17, 2013, from ec.europa.eu/research/horizon2020/

European Central Bank. (2015). *Building a Capital Markets Union – Eurosystem Contribution to the European Commission's Green Paper*. Retrieved from https://www.ecb.europa.eu/pub/pdf/other/150521_eurosystem_contribution_to_green_paper_-_building_a_cmuen.pdf

European Commission. (2008). *Report on the Operation of Regulation 1606/2002 on the Application of International Accounting Standards*. Retrieved from http://ec.europa.eu/finance/accounting/docs/ias/com-2008-0215_en.pdf

European Commission. (2010). *Summary Report of the Responses Received to the Commission's Consultations on the International Financial Reporting for Small and Medium-Sized Entities*. Retrieved from https://www.iasplus.com/en/binary/europe/1005smeconsultationsummary.pdf

European Commission. (2013). *Maystadt Report*. Retrieved from http://ec.europa.eu/internal_market/accounting/docs/governance/reform/131112_report_en.pdf

European Commission. (2015a). *Feedback Statement on the Green Paper "Building a Capital Markets Union"*. Retrieved from http://ec.europa.eu/finance/consultations/2015/capital-markets-union/docs/summary-of-responses_en.pdf
European Commission. (2015b). *Accounting Guide for SMEs – SME Accounting in Europe: Insights Provided by a Desk Research and a Survey*. Retrieved from https://ec.europa.eu/growth/content/accounting-guide-smes-sme-accounting-europe-insights-provided-desk-research-and-survey-0_en
European Commission. (2017a). *On the Mid-Term Review of the Capital Markets Union Action Plan*. Retrieved from https://ec.europa.eu/info/sites/info/files/communication-cmu-mid-term-review-june2017_en.pdf
European Commission. (2017b). *On the Mid-Term Review of the Capital Markets Union Action Plan*. Retrieved from https://ec.europa.eu/info/sites/info/files/staff-working-document-cmu-mid-term-review-june2017_en.pdf
European Commission. *What Is an SME?* Retrieved from http://ec.europa.eu/growth/smes/business-friendly-environment/sme-definition_en
European Commission. *International Accounting Standard 1*. Retrieved from http://ec.europa.eu/internal_market/accounting/docs/consolidated/ias1_en.pdf
European Commission. *Securities Market*. Explanatory Memorandum, p. 2. Retrieved from https://ec.europa.eu/info/business-economy-euro/banking-and-finance/financial-markets/securities-markets_en
European Commission. *Q&A Accompanying CMU Action Plan*. Retrieved from http://europa.eu/rapid/press-release_MEMO-15-5732_en.htm
European Commission. *Overview of Funding Programmes*. Retrieved from https://ec.europa.eu/info/funding-tenders/funding-opportunities/funding-programmes/overview-funding-programmes_en
European Commission. COM(2018a)109. *FinTech Action Plan: For a More Competitive and Innovative European Financial Sector*.
European Commission. COM(2018b)109. *FinTech Action Plan: For a More Competitive and Innovative European Financial Sector*, p. 6.
European Commission. COM(2018c)113. Proposal for a Regulation on European Crowdfunding Service Providers (ECSP) for Business.
European Commission. *Fintech Action Plan Fact Sheet*. Retrieved from https://ec.europa.eu/info/sites/info/files/180308-action-plan-fintech-factsheet_en.pdf
European Commission to the European Parliament and Council. (2015). *Evaluation of Regulation EC No 1606/2002 on Application of International Accounting Standards*. Retrieved June 18, 2015, from https://eur-lex.europa.eu/legal-content/EN/ALL/?uri=CELEX:32002R1606
European Court of Justice. *Charter of Fundamental Rights*.
European Investment Bank. Retrieved from http://www.eib.org/en/
European Investment Fund. Retrieved from www.eif.europa.eu
European Parliament. (2008). *Strong Criticism of the International Accounting Standards Board's Governance*. Retrieved from http://www.europarl.europa.eu/sides/getDoc.do?pubRef=-//EP//TEXT+IM-PRESS+20080410BRI26349+ITEM-024-EN+DOC+XML+V0//EN&language=SK

European Parliament. EP(2017)2772(RSP). *Motion for Resolution on Distributed Ledger Technologies and Blockchains: Building Trust with Disintermediation.*

European Parliament. EP(2017)2772(RSP). *Motion for Resolution on Distributed Ledger Technologies and Blockchains: Building Trust with Disintermediation*, p. 10.

European Voice. *Multiple Issues of the Newspaper.*

Eurostat. (2013). *Science, Technology and Innovation in Europe.* Luxembourg: Publications Office of the European Union.

EY. (2010). *IFRS for Small and Medium-Sized Entities a Comparison with IFRS – The Basics.* Retrieved from https://www.ey.com/Publication/vwLUAssets/IFRS_for_SMEs_Comparison/%24FILE/IFRS_for_SMEs_Comparison.pdf

EY. (2014, August). *The JOBS Act: 2014 Mid-Year Update—An Overview of Implementation and an Analysis of Emerging Growth Company Trends*, p. 13. Retrieved from http://www.ey.com/Publication/vwLUAssets/EY-the-JOBS-Act-2014/$FILE/EY-the-JOBS-Act-2014.pdf

EY. *IFRS for Small and Medium-Sized Entities.* Retrieved from http://www.ey.com/Publication/vwLUAssets/IFRS_for_SMEs_Comparison/$FILE/IFRS_for_SMEs_Comparison.pdf

Fagerberg, J., Mowery, D., & Verspagen, B. (2009). *The Focus on the Economic Exploitation of Knowledge. Innovation, Path Dependency, and Policy: The Norwegian Case* (p. 3). Oxford University Press.

FEI. (2013). *The Cost of IFRS Transition in Canada.* Retrieved from https://portal.feicanada.org/enews/file/CFERF%20studies/2012-2013/The%20cost%20of%20IFRS%20transition%20in%20Canada%20-%20July%204,%202013%20-%20final.pdf

Ferriss, T. *The 4 Hour Workweek.* Retrieved from https://fourhourworkweek.com/

Financial Times. *Multiple Issues of the Newspapers.*

FinTech Switzerland. *Top FinTech Books You Must Read.* Retrieved from http://fin-technews.ch/top-fintech-books/

FRC. (2015). *Consultation: Improving the Quality of Reporting by Smaller Listed and AIM Quoted Companies.* Retrieved from https://www.frc.org.uk/Our-Work/Publications/FRC-Board/Consultation-Improving-the-Quality-of-Reporting-b-File.pdf

Freedman, D., & Nutting, M. *Equity Crowdfunding for Investors: A Guide to Risks, Returns, Funding Portals, Due Diligence, and Deal Terms.* London: Wiley.

Fridson, M. (2001). *Financial Statement Analysis: A Practitioner's Guide.* Wiley.

Garengo, P., Biazzo, S., & Bititci, U. S. (2005). Performance Measurement Systems in SMEs: A Review for a Research Agenda. *International Journal of Management Review, 7*(1), 25–47.

Gassen, J. (2007). *Are Stewardship and Decision Usefulness Complementary of Conflicting Objectives of Financial Accounting?* Retrieved from http://sfb649.wiwi.hu-berlin.de/fedc/events/Motzen07/gassen.pdf

Gassen, J., & Fülbier, R. (2010). *IFRS for European Small and Medium-Sized Entities. A Theoretical and Empirical Analysis.* Retrieved from https://dgrv.de/webde.nsf/272e312c8017e736c1256e31005cedff/df403f6ea057d8dac12577c800441300/$FILE/DGRV_IFRS_fuer_KMU.pdf

Gertner, J. (2012a). *The Idea Factory: Bell Labs and the Great Age of American Innovation* (p. 352). New York: Penguin Books.

Gertner, J. (2012b). *The Idea Factory: Bell Labs and the Great Age of American Innovation* (pp. 18–19). New York: Penguin Books.

Gierczak, M. M., Bretschneider, U., Haas, P., Blohm, I., & Leimeister, J. M. (2016a). Crowdfunding: Outlining the New Era of Fundraising. In D. Bruntje & O. Gajda (Eds.), *Crowdfunding in Europe: State of the Art in Theory and Practice*. London: Springer.

Gierczak, M. M., Bretschneider, U., Haas, P., Blohm, I., & Leimeister, J. M. (2016b). Crowdfunding: Outlining the New Era of Fundraising. In D. Bruntje & O. Gajda (Eds.), *Crowdfunding in Europe: State of the Art in Theory and Practice* (p. 9). London: Springer.

Gill, I., & Raiser, M. (2012). *Golden Growth: Restoring the Lustre of the European Economic Model.* Washington, DC: World Bank Group Publications.

Goldin, C., & Katz, L. F. (2008). *The Race Between Education and Technology.* Cambridge, MA: Harvard University Press.

Grant Thornton. (2015). *The IFRS for SMEs.* Retrieved from https://www.grant-thornton.global/en/insights/articles/the-ifrs-for-smes/

Hall, P. (2001). *Varieties of Capitalism: Institutional Foundations of Comparative Advantage.* Oxford: Oxford University Press.

Hanke, B. (2009). *Debating the Varieties of Capitalism.* Oxford: Oxford University Press.

Haslam, C., et al. (2017). *The Routledge Companion to Critical Accounting, Stress Testing the Adoption of Fair Value Accounting (FVA): Fragility and Instability in Financialized Firms* (Routledge Companions in Business, Management and Accounting). London: Routledge.

Hausman, A. (2005). Innovativeness Among Small Businesses: Theory and Propositions for Future Research. *Industrial Marketing Management, 34*(8), 773–782.

Helwege, J., & Liang, N. (1996). Is There a Pecking Order? Evidence from a Panel of IPO Firms. *Journal of Financial Economics, 40*(3), 429–458.

Hippel, E., Ogawa, S., & De Jong, J. (2001). The Age of the Consumer-Innovator: Why It's Time to Rethink Product Development. *MIT Sloan Management Review, 53*(1, Fall 2011), 29. Their research also highlights a link with education policy and the importance of STEM fields of study. People with a higher educational background and a technical one are more likely to be consumer-innovators.

Hogarth-Scott, S., et al. (1996). Do Small Businesses Have to Practice Marketing to Survive and Grow? *Marketing Intelligence & Planning, 14*(1), 6–18.

ICAEW. (2007). *EU Implementation of IFRS and the Fair Value Directive.* Retrieved from http://ec.europa.eu/internal_market/accounting/docs/studies/2007-eu_implementation_of_ifrs.pdf

IFAC. (2016). *Research Insights—Accountancy Expertise and Business Performance.* Retrieved from https://www.ifac.org/global-knowledge-gateway/performance-financial-management/discussion/research-insights-accountancy

Ifo Institute, Center of Economic Studies, Dannreuther, C. (2007). *EU SMEs Policy*. Retrieved from https://www.cesifo-group.de/DocDL/forum2-07-focus2.pdf

IFRS. *Who Uses IFRS Standards*. Retrieved from www.ifrs.org/use-around-the-world/use-of-ifrs-standards-by-jurisdiction/

IFRS for SMEs Basis for Conclusions.

IFRS for SMEs Standard.

IFRS Standard (for the EU).

IFRS Standard (full).

Integrated Reporting. *Business Model*. Retrieved from http://integratedreporting.org/wp-content/uploads/2013/03/Business_Model.pdf

International Integrated Reporting Council. Retrieved from http://integratedreporting.org

Investiere. *Europe's Top 5 Crowdinvesting Platforms*. Retrieved from https://www.investiere.ch/sites/default/files/Top5platformsinEurope_PressRelease.pdf

Jeffrey Sachs Is the Prominent Scholar of the "Geography" Approach.

Jocumsen, G. (2004). How Do Small Business Managers Make Strategic Marketing Decisions?: A Model of Process. *European Journal of Marketing, 38*(5/6), 659–674.

Johnson, S. *Who Moved My Cheese*. Retrieved from http://jef.mentalis.org/hersenspinsels/downloads/WhoMovedMyCheese_DrSpencerJohnson.pdf

Kaminskaite, J. (2017). *Reducing the Failure Rate of SMEs*. Retrieved from https://www.theseus.fi/bitstream/handle/10024/129581/Reducing-the-failure-rate-of-SMEs-Julija-Kaminskaite-thesis.pdf?sequence=1

Kersten, R., Harms, J., Liket, K., & Maas, K. (2017). Small Firms, Large Impact? A System Review of the SME Finance Literature. *World Development, 97*, 330–348.

King, B. (2018). *Bank 4.0*. Marshall Cavendish International.

KPMG and University of Cambridge. (2016, October). *Global Insights from Regional Alternative Finance Studies*, p. 3. Retrieved from https://home.kpmg.com/content/dam/kpmg/uk/pdf/2016/10/global-alternative-finance-report-web.pdf

London Stock Exchange Group. *1000 Companies to Inspire Europe*. Retrieved from https://www.lseg.com/resources/1000-companies-inspire

Macenzi, B., et al. (2010). *Applying IFRS for SMEs*. Wiley.

Machado, H. (2016). *Growth of Small Businesses: A Literature Review and Perspectives of Studies*. Retrieved from http://www.scielo.br/pdf/gp/v23n2/en_0104-530X-gp-0104-530X1759-14.pdf

Machiavelli, N. *The Prince*. Retrieved from https://www.victoria.ac.nz/lals/about/staff/publications/paul-nation/Prince-Adapted2.pdf

Masiak, C., Moritz, A., Lang, F. (2017). *Financing Patterns of European SMEs Revisited: An Updated Empirical Taxonomy and Determinants of SME Financing Clusters*. EIF Working Paper, No. 2017/40, European Investment Fund (EIF), Luxembourg. Retrieved from http://www.eif.org/news_centre/publications/EIF_Working_Paper_2017_40.htm

Maystadt, P. (2013, October). *Should IFRS Standards Be More 'European'? Mission to Reinforce the EU's Contribution to the Development of International Accounting Standards*. Retrieved from http://ec.europa.eu/finance/accounting/docs/governance/reform/131112_report_en.pdf

Mazars. (2005). *The IFRS for SMEs Accounting Standard: Perceptions and Expectations Across Europe*. Retrieved from https://www.mazars.co.th/Home/News/Our-publications/Publications/Surveys/The-IFRS-for-SMEs-accounting-standard

Mazzucato, M. (2013a). *The Entrepreneurial State* (pp. 26–27). London: Anthem Press; and the Economics Department Lecture at the London School of Economics on 8 October 2013. Retrieved from www.richmedia.lse.ac.uk

Mazzucato, M. (2013b, August). Financing Innovation: Creative Destruction vs. Destructive Creation. *Industrial and Corporate Change, Oxford Journals, Oxford, 22*(4), 856.

Mazzucato, M. (2013c). Chapter 5: The State Behind the iPhone. In *The Entrepreneurial State* (pp. 87–112). London: Anthem Press.

McCartney, H. (2015). *Variegated Neoliberalism: EU Varieties of Capitalism and International Political Economy*. New York: Routledge.

Mintzberg, H. (1984). Who Should Control the Corporation. *California Management Review, 27*(1), 46–64.

Mokyr, J. (1990). *The Lever of Riches: Technological Creativity and Economic Progress*. Oxford: Oxford University Press.

Mokyr, J. (2017). *A Culture of Growth: The Origins of the Modern Economy*. Princeton, NJ: Princeton University Press.

Mullins, J. *How to Grow Your Business Without VCs*. Retrieved from https://www.london.edu/programmes/digital-learning/how-to-finance-your-startup-without-vc-online-course

Munro, D. (2013). *SME Financing*. Retrieved from https://www.palgrave.com/la/book/9781137375759

National Science Foundation. *On the Origins of Google*. Retrieved December 27, 2013, from http://www.nsf.gov/discoveries/disc_summ.jsp?cntn_id=100660

Nicole, T. (2016). 9 Different Kinds of SMEs Funding. *Entrepreneur*. Retrieved from https://www.entrepreneurmag.co.za/advice/funding/attracting-investors/sme-funding/

Nixon, R. (2015). *Remaining Relevant – The Future of the Accounting Profession*. Vivid Publishing.

North, D. (1991). *Institutions, Institutional Change and Economic Performance*. Cambridge: Cambridge University Press.

O'Dwyer, M., et al. (2009). Innovative Marketing in SMEs: An Empirical Study. *Journal of Strategic Marketing, 17*(5), 383–396.

OECD. (2004a). *OECD Compendium on International and Regional Bodies: Activities and Initiatives Related to Small and Medium-Sized Enterprises (SMEs)*. Retrieved from https://www.oecd.org/cfe/smes/2090691.pdf

OECD. (2004b). *Promoting Entrepreneurship and Innovative SMEs in Global Economy.* Retrieved from https://www.oecd.org/cfe/smes/31919278.pdf

OECD Innovation Strategy (Paris, 2010). (2005). *Oslo Guidelines for Collecting and Interpreting Innovation Data.* Retrieved December 15, 2013, from www.oecd.org

OECD/G20. (2015). *High Level Principles on SMEs Financing.* Retrieved from http://www.oecd.org/finance/G20-OECD-High-Level-Principles-on-SME-Financing.pdf

Parry, S. (2012). Marketing for Survival: A Comparative Case Study of SME Software Firms. *Journal of Small Business and Enterprise Development, 19*(4). Retrieved from https://www.researchgate.net/publication/262966360_Marketing_for_survival_A_comparative_case_study_of_SME_software_firms

Peacock, R. (2004). *Understanding Small Business: Practice, Theory and Research.* Adelaide: Scarman Publishing.

Phelps, E. (2013). *Mass Flourishing.* Princeton and Woodstock: Princeton University Press.

PKF. (2015). *IFRS for SMEs Illustrative Consolidated Financial Statements.* Retrieved from http://www.pkf.com/media/10031232/ifrs-for-smes-illustrative-financial-statements-standard-eff-1-january-2017.pdf

PwC. (2009). *IFRS for Small and Medium-Sized Entities Pocket Guide 2009.* Retrieved from https://www.pwc.com/gx/en/ifrs-reporting/pdf/ifrssme09.pdf

Quagli, A., et al. (2010). How Is the IFRS for SME Accepted in the European Context? An Analysis of the Homogeneity Among European Countries, Users and Preparers in the European Commission Questionnaire. *Advances in Accounting, 28*(1), 147–156.

Republic of Estonia, Information System Authority. Retrieved December 25, 2013, from www.x-road.eu

Sapir, A., & Veugelers, R. (2013). Manufacturing Europe's Growth. *European Voice,* October 31, p. 13.

Saucke, M. (2015). *Full IFRS and IFRS for SMEs Adoption by Private Firms: Empirical Evidence on Country Level.* Peter Lang GmbH.

Schumpeter, J. (1983). *Theory of Economic Development.* New York: Transaction Publishers.

Schumpeter, J. (2009). *Can Capitalism Survive? Creative Destruction and the Future of the Global Economy.* New York: Harper Collins Publishers. Originally published as *Capitalism, Socialism, and Democracy* by Harper & Row, New York, 1942.

Schwab, K. (2016). *The Fourth Industrial Revolution.* New York: Crown Business.

SEC. *Internal Control Over Financial Reporting in Exchange Act Periodic Reports of Non-Accelerated Filers.* Retrieved from https://www.sec.gov/rules/final/2010/33-9142.pdf

Semler, R. (1993). *Maverik.* Grand Central Publishing.

Semler, R. (2004). *The Seven Day Weekend.* Portfolio Hardcover.

Shepherd, J., & Wiklund, D. (2005). Entrepreneurial Orientation and Small Business Performance: A Configurational Approach. *Journal of Business Venturing, 20*(1), 71–91.

Smith, A. (2010). *The Wealth of Nations: The Economics Classic* (p. 298). Mankato: Capstone.

Storey, D. J. (1994). *Understanding the Small Business Sector*. University of Illinois at Urbana-Champaign's Academy for Entrepreneurial Leadership Historical Research Reference in Entrepreneurship. Retrieved from SSRN https://ssrn.com/abstract=1496214

Strouhal, J. (2011). *Harmonization of SME's Financial Reporting in Emerging CEE Countries*. WSEAS Press. Retrieved from http://www.wseas.us/e-library/conferences/2011/Strouhal/Strouhal.pdf

Torres, O. (2003). *A French Perspective of Research on Small Businesses: Denaturation and Proximity*. Retrieved from http://oliviertorres.net/travaux/pdf/ECSBLodz.pdf

Torres, O. (2006). *The Proximity Law of Small Business Finance*. Communication présentée à l'International Council of Small Business, Melbourne, Australia. Retrieved from http://oliviertorres.net/travaux/pdf/ICSB06.pdf

Torres, O., & Julien, P. A. (2005). Specificity and Denaturation of Small Business. *International Small Business Journal, 23*, 355–377.

UOB. (2018). *7 Ways SMEs Can Level Up with Budget. 2018 Measures*. Retrieved from https://www.uobgroup.com/business/inbusiness/article.html?id=7-ways-smes-can-level-up-with-budget-2018-measures

US Small Business Administration. *About the SBA*. Retrieved from https://www.sba.gov/about-sba

Villa, A., & Dario, A. (2009). *A Road Map to the Development of European SME Networks*. Retrieved from https://www.springer.com/us/book/9781848003415

Watson, J. (2010). *SME Performance: Separating Myth from Reality*. Edward Elgar Publishing Ltd.

World Federation of Exchanges. Retrieved from https://www.world-exchanges.org/home/index.php/research/wfe-research

Zabri, S., Yusoff, W., Ahmad, K., & Lean, J. (2017). *Literature Review on Financing Preferences Among Small and Medium Enterprises*. Conference: The 29th International Business Information Management Association Conference. Sustainable Economic Growth, Education Excellence, and Innovation Management Through Vision 2020. Retrieved from https://www.researchgate.net/publication/318315680_Literature_Review_on_Financing_Preferences_among_Small_And_Medium_Enterprises

Zhang, E., & Andrew, J. (2014). Financialisation and the Conceptual Framework. *Critical Perspectives on Accounting, 25*(1), 17–26.

Ziegler, P. (2010). *Edward Heath* (p. 71). London: Harper Press.

Index[1]

A
ACCA, 14
Accounting Directive, v, viii, 16, 96, 97, 118, 121
AIM, 118, 119, 121n6, 123
Alternative Investment Funds (AIFs), xviii
Autorité des Normes Comptables (ANC), 13, 127, 128

B
Basel III, xix, xxiii, 55, 57–58, 61, 64, 65, 69
Big 4, 13, 14
Big data, xxiv, 49, 103, 105, 166

C
Capital Markets Union (CMU), v–ix, xiii, xvii, xviii, xx, xxii, xxiii, xxv, xxvi, 40, 42, 51, 53, 54, 64, 69, 71–82, 108, 118, 119, 121, 122, 129, 162, 163
Capital Requirements Directive (CRD), xix, xxiii, 57, 76
COSME, 9, 60
Country by Country Reporting (CBCR), 100
Crowdfunding, vii, xviii, xxiv, 6, 9, 32, 44, 45, 50, 59, 71–82, 98, 100, 163

D
Distributed ledger technologies (DLT), 23–38, 64, 66, 70

E
Environmental, Social, and Governance (ESG), 99
European Central Bank (ECB), vi, xvi, 17, 78, 164
European Commission, v, xiii, xviii, 2, 8–10, 16, 17, 19, 28, 29, 34, 35, 37, 40, 53, 56, 60, 64, 69, 78–80, 99, 117, 118, 121, 123, 128, 129, 164

[1] Note: Page numbers followed by 'n' refer to notes.

E. Kaili et al. (eds.), *New Models of Financing and Financial Reporting for European SMEs*, https://doi.org/10.1007/978-3-030-02831-2

European Financial Reporting Advisory Group (EFRAG), 14, 15, 92
European Fund for Strategic Investments (EFSI), 9, 76
European Investment Bank (EIB), 2, 9, 52, 60
European Investment Fund (EIF), 9, 60
European Parliament, ix, xvi, xviii, xxiv, 10, 14, 17, 29, 60, 79, 81, 97
EuVECA, vi

F

Fair Value (FV), xiii, 87, 143–146, 149, 153–155
Financialisation, xiii, xx, 32, 87, 93
Financial Reporting Council (FRC), 120, 121n6, 123, 126–128
FinTech Action Plan, 78, 79
Fourth Industrial Revolution, xxiv, 72–75
Full IFRS, xvi, xx, xxi, xxv, 2, 11, 12n24, 14, 86, 108–110, 114, 120, 122–126, 128–130, 133, 135, 138, 140–158, 164

G

GDP, 39, 71, 75, 85
Generally Accepted Accounting Principles (GAAP), 11, 12, 110, 114, 136, 164

I

IFRS for SMEs, xiii, xvi, xx–xxii, xxv, 2, 10–17, 19, 86, 108, 112, 129–130, 133–159, 161, 164, 166
IFRS Foundation, xxv, 13, 107, 134, 137, 141, 159, 164
Information and Communication Technology (ICT), 24
Initial Coin Offerings (ICOs), xviii, xxiv, 3, 6, 31, 71–82, 161, 163
InnovFin, 9
Institute of Chartered Accountants in England and Wales (ICAEW), 13, 14, 19, 110, 161
Institute of Chartered Accountants of Scotland (ICAS), 124
Integrated financial viability statement (IFVS), 88, 89
Integrated reporting (<IR>), 92, 100–102
International Accounting Standard 1 (IAS1), 89, 93
International Accounting Standards Board (IASB), xx, 10–15, 17, 85–87, 93, 124–125, 128–131, 134, 136, 139, 147–149, 158, 159, 161, 164

L

Largest public interest entities (PIEs), 99

M

Maystadt report, 87, 108
Mini-bond, xxiii, 64, 65, 163
Multilateral Trading Facilities (MTFs), xv, xx, xxv, 5, 17, 109, 111, 115, 117, 118, 119n4, 127–129, 161, 164

N
Non-financial information (NFI), 95, 98–100, 102
Non-financial reporting, xxiv, 165, 166

S
Schumpeterian growth, 72
Second Machine Age, 72, 73
Single market, 29, 31, 97, 101
Smithian growth, 72
Supply Chain Finance (SFC), xxiii, 67, 163

U
Undertaking for Collectible Investment in Transferable Securities (UCITS), xviii
US Generally Accepted Accounting Principles (US GAAP), 110, 111

V
VentureEU, vi

GPSR Compliance

The European Union's (EU) General Product Safety Regulation (GPSR) is a set of rules that requires consumer products to be safe and our obligations to ensure this.

If you have any concerns about our products, you can contact us on ProductSafety@springernature.com

In case Publisher is established outside the EU, the EU authorized representative is:

Springer Nature Customer Service Center GmbH
Europaplatz 3
69115 Heidelberg, Germany

Batch number: 10844573

Printed by Printforce, the Netherlands